MHPG: Basic Mechanisms and Psychopathology

BEHAVIORAL BIOLOGY

AN INTERNATIONAL SERIES

Series editors

James L. McGaugh

Department of Psychobiology
University of California
Irvine, California

John C. Fentress

Department of Psychology
Dalhousie University
Halifax, Canada

Joseph P. Hegmann

Department of Zoology
The University of Iowa
Iowa City, Iowa

Holger Ursin, Eivind Baade, and Seymour Levine (Editors), Psychobiology of Stress: A Study of Coping Men

William W. Grings and Michael E. Dawson, Emotions and Bodily Responses: A Psychophysiological Approach

Enoch Callaway, Patricia Tueting, and Stephen H. Koslow (Editors), Event Related Brain Potentials in Man

Larry L. Butcher (Editor), Cholinergic–Monoaminergic Interactions in the Brain

Aryeh Routtenberg (Editor), Biology of Reinforcement: Facets of Brain-Stimulation Reward

Richard N. Aslin, Jeffrey R. Alberts, and Michael R. Petersen (Editors), Development of Perception: Psychobiological Perspectives. Vol. 1: Audition, Somatic Perception, and the Chemical Senses; Vol. 2: The Visual System

Joe L. Martinez, Jr., Robert A. Jensen, Rita B. Messing, Henk Rigter, and James L. McGaugh (Editors), Endogenous Peptides and Learning and Memory Processes

James W. Maas (Editor), MHPG: Basic Mechanisms and Psychopathology

T.M.
LCCC?

MHPG: Basic Mechanisms and Psychopathology

Edited by

JAMES W. MAAS

Department of Psychiatry, Yale University School of Medicine, New Haven, Connecticut

1983

ACADEMIC PRESS
A Subsidiary of Harcourt Brace Jovanovich, Publishers
New York   London
Paris   San Diego   San Francisco   São Paulo   Sydney   Tokyo   Toronto

ACADEMIC PRESS, INC.
111 Fifth Avenue, New York, New York 10003

United Kingdom Edition published by
ACADEMIC PRESS, INC. (LONDON) LTD.
24/28 Oval Road, London NW1 7DX

Library of Congress Cataloging in Publication Data

Main entry under title:

MHPG : Basic mechanisms and psychopathology.

(Behavioral biology)
Includes bibliographical references and index.
1. Methoxyhydroxyphenylglycol--Analysis. 2. Methoxy-
hydroxyphenylglycol--Diagnostic use. 3. Noradrenalin--
Metabolism. 4. Adrenergic mechanisms. I. Maas, James W.
II. Series: Behavioral biology (New York, N.Y. : 1978)
QP801.M42M46 1982   612'.814   82-11640
ISBN 0-12-462920-2

PRINTED IN THE UNITED STATES OF AMERICA

83 84 85 86   9 8 7 6 5 4 3 2 1

To the workers in the vineyard — patients and investigators alike

Contents

1. The Biochemical Pathways for Formation of 3-Methoxy-4-Hydroxyphenethyleneglycol in Man and Animals

B. Tabakoff and F. DeLeon-Jones

2. Neuronal Activity, Impulse Flow, and MHPG Production

Robert H. Roth

6. Preliminary Characterization of Plasma MHPG in Man

James F. Leckman and James W. Maas

7. Relationship between Psychiatric Diagnostic Groups of Depressive Disorders and MHPG

Joseph J. Schildkraut, Paul J. Orsulak, Alan F. Schatzberg,
and Alan H. Rosenbaum

8. Sources of Variance in Clinical Studies of MHPG

William Z. Potter, Giovanni Muscettola, and Frederick K. Goodwin

9. Urinary MHPG and Treatment Response: A Review

Daniël P. van Kammen

10. Clinical Studies of MHPG in Childhood and Adolescence

J. Gerald Young, Donald J. Cohen, Bennett A. Shaywitz, George M. Anderson, and James W. Maas

Contributors

Numbers in parentheses indicate the pages on which the authors' contributions begin.

GEORGE M. ANDERSON (193), Department of Laboratory Medicine, and Child Study Center, Yale University School of Medicine, New Haven, Connecticut 06510

DONALD J. COHEN (193), Child Study Center, Yale University School of Medicine, New Haven, Connecticut 06510

JOHN M. DAVIS (45), Department of Psychiatry, University of Illinois, and Illinois State Psychiatric Institute, Chicago, Illinois 60612

F. DeLEON-JONES[1] (1), Department of Psychiatry and Psychopharmacology, University of Illinois, College of Medicine at Chicago, Chicago, Illinois 60612

FREDERICK K. GOODWIN (145), Intramural Research Program, National Institute of Mental Health, Bethesda, Maryland 20205

SUSAN E. HATTOX[2] (69), Department of Psychiatry and Pharmacology, Yale School of Medicine, New Haven, Connecticut 06510

J. I. JAVAID (45), Research Department, Illinois State Psychiatric Institute, Chicago, Illinois 60612

JAMES F. LECKMAN (33, 107), Child Study Center, Yale University School of Medicine, New Haven, Connecticut 06510

JAMES W. MAAS[3] (33, 107, 193), Department of Psychiatry, Yale University School of Medicine, New Haven, Connecticut 06510

GIOVANNI MUSCETTOLA (145), Department of Psychiatry, The Second Medical School, University of Naples, Naples, Italy

PAUL J. ORSULAK (129), Psychiatric Chemistry Laboratory, Department of Psychiatry, Harvard Medical School,

[1]Present address: VA West Side Medical Center, Chicago, Illinois 60612.
[2]Present address: Boehringer Ingelheim, Ltd., Ridgefield, Connecticut 06877.
[3]Present address: The University of Texas Health Science Center at San Antonio, Department of Psychiatry, San Antonio, Texas 78284.

Massachusetts Mental Health Center, Boston, Massachusetts 02115

WILLIAM Z. POTTER (145), Clinical Psychobiology Branch, National Institute of Mental Health, Bethesda, Maryland 20205

ALAN H. ROSENBAUM (129), Henry Ford Hospital, Detroit, Michigan 48202

ROBERT H. ROTH (19), Departments of Pharmacology and Psychiatry, Yale University School of Medicine, New Haven, Connecticut 06510

JOAN RUBINSTEIN (45), University of Chicago, Pritzker School of Medicine, Chicago, Illinois 60637

ALAN F. SCHATZBERG (129), Harvard Medical School, and Affective Disease Program, McLean Hospital, Belmont, Massachusetts 02178

JOSEPH J. SCHILDKRAUT (129), Harvard Medical School, and Neuropsychopharmacology Laboratory, Massachusetts Mental Health Center, and Psychiatric Chemistry Laboratory, New England Deaconess Hospital, Boston, Massachusetts 02115

BENNETT A. SHAYWITZ (193), Department of Neurology, Yale University School of Medicine, New Haven, Connecticut 06510

B. TABAKOFF (1), Alcohol and Drug Abuse Research and Training Program, Department of Physiology and Biophysics, University of Illinois Medical Center, and Westside Veterans Administration Medical Center, Chicago, Illinois 60612

DANIËL P. VAN KAMMEN (167), Biological Psychiatry Branch, National Institute of Mental Health, Bethesda, Maryland 20205

J. GERALD YOUNG[4] (193), Child Study Center, Yale University School of Medicine, New Haven, Connecticut 06510

[4]Present address: The Mount Sinai Medical Center, Division of Child and Adolescent Psychiatry, New York, New York 10029.

Preface

In a sense this book is a history of the emergence of increasingly close and fruitful interactions between investigators in clinical biological psychiatry and basic neuropsychopharmacology. Interest in 3-methoxy-4-hydroxyphenethyleneglycol (MHPG) was originally sparked by attempts to begin clinical investigations dealing with the possibility that there might be alterations of norepinephrine (NE) metabolism and/or disposition in the brains of patients who had depression or mania. This possibility rested primarily upon experimental results with animals that indicated that antidepressant and euphoriant-type drugs altered storage, release, and reuptake of biogenic amines such as NE in brain. In attempts to pursue clinical studies dealing with CNS NE metabolism and the affective disorders, a marker for the metabolism of brain NE was sought. When early experimental work with dogs, and later monkeys, suggested that urinary MHPG might provide such a probe, a series of clinical investigations dealing with urinary MHPG in depression and mania was launched by several different laboratories. As this process went forward it soon became apparent that major areas of ignorance existed in terms of our knowledge of norepinephrine metabolism and noradrenergic function. These deficits, coupled with the possibility that MHPG might provide information regarding the pathogenesis of depressive illness and perhaps even identify biochemically definable subtypes of the illness, gave further impetus to continuing and evolving work by both basic and clinical investigators. Each of the chapters in this book provides a current summary of information from the different areas of investigations that have been pursued.

In addition to the substantive content of the chapters in this book, however, if one takes the historical perspective, it may be noted that there is a thematic aspect to the chapters in that each of them summarizes work that has relevance to attempts of clinical investigators and basic neuropsychopharmacologists, separately and together, to understand the possible role of brain noradrenergic systems in psychiatric disorders, in particular, depression and mania.

Similar developments have occurred in other areas of biological psychiatry, the neurosciences, and neuropsychopharmacology, and in the editor's opinion, this book is indicative of the likelihood that slowly, but surely, an understanding of neurobiological processes that underlie psychopathological states will emerge.

The Biochemical Pathways
for Formation of
3-Methoxy-4-Hydroxyphenethylenegylcol
in Man and Animals*

B. TABAKOFF

F. DELEON-JONES

Veterans Administration West Side Medical Center and University of Illinois Medical Center, Chicago

I. Introduction

The measurement of urinary levels of 3-methoxy-4-hydroxyphenethyleneglycol (MHPG) has become a commonly used method for ascertaining brain norepinephrine (NE) metabolism in humans and for

*Supported by the Medical Research Service of the Veterans Administration and grants from NIAAA, NIDA, and the State of Illinois DMH&DD.

1

deriving conclusions regarding the functional state of brain noradrenergic neurons. The use of this measure as a means of monitoring
the function of brain NE neurons is not without controversy, much of
which has centered around the question of what proportion of urinary
MHPG is derived from the central nervous system (CNS) metabolism of
NE. Questions have also been raised as to whether discrete changes in
CNS NE metabolism, which produce significant changes in behavior,
would produce noticeable changes in urinary output of MHPG. The
discussion of the applicability of MHPG measurements to an understanding of pathological processes in the CNS will be the subject of
several of the succeeding chapters. This chapter will be directed toward
characterizing the enzyme systems that produce MHPG in the brain and
periphery because understanding of the features of these enzymes may
be utilized to reconcile several contradictions appearing in the literature
with regard to the origin of urinary MHPG.

It is currently accepted that an increase in the firing rate of a noradrenergic neuron will result in an increased release of NE from that
neuron (see Roth, this volume) and that stimulation of NE-containing
neurons in brain has been shown to lower NE levels and concomitantly
increase MHPG levels in brain areas innervated by such neurons (Ader
et al., 1978; Korf *et al.*, 1973; Weiner *et al.*, 1972). The stimulus–secretion-coupled release of NE in peripheral adrenergic neurons
and in the brain results in the exposure of sequestered stores of NE to
the intra- and extraneuronal degradative enzymes (Fig. 1). The peripheral noradrenergic systems have also been used to demonstrate that
the intraneuronal pool of readily metabolizable amine (extravesicular
pool) is derived, in part, from newly synthesized amine which is not
sequestered in vesicles (Weiner and Bjur, 1972), as well as amine that is
actively taken up from the synapse by specific uptake systems (Iversen,
1973). Thus the intraneuronal metabolism of NE serves to inactivate
released neurotransmitter and to regulate the size of the intracellular
pool of NE, which acts in the feedback control of the enzymes that
synthesize this amine (Weiner, 1970).

II. Sources of Urinary MHPG

Urinary metabolites of epinephrine and NE are derived both from
neuronally released and metabolized catecholamines and from epinephrine and the small amount of norepinephrine released into the

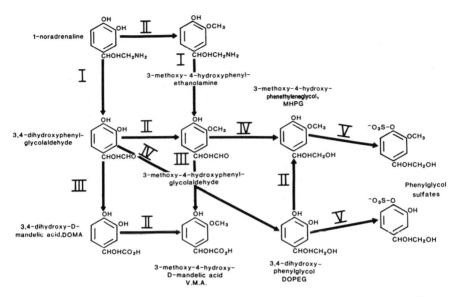

Fig. 1. Central nervous system metabolism of norepinephrine: I. Monoamine oxidase (MAO; amine : oxygen oxidoreductase [deaminating] EC 1.4.3.4); II. Catechol-*O*-methyltransferase (COMT; *S*-adenosyl-L-methionine : catechol-*O*-methyltransferase EC 2.1.1.6); III. Aldehyde dehydrogenase (aldehyde : NAD(P) oxidoreductase EC 1.2.1.3); IV. Aldehyde reductase (alcohol : NAD(P) oxidoreductase EC 1.1.1.2); V. Phenol sulfotransferase (PST; 3′-phosphoadenylsulfatophosphate : phenol sulfotransferase EC 2.8.2.1).

circulation from the adrenal medulla. Labeled NE introduced into the circulatory system of man is metabolized primarily to the acid excretion product vanillylmandelic acid (VMA) (Davis *et al.*, 1967). However, studies using combined gas chromatographic and mass spectroscopic techniques have unambiguously demonstrated MHPG to be the major endogenous NE metabolite in brains of both humans (Karoum *et al.*, 1976; Karoum *et al.*, 1977; Maas *et al.*, 1976) and rats. These studies also substantiated previous observations that MHPG in rat brain is present almost totally in the form of the sulfate conjugate of MHPG (Schanberg *et al.*, 1968), whereas most of the MHPG in human brain is present in its unconjugated form (Karoum *et al.*, 1977; Maas *et al.*, 1976; also see Hattox, Chapter 5, this volume). The glucuronide conjugate of MHPG has also been detected in human brain by GC–MS techniques (Karoum *et al.*, 1977), but the low levels of this MHPG conjugate support earlier studies that indicate that little glucuronide conjugation takes place in the CNS (Schanberg *et al.*, 1968). Three things can be explained by considering the inherent characteristics of the amine-catabolizing enzymes that reside in the brain and peripheral organs of humans and animals: the species-specific differences in the quantity of sulfate-conjugated MHPG in brain, the observation that MHPG is the major metabolite of NE in the CNS while being a lesser metabolite in the periphery, and the observation that MHPG constitutes a greater proportion of urinary epinephrine and NE metabolites in the rat compared to man (Hassan, 1971; Karoum *et al.*, 1973). The following paragraphs will (1) outline the pathways of NE and epinephrine catabolism, (2) emphasize the features of the enzymes that determine which catabolite will predominate in the CNS or peripheral organs, and (3) summarize the enzymatic features that contribute to species differences in metabolite excretion patterns.

III. Oxidative Deamination and O-Methylation of NE

Two types of enzymes compete for the initial catabolism of NE or epinephrine. These enzymes are monoamine oxidase (MAO; amine : oxygen oxidoreductase [deaminating] EC 1.4.3.4) and catechol O-methyltransferase (COMT; 5-adenosyl-L-methionine : catechol O-methyltransferase, EC 2.1.1.6). The metabolism of the amine by one enzyme does not preclude its further metabolism by the other enzyme. Thus deaminated catecholamines are good substrates for COMT (Guldberg and Marsden, 1975) and O-methylated catecholamines are good substrates for MAO (Houslay and Tipton, 1976).

The COMT present *in brain* is immunologically similar to the enzyme ubiquitously distributed in various peripheral organs (Axelrod, 1971; Borchardt and Cheng, 1978), and little evidence exists for the presence of multiple forms of COMT in a particular species (Borchardt and Cheng, 1978; Rock *et al.*, 1970). Although most COMT is located in the cytosol, rat brain does contain a significant amount of COMT that is recovered with the microsomal fraction (Borchardt and Cheng, 1978). The cytosolic and extraneuronal localization of COMT (Axelrod, 1971; Borchardt and Cheng, 1978) allows for O-methylation of released NE, both outside the neuron and after reuptake into the neuron terminal. The membrane-bound enzyme activity has approximately a threefold lower K_m for norepinephrine than does the soluble form of the enzyme (Borchardt and Cheng, 1978). Whether the membrane-bound COMT is a physiologically important form of this enzyme has yet to be established.

Partially purified COMT from the cytosol of human brain has been found to demonstrate a significantly lower K_m for dihydroxybenzoic acid compared with the K_m for dopamine (White and Wu, 1975), and this kinetic behavior has led to speculation that, within neurons, the deamination of catecholamines may normally precede metabolism by COMT. S-Adenosylmethionine (SAM) is an obligatory cosubstrate for the O-methylation of a large number of structurally different catechols by COMT, and the O-methylation of epinephrine and norepinephrine results primarily in the formation of the m-methoxy derivative of these catecholamines (White and Wu, 1975; Flohe and Hennies, 1977). COMT exhibits a low K_m for SAM, but S-adenosylhomocysteine (SAH), which is one of the reaction products, is a potent inhibitor of COMT activity (Flohe and Schwabe, 1972). Because approximately equal concentrations of SAM and SAH are present in most tissues (Salvatore et al., 1971), COMT activity would be strongly influenced by the ratio of SAM to SAH at any particular time.

Peripherally administered catecholamines are rapidly metabolized by COMT, primarily in liver (Axelrod, 1971), but controversy still exists regarding the role played by brain COMT in the inactivation of the neuronally released NE. The administration of pyrogallol, a competitive inhibitor of COMT, did not increase brain catecholamine levels, but administration of another type of COMT inhibitor (U-0521) was reported to increase brain NE levels (Crout et al., 1961; Giles and Miller, 1967). Moreover, levels of *normetanephrine* in brain are increased after inhibition of MAO (Giles and Miller, 1967). Thus COMT activity does play a role in the intraneuronal NE metabolism if the competing enzyme MAO is inhibited (Borchardt and Cheng, 1978). The inability to increase amine levels with the use of certain COMT inhibitors *in vivo* may be a consequence of the competition between COMT and MAO for NE within the neuron terminal and of differences between *in vitro* and *in vivo* accessibility of inhibitors to COMT located within the NE neuron terminals.

O-Methylation of NE may also occur in the extraneuronal compartments of brain. A paper by Kaplan et al. (1979) demonstrated by use of immunohistochemistry that ventricular ependymal cells and the choroid plexus contained the greatest amounts of COMT in brain. Glial elements also demonstrated significant amounts of immunoreactive COMT, but neurons were shown to contain little or no COMT activity. Although this work does not exclude the presence of small amounts of COMT in neurons, other evidence points to extraneuronal compartments as major sites of normetanephrine production and its further metabolism.

The O-methylated derivative of norepinephrine is a poor substrate for "Uptake$_1$", which is the system responsible for neuronal NE reuptake (Iversen, 1973). Normetanephrine is, however, rapidly accumulated in brain slices by an extraneuronal uptake system (Hendley et al., 1970), which has characteristics similar to the "Uptake$_2$" systems described by Iversen (Iversen, 1973). Monoamine oxidases, as well as enzymes that further metabolize the aldehyde produced from NE, are present in both neuronal and extraneuronal (e.g., glial) compartments in brain (Duncan et al., 1972). Therefore, normetanephrine, whether formed in the neuron or taken up into extraneuronal sites, will be available for further metabolism by MAO and aldehyde dehydrogenases and reductases.

MAO is located on the outer membrane of mitochondria (Tipton, 1967), and two forms of MAO have been shown to occur in brain and have been labeled types A and B (Johnson, 1968). These forms are distinguished primarily by their substrate specificity and relative sensitivity to the MAO inhibitors clorgyline and deprenyl (Knoll and Maygar, 1972). Norepinephrine and normetanephrine are oxidatively deaminated primarily by type A MAO (Houslay and Tipton, 1974). It is this form of the enzyme that is significantly more sensitive to inhibition by clorgyline in vitro. The two MAO enzyme forms may, however, not represent distinct proteins, but may represent a single enzyme within different lipid domains in the mitochondrial outer membrane. Houslay and Tipton (1973) have demonstrated that the substrate preferences and inhibitor characteristics of electrophoretically separable forms of MAO (Collins et al., 1970) can be eliminated by treating the membrane-bound enzyme with chaotropic agents which disrupt protein–lipid aggregates.

Evidence has been presented to indicate that type A and B forms of MAO are located within different mitochondrial subtypes (Kroon and Valdstra, 1972; Owen et al., 1977) and that various parts of human brain may have different proportions of type A and B MAO activity (Owen et al., 1979). The relative distribution of type A MAO, estimated by in vitro assays, roughly correlates with the anatomical distribution of NE. Areas containing high concentrations of NE, such as the hypothalamus and hippocampus, have been shown to contain high amounts of type A MAO activity compared with other brain areas, but the human hippocampus also contains a high amount of type B MAO activity, which preferentially deaminates amines such as phenylethylamine and possibly dopamine (Glover et al., 1977; Owen et al., 1979). Although NE is one of the preferred substrates for type A MAO, it is at present premature to conclude that NE is deaminated in vivo by only type A MAO (Fowler and Callingham, 1978), and thus the functional significance of the various types of MAO *in vivo* has yet to be fully clarified. It is, however, clear that normetanephrine and metanephrine are converted by the mitochondrial MAO to a single product, i.e., the aldehyde derivative of these amines 3-methoxy-4-hydroxyphenylglycolaldehyde.

In blood, the action of several amine oxidases also result in the formation of aldehyde derivatives of normetanephrine and other amines. Bond and Cundall (1977) have recently characterized amine oxidase activity in human plasma, platelets, lymphocytes, and granulocytes. Platelets were shown to contain an amine oxidase quite similar to type B MAO from other organs. On the other hand, plasma contains an amine oxidase referred to as "benzylamine oxidase" (McEwen, 1971). Benzylamine oxidase utilizes pyridoxal as its prosthetic group, whereas the flavin moiety is utilized by mitochondrial MAO (McEwen *et al.*, 1966; Tipton, 1968). The difference in prosthetic groups between the mitochondrial type and plasma type amine oxidases also allows for a distinction between the enzymes by use of inhibitors that react with the prosthestic groups. Semicarbazide inhibits the plasma amine oxidase (McEwen, 1965), but clorgyline and deprenyl have little effect on the plasma amine oxidase activity (Bond and Cundall, 1977). Although normetanephrine is not a preferred substrate for the plasma amine oxidase, it is metabolized by this enzyme (McEwen, 1972), and significant deamination of this amine may take place within the blood. On the other hand, epinephrine, which possesses a secondary amine group, would not be a substrate for plasma amine oxidase (McEwen, 1972); and thus, circulating epinephrine would be oxidatively deaminated primarily by mitochondrial MAO in organs such as the liver.

IV. Enzymes Active in Producing the Alcohol Metabolites of NE

The deamination of NE, epinephrine, or normetanephrine by MAO plays little role in determining whether the final product of the metabolism of a biogenic amine will be an acid or an alcohol (e.g., MHPG or VMA). The final product of NE or epinephrine catabolism is determined by the characteristics of the enzymes that oxidize or reduce the aldehyde intermediates produced in the reaction catalyzed by MAO. Because many of the characteristics of these dehydrogenases and reductases have only recently been determined, a more extensive discussion of these enzymes is included in this chapter.

The finding that NADPH, rather than NADH, was the preferred cofactor for the reduction of "biogenic aldehydes" to their alcohol derivatives by brain tissue (Eccleston *et al.,* 1966; Feldstein and Williamson, 1968) casts doubt on the earlier contention that formation of the alcohol derivatives (e.g., MHPG) of the biogenic amines was catalyzed by an alcohol dehydrogenase similar to that found in liver. NADH is the preferred cofactor for alcohol dehydrogenase and pyrazole is a characteristic and potent inhibitor of alcohol dehydrogenase, but the inclusion of pyrazole in reaction mixtures containing rat brain homogenate did not affect the production of MHPG by these homogenates (Anderson *et al.,* 1976). Furthermore, although human liver alcohol dehydrogenase will metabolize the aldehyde derivatives of NE (Wermuth and Munch, 1979), the alcohol dehydrogenase derived from liver of other species (e.g., horse) does not seem to catalyze readily the reduction of 3,4-dihydroxyphenylglycolaldehyde (Duncan, 1975). Thus the small amount of alcohol dehydrogenase present in brain (Raskin and Sokoloff, 1972) does not play a major role in production of MHPG, although it may be of possible importance in an as-yet-undetermined biological function.

On the other hand, an NADPH-dependent enzyme that could reduce a wide variety of aromatic and aliphatic aldehydes to their alcohol derivatives has been isolated from bovine brain (Tabakoff and Erwin, 1970). The hypothalamus and brain stem contained the highest amounts of this enzyme activity (Tabakoff and Erwin, 1970), and the aldehyde derivatives of catecholamines and indoleamines were found to be some of the substrates metabolized by this enzyme (Tabakoff *et al.,* 1973). This enzyme was also found to be sensitive to inhibition by barbiturates (Erwin *et al.,* 1971) and phenothiazines (Bronaugh and Erwin, 1972) but was not inhibited by pyrazole (Tabakoff and Erwin, 1970). In the course of the studies of bovine brain a second enzyme that metabolized aldehydes to alcohols, using either NADH or NADPH as a cofactor, was also noted (Tabakoff and Erwin, 1970). This enzyme activity was separable from the NADPH-dependent enzyme and was partially purified and characterized by Erwin *et al.* (1972). Studies using pig brain (Turner and Tipton, 1972) and rat brain (Ris and von Wartburg, 1973) similarly established the presence of two enzyme forms that were capable of reducing biogenic aldehydes. These brain enzymes were classified as alcohol : NAD(P) oxidoreductases (EC 1.1.1.2) (aldehyde reductases) (Tabakoff and Erwin, 1970). Turner and Tipton (1972), after establishing that one form of aldehyde reductase exhibited much lower Michaelis constants (K_m values) for various aldehydes than the second form, designated the two enzyme forms as the "low K_m" and "high K_m" enzymes. The two enzyme forms isolated from rat brain by Ris and von Wartburg

(1973) and labeled as enzyme 4.1 and 4.2 have, respectively, strong similarities with the high K_m and low K_m forms isolated from pig brain by Turner and Tipton (1972). The brain "aldose reductases" isolated by Dons and Doughty (1976) also have many properties in common with the previously mentioned enzymes and may be equivalent to the aldehyde reductases. In further discussion we shall use the designation "Form 1" to refer to the "NADPH-dependent aldehyde reductase," the high K_m enzyme and rat brain enzyme form 4.1, because these forms of aldehyde reductase seem to be equivalent. "Form 2" will be used in reference to the low K_m enzyme and the rat brain enzyme form 4.2 due to their many similarities (e.g., their ability to use either NADH or NADPH as a cofactor). It should be noted at this point, however, that human brain has been shown (Ris and von Wartburg, 1973) to have four separable forms of aldehyde reductase. One form, labeled AR-3 by Ris and von Wartburg (1973), closely resembles Form 1 derived from other mammalian species, whereas a second form of the human brain reductase, AR-2 (Ris and von Wartburg, 1973), has certain properties in common with Form 2 reductase found in rat and pig brain. The remaining two forms of human brain aldehyde reductases correspond to an aromatic ketone reductase found in various tissues of mammals (Sawada and Hara, 1978) and a reductase of narrow substrate specificity, which reduces succinic semialdehyde to γ-hydroxybutyrate (Anderson *et al.*, 1977; Hoffman *et al.*, 1980).

Form 1 and Form 2 aldehyde reductases are those primarily responsible for reduction of aldehydes derived from NE but Forms 1 and 2 aldehyde reductases do differ in substrate and cofactor specifities and sensitivity to various inhibitors. Form 1 enzyme isolated from bovine, rat, and pig brain and the AR-3 form (Form 1) of human brain reductase are relatively specific in their use of NADPH as a cofactor (Tabakoff and Erwin, 1970; Turner and Tipton, 1972; Ris and von Wartburg, 1973). Form 2 brain aldehyde reductase can utilize NADH, as well as NADPH (Turner and Tipton, 1972; Ris and von Wartburg, 1973), and in fact, NADH is the preferred cofactor for reduction of aldehydes by Form 2 enzyme from bovine brain (Erwin *et al.*, 1972). Both forms of aldehyde reductase possess a broad substrate specificity, which includes aromatic and aliphatic aldehydes (Tabakoff and Erwin, 1970; Turner and Tipton, 1972; Ris and von Wartburg, 1973). The enzymes have been shown to catalyze the reduction of a number of aldehyde derivatives of the biogenic amines; the aldehydes that have an α-hydroxy group are preferred substrates (Tabakoff *et al.*, 1973).

Many psychoactive drugs have been shown to inhibit aldehyde reductases from brain. It is worth noting that most of the drugs are better inhibitors of Form 1 aldehyde reductase than of Form 2. Barbituric acid derivatives carrying substituents at the 5 position have been shown to be noncompetitive inhibitors of Form 1 aldehyde reductase from bovine (Erwin *et al.,* 1971), pig (Turner and Tipton, 1972), human (Ris and von Wartburg, 1973), and rat brain (Tabakoff *et al.,* 1973), with the K_i values ranging from 0.03 to 4 mM (Erwin *et al.,* 1971; Tabakoff *et al.,* 1973). The ionized form of the barbiturates was found to be the actual inhibitor of aldehyde reductase (Erwin *et al.,* 1971) and the metabolites of the barbiturates, which have little or no sedative properties (Sharpless, 1970), were found to be poor inhibitors of Form 1 enzyme (Erwin *et al.,* 1971). On the other hand, even the physiologically active barbiturates are relatively poor inhibitors of Form 2 aldehyde reductase from various species (Erwin *et al.,* 1972; Ris and von Wartburg, 1973). Concentrations of barbiturate producing nearly total inhibition of Form 1 aldehyde reductase from rat brain inhibited the activity of Form 2 enzyme by only 30% (Ris and von Wartburg, 1973). Several other groups of compounds have been found to inhibit differentially the two forms of aldehyde reductase from mammalian brain (Erwin and Deitrich, 1973; Ris *et al.,* 1975). The structural feature that seems to be important for producing a potent inhibitor of Form 1 enzyme, but having little inhibitory effect on Form 2, is the presence of the —CONHCO—grouping within the structure of the drug and a minimal lipophilic substitution (Erwin and Deitrich, 1973; Ris *et al.,* 1975). Compounds such as phenothiazines, which do not contain this "pharmacophoric" grouping, although inhibiting aldehyde reductase activity (Bronaugh and Erwin, 1972), do not exhibit differential effects on the two forms of the reductase derived from mammalian brain (Ris and von Wartburg, 1973).

As already mentioned, the major feature distinguishing brain aldehyde reductases from alcohol dehydrogenase of the type found in liver is the insensitivity of the reductases to inhibition by pyrazole (Tabakoff and Erwin, 1970). Several other major differences are also evident in the characteristics of brain aldehyde reductases when compared with liver alcohol dehydrogenase. These differences include the cofactor specificity, the number of subunits (brain reductases exist as active monomers whereas liver alcohol dehydrogenase is a dimer), the molecular weight, and the reaction mechanism (Wermuth *et al.,* 1977). Wemuth, Munch, and von Wartburg (1977) have suggested, however, that the monomeric reductases served as evolutionary precursors of the diversified oligomeric dehydrogenases.

When the subcellular distribution of Form 1 and Form 2 aldehyde reductase was examined in rat brain, the Form 1 enzyme was found to reside primarily in the cytosol, whereas the Form 2 enzyme was localized primarily to the mitochondrial fraction (Anderson *et al.*, 1976). By use of selective inhibitors, Anderson *et al.* (1976) demonstrated that, in rat brain, Form 2 aldehyde reductase was primarily responsible for the production of MHPG from the aldehyde derived from nor-metanephrine. One may conclude that both the production of biogenic aldehydes by monoamine oxidase and their subsequent metabolism to their alcohol derivatives within the neuron would take place on or within the mitochondria.

When considering differences between CNS and peripheral metabo-lism of NE, the tissue distribution of Form 1 and Form 2 aldehyde reductase becomes an important issue. In several studies of livers of humans (Wermuth *et al.*, 1977) and other animals (Feldsted *et al.*, 1977; Tulsiani and Touster, 1977), no evidence for the presence of Form 2 aldehyde reductase was gathered, although Form 1 enzyme was clearly shown to be present in liver and other peripheral tissues (Bosron and Prairie, 1973). Human liver also contains substantial amounts of alcohol dehydrogenase (EC 1.1.1.1), which can metabolize 3-methoxy-4-hy-droxyphenylglycolaldehyde to MHPG (Wermuth and Munch, 1979). Under normal physiological conditions, the high NAD/NADH ratios found in liver (Schulman *et al.*, 1974), however, prevent the liver alcohol dehydrogenase from catalyzing the reduction of various aldehydes pre-sent at low concentrations in this organ. The absence of Form 2 al-dehyde reductase in liver and the ability of the *aldehyde dehydrogenase* in this tissue to compete effectively for aldehyde substrates are, therefore, important features that determine the path of biogenic aldehyde metab-olism in the periphery.

V. Enzymes Active in Producing the Acid Metabolites of NE

The oxidation of aldehydes in brain and other tissues depends pri-marily on the activity of NAD-dependent aldehyde dehydrogenases (al-dehyde : NAD oxidoreductases EC 1.2.1.3) (Deitrich, 1966; Racker, 1949). The aldehyde dehydrogenases that catalyze the oxidation of bio-genic aldehydes to the acid excretion products possess a broad substrate specificity and occur in various tissues in multiple molecular forms, which are selectively distributed in the cytosol or mitochondria (Siew *et al.*, 1976; Tottmar and Marchner, 1976). Two forms of aldehyde de-hydrogenase may be present in mitochondria derived from liver (Siew *et al.*, 1976). The enzyme form found in the mitochondrial matrix in the rat exhibits a particularly low K_m value for a variety of aldehydes and is quite sensitive to inhibition by disulfiram and cyanamid (Deitrich *et al.*, 1976; Siew *et al.*, 1976). Although there is growing evidence that liver and brain aldehyde dehydrogenases are not identical (Deitrich *et al.*, 1976), brain mitochondria also contains an aldehyde dehydrogenase that has a high affinity for a variety of aldehyde substrates (Erwin and Deitrich, 1966; Duncan *et al.*, 1971). Brain aldehyde dehydrogeanse, however, displays a substantially higher K_m for α-hydroxy-substituted aldehydes compared with aldehydes lacking the α-hydroxy substituent (Duncan and Sourkes, 1974). The aldehyde derivative of dopamine is, therefore, a significantly better substrate for brain mitochondrial aldehyde dehydrogenase than the aldehyde derivative of normetanephrine (Duncan and Sourkes, 1974). As previously stated, Form 2 aldehyde reductase, which is also located in brain mitochondria, exhibits a lower K_m and a substantially higher maximum velocity with the α-hydroxy-substituted aldehydes derived from normetanephrine, as compared with the aldehyde derivative of dopamine. The ability of Form 2 aldehyde reductase to compete effectively with brain aldehyde dehydrogenases for the aldehyde derivative of normetanephrine may be the determining feature of why NE is primarily metabolized to its alcohol derivative in brain.

Aldehyde dehydrogenase activity is found in all brain areas, but a greater amount of enzyme activity has been noted in areas such as the striatum (Erwin and Deitrich, 1966). This anatomical distribution of brain aldehyde dehydrogenase may be responsible for the greater amounts of VMA found in the striatum of rat brain, as compared with other brain areas (Karoum *et al.*, 1976), even though the actual source of brain VMA remains an enigma (Ader *et al.*, 1978). VMA is distributed in brain in a manner that does not correspond to the distribution of NE (Karoum *et al.*, 1976), and stimulation or destruction of NE neurons in brain does not produce changes in brain VMA levels (Ader *et al.*, 1978).

In the liver Form 1 aldehyde reductase will to a certain extent compete with aldehyde dehydrogenase for metabolism of the aldehyde derivatives of the adrenergic amines. The extent of this competition in a particular species will depend on the relative activities of the dehydrogenases and reductases in the peripheral organs and the distribution of these enzymes in the subcellular compartments of an organ such as the liver. The mitochondrial localization of at least a portion of the dehydrogenase activity may provide greater access for this enzyme to aldehydes produced by the MAO reaction sequence. Biogenic amines deaminated by plasma MAO may also be oxidized by the recently described aldehyde dehydrogenase present in plasma and erythrocytes in humans (Pietruszko and Vallari, 1978). No aldehyde dehydrogenase activity was noted in rat blood (Deitrich, 1966), and this difference between rat and human may account for the fact that VMA constitutes a lesser portion of urinary NE and epinephrine metabolites in rat than in man. Although some aldehyde reductase activity may be present in platelets (Pletscher, 1968), norepinephrine and epinephrine would be excluded from metabolism within this physiologic compartment because of the lack of specific uptake systems for catecholamines in platelets (Pletscher, 1968). The metabolism of epinephrine and norepinephrine released into the circulatory system of humans would be, therefore, weighted toward the production of the acid excretion product, both within the blood and within the liver. Only under conditions in which the low K_m aldehyde dehydrogenase activity of organs such as the liver is inhibited would the alcohol derivative of peripherally derived NE or epinephrine constitute a major catabolic product of these amines. The administration of disulfiram to humans was shown to shift the catabolism of NE toward the reductive pathway (Smith *et al.*, 1966), and the introduction of a competitive substrate for the aldehyde dehydrogenase, such as acetaldehyde, also produced a similar shift in metabolism of NE (Davis *et al.*, 1976; Majchrowicz, 1975).

VI. Enzymes Active in Producing the Sulfate or Glucuronide Conjugates of MHPG

MHPG appears in the urine of humans primarily as a sulfate or glucuronide conjugate (Karoum *et al.*, 1973). Little if any MHPG has been found conjugated with glucuronide in the brain of several animal species (Karoum *et al.*, 1977; Maas *et al.*, 1976), and, therefore, glucuronide conjugation is most probably a feature of peripheral MHPG metabolism. In human brain, less than 25% of the MHPG is present as the sulfate conjugate (see Hattox, Chapter 5, in this volume). On the other hand, MHPG in rat brain is present nearly totally as its sulfate ester (Karoum *et al.*, 1976; Schanberg *et al.*, 1968). The enzyme responsible for the conjugation of MHPG with sulfate is phenol sulfotransferase (PST; 3'-phosphoadenylsulfatophosphate : phenol sulfotransferase EC 2.8.2.1). This enzyme, which uses adenosine 3'-phosphate-5'-sulfophosphate as the sulfate donor (Pennings *et al.*, 1977), is localized in the cytosol of cells (Jansen *et al.*, 1974) and is unevenly distributed in various parts of brain, with the hypothalamus having a substantially greater amount of enzyme activity than other parts of the brain (Foldes and Meek, 1974). Denervation studies indicate that PST is not localized primarily in noradrenergic neurons (Foldes and Meek, 1974). There is, however, good correlation between the absolute levels of PST present in brain of a particular animal species and the proportion of MHPG appearing in the free or sulfate-conjugated form in brain. Thus human brain has substantially less enzyme activity per gram than rat brain (Foldes and Meek, 1974), and as previously mentioned, the major portion of MHPG in brain appears in the free form (Karoum *et al.*, 1977). The formation of the sulfate conjugate of MHPG in brain allows for the active transport of this metabolite out of the CNS by the probenecid-sensitive organic acid transport system (Meek and Neff, 1972), whereas free MHPG is probably removed by passive diffusion into the plasma. Brain levels of free MHPG are little affected by pretreatment of animals with probenecid. The MHPG appearing in the plasma can be sulfate-conjugated by PST that is present in organs other than brain (Foldes and Meek, 1974), or it may be converted to its glucuronide conjugate.

Although it is clear that the presence and specificity of the various aldehyde reductases and dehydrogenases in different organs of the body determine the catabolic pathway that a particular amine such as NE will follow in that organ, several other considerations enter into the calculation of the proportion of urinary metabolites of a biogenic amine that are derived from an organ such as the brain. One must have knowledge regarding the *rates* of formation and elimination of NE metabolites from various organs. This factor is particularly important when one considers that MHPG produced at one locus, e.g., brain, may be transported to another tissue, such as liver, and reoxidized to an aldehyde and then further oxidized to VMA (Blombery *et al.*, 1980). The amount of any metabolite formed is also dependent on the pool size of epinephrine and norepinephrine available for metabolism at any particular time. Less than 10% of brain MAO, COMT, and aldehyde reductase activity has been localized in synaptosomes prepared from brain (Anderson *et al.*, 1976; Borchardt and Cheng, 1978; Tabakoff *et al.*, 1974), but the activity of these enzymes under physiological conditions in this compartment would be several times higher than necessary to account for the measured turnover rates for amines such as NE (e.g., <1 nmol/h/gm rat brain) (Neff *et al.*, 1970), and thus the rate-limiting process is the release of the amines into the catabolic pool.

VII. Estimates of CNS NE Metabolism by Measures of Urinary MHPG

By measuring venous–arterial differences in the concentration of MHPG, Maas *et al.* (1977, 1979) have estimated that approximately 60% of MHPG found in human urine is derived from CNS NE metabolism. Previous studies in which CNS NE neurons of monkeys were lesioned with 6-hydroxydopamine (6-OHDA) also indicated that a substantial amount of urinary MHPG in primates is derived from the CNS (Maas *et al.*, 1972). On the other hand, the intraventricular administration of 6-OHDA, which produced approximately a 65% depletion of brain NE in rats, had little effect on urinary MHPG excretion in this species (Bareggi *et al.*, 1974). If one calculates the production and excretion of MHPG by rat brain using the data provided by Karoum *et al.* (1976), one finds that in rat only 4–5% of urinary MHPG (Bareggi *et al.*, 1974) can be ascribed to brain metabolism of NE. On the other hand, if one extrapolates to humans from the data on brain MHPG elimination rates in nonhuman primates or uses data derived directly from human subjects (Maas *et al.*, 1977, 1979), one can calculate that approximately 50% of human urinary MHPG is derived from the CNS within a 24-h period. This value could be diminished if MHPG produced in brain is per chance oxidized in peripheral organs or blood. The determinant features of species differences in MHPG excretion, therefore, are (1) the relative rates of NE and epinephrine turnover in the brain and periphery of a particular species and (2) the distribution and the characteristics of the aldehyde dehydrogenases, reductases, and other amine catabolizing enzymes in the species under investigation.

VIII. Summary

Substantial species specific differences exist in the quantities of urinary MHPG that can be traced to the CNS metabolism of NE. The determinants of these differences are related to the rates of NE turnover and the biochemical profiles of the amine-catabolizing enzymes in the CNS and peripheral organs of each species. The enzymes primarily responsible for determining whether a particular biogenic amine transmitter (e.g., NE) is metabolized to its acid or alcohol excretion product are the aldehyde reductases and aldehyde dehydrogenases. The characteristics and tissue distributions of these enzymes as well as the characteristics of MAO, COMT, and conjugating enzymes are described in this chapter, and it is concluded that an understanding of all the catabolic enzymes is necessary for the proper interpretation of the sources of urinary MHPG in a given species.

References

Ader, I. P., Muskiet, F. A. J., Ieuring, H. J., and Korf, J. 1978. *J. Neurochem.* **30**, 1213–1216.

Anderson, R. A., Meyerson, L. R., and Tabakoff, B. 1976. *Neurochem. Res.* **1**, 525–540.

Anderson, R. A., Ritzmann, R. F., and Tabakoff, B. 1977. *J. Neurochem.* **28**, 633–639.

Axelrod, J. 1971. *Science* **173**, 597–606.

Bareggi, S. R., Marc, V., and Morselli, P. L. 1974. *Brain Res.* **75**, 177–180.

Blombery, A., Kopin, I. J., Gordon, E. K., Markey, S. P., and Ebert, M. H. 1980. *Arch. Gen. Psychiatry* **37**, 1095–1098.

Bond, P. A., and Cundall, R. L. 1977. *Clin. Chim. Acta.* **80**, 317–326.

Borchardt, R., and Cheung, C. F. 1978. *Biochem. Biophys. Acta* **522**, 49–62.

Bosron, W. F., and Prairie, R. L. 1973. *Arch. Biochem. Biophys.* **154**, 166–172.

Bronaugh, R. L., and Erwin, V. G. 1972. *Biochem. Pharmacol.* **21**, 1457–1465.

Collins, G. G. S., Sandler, M., Williams, E. D., and Youdim, M. B. H. 1970. *Nature* **255**, 817–820.

Crout, J. R., Creveling, C. R., and Udenfriend, S. 1961. *J. Pharmacol. Exp. Ther.* **132**, 269–277.

Davis, V. E., Brown, H., Huff, J. A., and Cashaw, J. E. 1967. *J. Lab. Clin. Med.* **69**, 787–799.

Deitrich, R. A. 1966. *Biochem. Pharmacol.* **15**, 1911–1922.

Deitrich, R. A., Troxell, P. A., and Worth, W. S. 1976. *Biochem. Pharmacol.* **25**, 2733–2737.

Dons, R. F., and Doughty, C. C. 1976. *Biochem. Biophys. Acta* **452**, 1–12.

Duncan, R. J. S. 1975. *Can. J. Biochem.* **53**, 920–922.

Duncan, R. J. S., and Sourkes, T. L. 1974. *J. Neurochem.* **22**, 663–669.

Duncan, R. J. S., Sourkes, T. L., Boucher, R., Poirier, L. J., and Roberge, A. 1972. *J. Neurochem.* **19**, 2007–2010.

Duncan, R. J. S., and Tipton, K. F. 1971. *J. Biochem.* **22**, 257–262.

Eccleston, D., Moir, A. T. B., Reading, H. W., and Ritchie, I. M. 1966. *Br. J. Pharmacol. Chemother.* **28**, 367–377.

Erwin, V. G., and Deitrich, R. A. 1966. *J. Biol. Chem.* **241(15)**, 3533–3539.

Erwin, V. G., and Deitrich, R. A. 1973. *Biochem. Pharmacol.* **22**, 2615–2524.

Erwin, V. G., Heston, W. D. W., and Tabakoff, B. 1972. *J. Neurochem.* **19**, 2269–2278.

Erwin, V. G., Tabakoff, B., and Bronaugh, R. L. 1971. *Mol. Pharmacol.* **7(2)**, 169–176.

Felsted, R. L., Gee, M., and Bachur, N. R. 1974. *J. Biol. Chem.* **249**, 3672–3677.

Felsted, R. L., Richter, D. R., and Bachur, N. R. 1977. *Biochem. Pharmacol.* **26**, 1117–1124.

Feldstein, A., and Williamson, O. 1968. *Br. J. Pharmacol.* **34**, 38–42.

Flohe, L., and Hennies, H. H. 1977. *Structure and Function of Monoamine Enzymes* (E. Usdin, N. Weiner, and M. B. H. Youdim, eds.), pp. 675–706. Marcel-Decker, New York.

Flohe, L., and Schwabe, K. P. 1972. Hoppe-Seyler's, Z. *Physiol. Chem.* **353**, 463–475.
Foldes, A., and Meek, J. L. 1974. *J. Neurochem.* **23**, 303–307.
Fowler, C. J., and Callingham, B. A. 1978. *Biochem. Pharmacol.* **27**, 97–101.
Giles, R. E., and Miller, J. W. 1967. *J. Pharm. Exper. Ther.* **158**, 189–194.
Glover, V., Sandler, M., Owen, F., and Riley, G. J. 1977. *Nature* **265**, 80–81.
Guldberg, H. C., and Marsden, C. A. 1975. *Pharmacol. Rev.* **27**, 135–206.
Hassan, A. 1971. *Biochem. Pharmacol.* **20**, 2299–2308.
Hendley, E. D., Taylor, K. M., and Snyder, S. H. 1970. *Eur. J. Pharmacol.* **12**, 167–179.
Hoffman, P. L., Wermuth, B., and von Wartburg, J. P. 1980. *J. Neurochem.* **35**, 354–366.
Houslay, M. D., and Tipton, K. F. 1973. *Biochem. J.* **135**, 173–186.
Houslay, M. D., and Tipton, K. F. 1974. *Biochem. J.* **139**, 645–652.
Houslay, M. D., and Tipton, K. F. 1976. *Life Sci.* **19**, 467–478.
Iversen, L. L. 1973. *Br. Med. Bull.* **29**, 130–135.
Jansen, G. S. I. M., Vrensen, G. F. J. M., and Van Kempen, G. M. J. 1974. *J. Neurochem.* **23**, 329–335.
Johnston, J. P. 1968. *Biochem. Pharmacol.* **17**, 1285–1297.
Kaplan, G. P., Hartman, B. K., and Creveling, C. R. 1979. *Brain Res.* **167**, 241–250.
Karoum, F., Lefevre, H., Bigelow, L. B., and Costa, E. 1973. *Clin. Chim. Acta.* **43**, 127–137.
Karoum, F., Moyer-Schwing, I., Potkin, S. G., and Wyatt, R. J. 1977. *Brain Res.* **125**, 333–339.
Karoum, F., Neff, N. H., and Wyatt, R. J. 1976. *J. Neurochem.* **27**, 33–35.
Knoll, J., and Magyar, K. 1972. *Adv. Biochem. Psychopharmacol.* **5**, 393–408.
Korf, J., Aghajanian, G. K., and Roth, R. H. 1973. *Eur. J. Pharmacol.* **21**, 302–310.
Kroon, M. C., and Veldstra, H. 1972. *FEBS Lett.* **24**, 173–176.
Maas, J. W., Dekirmenjian, H., Garver, D., Redmond, Jr., D. E., and Landis, D. H. 1972. *Brain Res.* **41**, 507–511.
Maas, J. W., Hattox, S. E., Landis, D. H., and Roth, R. H. 1977. *Eur. J. Pharmacol.* **6**, 221–228.
Maas, J. W., Hattox, S. E., Greene, N. M., and Landis, D. H. 1979. *Science* **205**, 1025–1027.
Maas, J. W., Landis, D. H., and Dekirmenjian H. 1976. *Psychoparmacol. Commun.* **2**, 403–410.
Majchrowicz, E. 1975. *Adv. Exp. Med. Biol.* **56**, 111–134.
McEwen, Jr., C. M. 1965. *J. Biol. Chem.* **240**, 2003–2010.
McEwen, Jr., C. M. 1971. *Methods Enzymol.* **178B**, 692–698.
McEwen, Jr., C. M. 1972. *Adv. Biochem. Psychopharmacol.* **5**, 151–165.
McEwen, Jr., C. M., Cullen, K. T., and Sober, A. J. 1966. *J. Biol. Chem.* **241**, 4544–4556.
Meek, J. L., and Neff, N. H. 1972. *J. Pharmacol. Exp. Ther.* **181**, 457–461.
Neff, N. H., Spano, P. F., Groppetti, A., Wang, C. T., and Costa, E. 1970. *J. Pharmacol. Exper. Ther.* **176**, 701–710.
Owen, F., Bourne, R. C., Lai, J. C. K., and Williams, R. 1977. *Biochem. Pharmacol.* **26**, 289–293.
Owen, F., Cross, A. J., and Lofthouse, R. 1979. *Biochem. Pharmacol.* **28**, 1077–1080.
Pennings, E. J. M., Vrielink, R., and Van Kempen, G. M. J. 1977. *Biochem. J.* **307**, 299–307.
Pietruszko, R., and Vallari, R. C. 1978. *FEBS Lett.* **92**, 89–91.
Pletscher, A. 1968. *Br. J. Pharmacol. Chemother.* **32**, 1–16.
Racker, E. 1949. *J. Biol. Chem.* **177**, 883–892.
Raskin, N. H., and Sokoloff, L. 1972. *J. Neurochem.* **19**, 273–282.
Ris, M. M., Deitrich, R. A., and von Wartburg, J. P. 1975. *Biochem. Pharmacol.* **24**, 1865–1869.
Ris, M. M., and von Wartburg, J. P. 1973. *Eur. J. Biochem.* **27**, 69–77.

Rock, G. D., Tong, J. H., and D'Iorio, A. D. 1970. *Can. J. Biochem.* **48,** 1326–1331.

Salvatore, F., Utili, R., Zappia, V., and Shapire, S. K. 1971. *Anal. Biochem.* **41,** 16–28.

Sawada, H., and Hara, A. 1978. *Biochem. Pharmacol.* **28,** 1089–1094.

Schanberg, S. M., Schildkraut, J. J., Breese, G. R., and Koplin, I. J. 1968. *Biochem. Pharmacol.* **17,** 247–254.

Schulman, M. P., Gupta, N. K., Omachi, A., Hoffman, G., and Marshall, W. E. 1974. *Anal. Biochem.* **60,** 302–311.

Sharpless, S. K. 1970. *The Pharmacological Basis of Therapeutics* (I. S. Goodman, and A. Gilman, eds.) pp. 98–120. Macmillan, New York.

Siew, C., Deitrich, R. A., and Erwin, V. G. 1976. *Arch. Biochem. Biophys.* **176I,** 638–649.

Smith, A. A., and Gitlow, S. 1966. *Biochemical Factors in Alcoholism* (R. P. Maickel, eds.) p. 53. Pergamon Press, Oxford.

Tabakoff, B., Anderson, R., and Alivisatos, S. G. A. 1973. *Mol. Pharmacol.* **9(4),** 428–437.

Tabakoff, B., and Erwin, V. G. 1970. *J. Biol. Chem.* **216(12),** 3263–3268.

Tabakoff, B., Meyerson, L., and Alivisatos, S. G. A. 1974. *Brain Res.* **66,** 491–508.

Tipton, K. F. 1967. *Biochem. Biophys. Acta* **135,** 910–920.

Tipton, K. F. 1968. *Biochem. Biophys. Acta* **159,** 451–459.

Tottmar, O., and Marchner, H. 1976. *Acta Pharm. Toxicol.* **38,** 366–375.

Tulsiani, D. R. P., and Touster, O. 1977. *J. Biol. Chem.* **252,** 2545–2550.

Turner, A. J., and Tipton, K. F. 1972a. *Biochem. J.* **130,** 765–772.

Turner, A. J., and Tipton, K. F. 1972b. *Eur. J. Biochem.* **30,** 361–368.

Weiner, N. 1970. *Ann. Rev. Pharmacol.* **10,** 273–290.

Weiner, N., and Bjur, R. 1972. *Adv. Biochem. Psychopharmacol.* **5,** 409–419.

Wemuth, B., and Munch, J. D. B. 1979. *Biochem. Pharmacol.* **28,** 1431–1433.

Wermuth, B., Munch, J. D. B., and von Wartburg, J. P. 1977. *J. Biol. Chem.* **252,** 3821–3828.

White, H. L., and Wu, J. C. 1975. *Biochem. J.* **145,** 135–143.

2

Neuronal Activity, Impulse Flow, and MHPG Production

ROBERT H. ROTH

Yale University School of Medicine, New Haven

I. Introduction

Since the mid-1960s it has been appreciated that stimulation of peripheral sympathetic noradrenergic neurons causes an increase in the release, turnover, and catabolism of norepinephrine (NE) as well as an acceleration of NE biosynthesis in the terminals of the stimulated neurons (see Salzman and Roth, 1979). The increase in NE synthesis appears to be due to an acceleration of the enzymatic hydroxylation of tyrosine by tyrosine hydroxylase, whereas the increase in metabolite levels occurs as a result of enhanced transmitter release and the consequent exposure of NE to degradative enzymes. Short-term stimulation (minutes) of peripheral sympathetic nerves does not produce alterations in the activity of degradative enzymes.

This initial work on catecholamine neurons in the peripheral nervous system laid the groundwork and supplied the impetus for similar experi-

19

MHPG: BASIC MECHANISMS
AND PSYCHOPATHOLOGY

ments to be conducted on the CNS. Studies on central NE neurons prior to the mid-1960s suffered from the lack of a well-defined anatomical description of central monoaminergic pathways. Prior to mapping out these neurons it was impossible to carry out electrophysiological studies on these systems in the brain. Biochemical studies were also greatly hampered. In fact, without a detailed anatomical map it was impossible to assess where to attempt stimulation of NE neurons or where to look for biochemical effects occurring in NE nerve terminals following experimental or pharmacological treatments. Despite these difficulties, several studies conducted in the late 1950s and early 1960s demonstrated that conditions such as stress, which were believed to cause an increase in the activity of central NE neurons, did lead to changes in the steady-state levels and in the turnover and catabolism of NE (Barchas and Freedman, 1963; Bliss *et al.*, 1968; Corrodi *et al.*, 1968; Paulsen and Hess, 1963).

II. Anatomy of NE Systems

With the advent of the fluorescent histochemical method for visualizing catecholamines within tissue sections and the subsequent mapping of central catecholamine neuroanatomy, the CNS, albeit more complex than the peripheral NE system, became increasingly more amenable to study. Subsequent to the anatomical mapping of NE systems the majority of *in vivo* studies on NE neurons in brain have focused on the noradrenergic neurons originating in the nucleus locus coeruleus. The locus coeruleus in the rat is located bilaterally beneath the floor of the fourth ventricle and consists almost exclusively of noradrenergic cell bodies. These cell bodies send out axonal processes to the cerebellum and forebrain regions as well as to the brain stem and spinal cord (cf. Fig. 1). The noradrenergic terminals in the cortex and hippocampus of the rat are largely supplied by the noradrenergic cell bodies originating in this nucleus. In the rat the locus coeruleus comprises a highly compact group of cells, which make it possible to stimulate effectively the efferent noradrenergic neurons by placing a stimulating electrode within or in close proximity to this nucleus (Fig. 2). Because of the anatomy it is also possible to destroy this system by placement of discrete electrolytic lesions in the locus coeruleus, by stereotaxic injection of 6-hydroxydopamine into the NE fiber bundles, or by transection of the NE fiber bundles. Although a small number of NE fibers originating from this

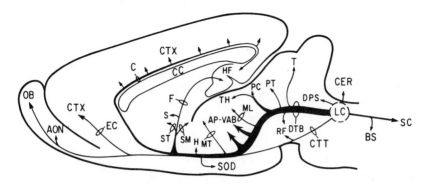

Fig. 1. Diagram of the projections of the locus coeruleus in the rat viewed in the sagittal plane. Abbreviations: AON, anterior olfactory nucleus; AP-VAB, ansa peduncularis-ventral amygdaloid bundle system; BS, brainstem, nuclei; C, cingulum; CC, corpus callosum; CER, cerebellum; CTT, central tegmental tract; CTX, cerebral neocortex; DPS, dorsal periventricular system; DTB, dorsal catecholamine bundle; EC, external capsule, F, fornix; H, hypothalamus; HF, hippocampal formation; LC, locus coeruleus; ML, medial lemniscus; MT, mammillothalamic tract; OB, olfactory bulb; PC, posterior commissure; PT, pretectal area; RF, reticular formation; S, septal area; SC, spinal cord; SM, stria medullaris; SOD, supraoptic decussations; ST, stria terminalis; T, tectum; TH, thalamus. (Diagram compiled by R. Y. Moore. Reproduced with permission from Cooper, Bloom, and Roth, 1978, Oxford Press.)

nucleus may cross the midline and innervate contralateral brain regions, the majority of the projections from this system are to ipsilateral structures.

Subsequent to mapping out the noradrenergic systems in the rodent brain, fluorescent histochemical techniques were also employed to disclose the anatomy of central monoamine systems in primates. It is interesting to note that the anatomy of central adrenergic systems in primate brain is quite similar to the anatomy of noradrenergic systems in rat brain (Bowden *et al.*, 1978; Fujita and Tanaka, 1974; Garver and Sladek, 1976; Gatter and Powell, 1977).

III. Impulse Flow and Transmitter Metabolism

Over the past decade a great deal of research has been directed at understanding the relationship between alterations in impulse flow and transmitter dynamics in chemically defined neurons in the central ner-

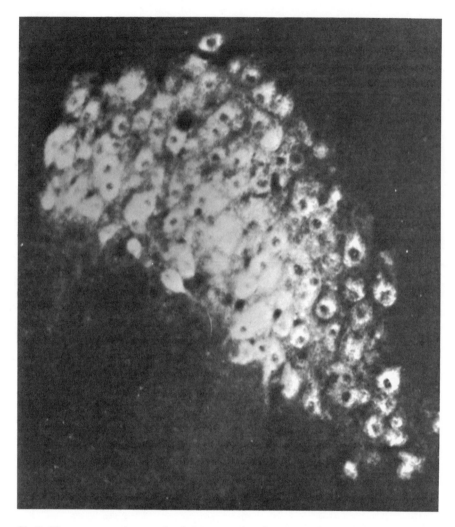

Fig.2. Fluorescence micrograph of the rat nucleus locus coeruleus. This frontal section through the principal portion of the nucleus illustrates the intensely fluorescent NE neurons clustered closely together. Within the neurons, the nucleus, which is not fluorescent after formaldehyde treatment, appears dark except for the nucleolus. (Reproduced with permission from Cooper, Bloom, and Roth, 1978, Oxford Press.)

vous system. Results indicate that monoamine systems in general appear to respond to alterations in impulse flow in a rather predictable fashion (see Roth et al., 1978; Salzman and Roth, 1979). The synthesis, release, and catabolism of transmitter are increased during periods of elevated physiological activity that require increased transmitter utilization. During periods of quiescence or reduced neuronal activity, when the demand for transmitter is diminished, transmitter synthesis, release, and catabolism are decreased. There are, of course, exceptions to this very broad generalization, the most notable being the response of central dopaminergic systems to a blockade of impulse flow. In dopamine systems such as the nigrostriatal and mesolimbic systems a cessation of impulse flow results in a decrease in the release and catabolism of dopamine but a paradoxical increase in dopamine biosynthesis. This increase in dopamine biosynthesis is mediated at the level of tyrosine hydroxylation and appears to be regulated by dopamine autoreceptors located on the dopaminergic nerve terminals (Nowycky and Roth, 1978). These dopaminergic autoreceptors also appear to control transmitter release. Similar autoreceptors are present on noradrenergic nerve terminals where they appear to be involved in the modulation of NE release. However, whether these noradrenergic autoreceptors play a role in the modulation of NE synthesis is at present uncertain.

In the last 10 years, it has been possible by the application of sophisticated methodologies to investigate carefully the dynamics of central catecholamine systems and their biochemical and electrophysiological responsiveness to experimental and pharmacological manipulations. In recent years there has been considerable interest in discovering a noninvasive technique for evaluating changes in functional activity of chemically defined neurons in the CNS of animals and man. In most instances, transmitter turnover measures have provided reliable techniques for measurement of changes in neuronal activity within chemically defined neuronal systems. However, many of the experimental techniques used to measure transmitter turnover in the CNS are not readily extrapolated to in vivo use in animals and man in a noninvasive manner. Thus, the emphasis has been to determine whether the transmitter in question, or a metabolite found in brain but egressing to an accessible body fluid such as blood or CSF, might provide some insight concerning changes in the overall function of central neurotransmitter systems. Implicit in this approach is the assumption that transmitter metabolite levels in brain or released transmitters do indeed reflect alterations in the functional activity of the transmitter system under study.

This chapter focuses on the relationship between altered neuronal activity and transmitter dynamics in central noradrenergic neurons with a particular emphasis on an examination of how the norepinephrine metabolite, 3-methoxy-4-hydroxyphenethylene glycol (MHPG), reflects changes in functional activity of noradrenergic systems in brain.

IV. Norepinephrine Metabolism

The biochemical pathways through which NE is metabolized are described in detail in the chapter by Tabakoff and DeLeon-Jones (Chapter 1), but for the purposes of this chapter may be briefly described as follows. Norepinephrine in the brain is catabolized by several enzymes: monoamine oxidase, catechol O-methyltransferase, aldehyde reductase, and aldehyde dehydrogenase. The catabolism of norepinephrine is depicted in Fig. 3. Norepinephrine as well as its metabolites can also be conjugated in the brain by the enzyme phenolsulfotransferase. In some animals, such as the rat, the major metabolites of NE found in the CNS exist in the conjugated form. In most animal species including man the primary NE metabolites found in the central nervous system are the O-methylated, deaminated reduced metabolite MHPG and the deaminated reduced metabolite 3,4-dihydroxyphenethylene glycol (DHPG). In rat brain MHPG occurs primarily in the conjugated form as the O-sulfate (Schanberg et al., 1968), whereas in brains of human and most nonhuman primates it exists primarily in the free, unconjugated form (Maas et al., 1976b; Karoum et al., 1977). Acidic metabolites of NE provide only a minor contribution to the total pool of noradrenergic metabolite found in brain of rat and primates (Ader et al., 1979; Karoum et al., 1976; Sjoqvist, 1975).

V. Impulse Flow and Transmitter Turnover

During the late 1960s and early 1970s several laboratories demonstrated that the changes in NE turnover in central NE neurons following alterations in impulse flow paralleled those observed earlier in the periphery. Thus, an increase in impulse flow in central NE neurons was associated with an apparent increase in NE turnover, and a decrease in impulse flow was associated with a reduction in NE turnover. For example, Arbuthnott et al. (1970) demonstrated that electrical stimulation of the central ascending NE pathway induced a increase in NE turnover as

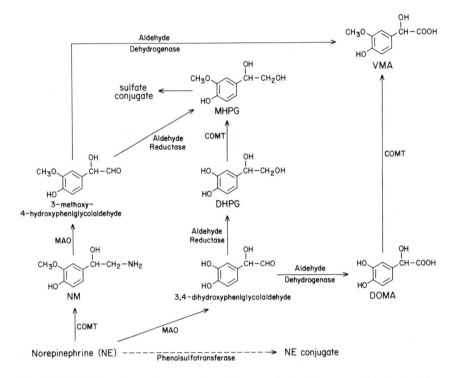

Fig. 3. Metabolic pathways for norepinephrine metabolism in mammalian brain. The following abbreviations are used in this figure: monoamine oxidase (MAO); catechol *O*-methyltransferase (COMT); norepinephrine (NE); 3-methoxy-4-hydroxyphenethylene-glycol (MHPG); vanillylmandelic acid (VMA); 3,4-dihydroxyphenylglycol (DHPG); nor-metanephrine (NM); 3,4-dihydroxymandelic acid (DOMA).

judged by decreases in the histofluorescence of NE terminals after α-methyltyrosine administration. Andén and co-workers (1965) demonstrated that acute transection of the spinal cord induces a decrease in NE turnover and that stimulation of the medulla oblongata causes an increase in NE turnover in the spinal cord.

VI. Impulse Flow and MHPG Production

In 1973 two laboratories (Korf *et al.*, 1973a; Walter and Eccleston, 1973) independently demonstrated that electrical stimulation of the locus coeruleus resulted in an increase in the steady-state levels of

MHPG conjugate, the major NE metabolite found in rat brain (Schanberg *et al.*, 1968; Nielsen and Braestrup, 1976). The increase observed
during stimulation appeared to show a time dependency and appeared
to be related to the frequency of depolarization of the noradrenergic
neurons. The increases in cortical MHPG produced by stimulation in the
locus coeruleus could be prevented by transection of the NE neurons
projecting from the locus coeruleus to he cerebral cortex, suggesting
that the observed changes were due to changes in the activity of noradrenergic neurons originating in the locus coeruleus. These observations have been confirmed by others (Ader and Korf, 1979; Crawley *et
al.*, 1978, 1979b, 1980).

Other studies demonstrated that if impulse flow in central NE projections to the cortex was blocked by transection of the dorsal NE fiber
bundle or by destruction of the locus coeruleus, NE turnover and
steady-state levels of MHPG in the cortex were reduced (Arbuthnott *et
al.*, 1970; Korf *et al.*, 1973a,c). The modest reduction in NE turnover
and steady-state levels of MHPG that was observed following total blockade of impulse flow is probably related to the fact that the normal firing
rate of locus coeruleus cells is about 1 impulse/s (Bunney *et al.*, 1975).
Thus, reduction of the spontaneous rate of firing from 1 impulse/s to
zero has much less consequence than increasing the firing rate to 20
impulses/s, the conditions of the electrical stimulation studies. The observed demonstration of a correlation between changes in noradrenergic neuronal activity and the levels of MHPG has suggested that
changes in the levels of MHPG within selected brain regions may provide a useful index of alterations in the functional activity of central
noradrenergic systems. Indeed, numerous pharmacological studies have
demonstrated that there is a good correlation between drug-induced
and experimentally induced changes in the firing rate of locus coeruleus
neurons and alterations in brain levels of MHPG (Table I). For example,
drug-induced suppression of central noradrenergic activity produced by
administration of clonidine or tricyclic antidepressants is accompanied
by a reduction in the levels of MHPG. Drugs such as piperoxane or
yohimbine, or experimental conditions such as stress (Cedarbaum and
Aghajanian, 1976; Korf *et al.*, 1974; Svensson and Usdin, 1978), or
naloxone-precipitated withdrawal (Aghajanian, 1978), all of which cause
an increase in noradrenergic activity, produce an increase in the brain
levels of MHPG (Korf *et al.*, 1973b; Crawley *et al.*, 1979a). However, this
correlation is not absolute. For example, drugs like MAO inhibitors,
which block the formation of MHPG, do not have reproducible inhibitory effects on NE cell firing. Likewise, doses of morphine, which cause a
suppression of NE unit activity (Korf *et al.*, 1974), increase rather than
decrease endogenous brain levels of MHPG (Lo Pachin and Reigle,

TABLE I

Correlation between Brain Levels of MHPG and Electrophysiological Activity of NE Neurons in the Locus Coeruleus

Drug or experimental treatment	Change in LC unit activity	Citation	Change in brain MHPG	Citation
Clonidine	Decrease	Svensson et al., 1975	Decrease	Tang et al., 1979; Braestrup, 1974; Elsworth et al., 1980
Yohimbine	Increase	Svensson and Usdin, 1978	Increase	Roth, Gysling and Reinhard, unpublished
Piperoxane	Increase	Cedarbaum and Aghajanian, 1976	Increase	Roth and Maas, 1975; Hattox and Crawley, 1979; Redmond et al., 1979; Crawley et al., 1980
Desipramine	Decrease	Nyback et al., 1975	Decrease	Bareggi et al., 1978c; Nielsen and Braestrup, 1977
Stress	Increase	Korf et al., 1974; Cedarbaum and Aghajanian, 1977; Bunney et al., 1975	Increase	Korf et al., 1973a; Stone, 1975
Electrical stimulation LC	Increase		Increase	Korf et al., 1973a; Crawley et al., 1978; Walter and Eccleston, 1973
Transection dorsal NE bundle	Decrease		Decrease	Korf et al., 1973a; Ader and Korf, 1979; Arbuthnott et al., 1973
Amphetamine	Decrease	Bunney et al., 1973, 1975	Decrease	Calderini et al., 1975
			Increase	Bareggi et al., 1978b; Roffman et al., 1975
Morphine	Decrease	Korf et al., 1974	Increase	Lo Pachin and Reigle, 1978; Roffman et al., 1975; 1979
Naloxone precipitated morphine withdrawal	Increase	Aghajanian, 1978	Increase	Crawley et al., 1979a; Redmond et al., 1979

1978; Roffman *et al.,* 1979). This is probably a result of morphine's ability to enhance catecholamine synthesis rather than being related to its effects on NE single-cell activity. Also, depending on the dose and time course investigated, amphetamine, a drug that inhibits locus coeruleus single-cell activity (Bunney *et al.,* 1975) can either increase or decrease the steady-state levels of MHPG (Bareggi *et al.,* 1978). This biphasic effect is due in part to the multiple pharmacological actions of amphetamine; most notable is its ability to cause the release of catecholamine as well as block reuptake and inhibit the firing of NE neurons. In high doses amphetamine also inhibits MAO, one of the primary enzymes involved in MHPG formation (Fig. 3). The latter studies serve as a caveat to those who would argue that MHPG levels always reflect changes in the functional activity of central NE neurons. It is quite clear that numerous pharmacological agents can influence MHPG disposition without having a predictable effect on impulse flow in central NE systems.

Monitoring the changes in the brain levels of another NE metabolite, normetanephrine, also provides an indication of changes in the metabolism of norepinephrine in the central nervous system. In most animals, however, normetanephrine is a minor brain metabolite of norepinephrine; and unless a monoamine oxidase inhibitor is administered to prevent the deamination of normetanephrine, this metabolite does not accumulate to a substantial degree in brain. Thus, measurement of endogenous levels of normetanephrine in the absence of appropriate drugs is more difficult than measurement of MHPG. Also, because most investigators would like to avoid the confounding problems associated with multiple drug administration, MHPG is usually selected as the metabolite of choice when attempts are made to gain insight concerning metabolism of norepinephrine in the central nervous system.

VII.   Plasma and CSF MHPG

The relatively good correlation between alterations in impulse flow in the CNS and levels of brain MHPG previously described has encouraged many researchers to investigate whether changes in this metabolite in accessible body fluids, such as CSF or plasma, might be useful in predicting changes in CNS metabolism of NE. Recent experiments in laboratory animals and in man have suggested that MHPG measurements may provide useful information concerning the global function of central noradrenergic neurons under carefully defined experimental conditions. For example, stimulation of rat locus coeruleus, which causes an increase in brain levels of MHPG, results in an increase in the output of MHPG into the ventricular-cisternal perfusate (Ader *et al.*, 1979). MHPG levels in plasma are also elevated following stimulation of the locus coeruleus, and there is a good correlation between brain and plasma changes in MHPG (Crawley *et al.*, 1979b). However, in the rat only about 30% of the plasma increase in MHPG observed following stimulation of the locus coeruleus appears to originate from brain. In nonhuman primates, in which a greater proportion of plasma MHPG appears to derive from the CNS (Maas *et al.*, 1976a, 1977), there is an excellent correlation between drug-induced changes elicited in brain and the changes found in both plasma and CSF (Elsworth *et al.*, 1980, 1981). In man (normal human volunteers) there is also a highly significant correlation between levels of MHPG found in CSF and plasma (Jimerson *et al.*, 1977). Although variable estimates have been made concerning the actual percentage of MHPG found in plasma that originates in brain, the high correlation found between brain and plasma levels and CSF and plasma levels of this metabolite, especially in primates, strengthens the belief that plasma levels of MHPG may provide a useful index of CNS NE metabolism and central noradrenergic function. However, even under the most rigorously controlled experimental conditions plasma levels of MHPG can, at best, provide information concerning norepinephrine metabolism in the entire CNS only. Information on regional alterations in central noradrenergic activity cannot be obtained by this approach.

VIII. Summary

Numerous basic studies demonstrate that under experimentally defined and controlled conditions there is a good correlation between changes in impulse flow in central noradrenergic neurons of the locus coeruleus and MHPG levels measured in brain. However, this correlation is not absolute, and mention is made of several pharmacological treatments under which this correlation breaks down. Because a significant proportion of MHPG generated by brain egresses to the circulation (the percentage is largest in primates), plasma measures of this metabolite may provide a useful measure of central NE metabolism, which is probably reflective of central noradrenergic activity. This possibility and the use of plasma and CSF measures of MHPG in clinical studies are rigorously explored in later chapters.

References

Ader, J.-P, and Korf, J. 1979. *J. Neurochem.* **32**, 1761–1768.

Ader, J.-P., Aizenstein, M. L., Postema, F., and Korf, J. 1979. *J. Neural Transm.* **46**, 279–290.

Aghajanian, G. K. 1978. *Nature (Lond.)* **276**, 186–188.

Andén, N.-E., and Grabowska, M. 1975. *6-Hydroxydopamine as Denervation Tool in Catecholamine Research* (G. Johnson, T. Malmfors, and C. Sachs, eds.), pp. 143–150. American Elsevier, New York.

Andén, N.-E., Carlsson, A., Hillarp, N.-A., and Magnusson, T. 1965. *Life Sci.* **4**, 129–132.

Andén, N.-E., Corrodi, H., Fuxe, K., and Hökfelt, T. 1967. *Eur. J. Pharmacol.* **2**, 59–64.

Andén, N.-E., Grabowska, M., and Strombom, U. 1976. *Naunyn–Schmiedeberg's Arch. Pharmacol.* **292**, 43–52.

Arbuthnott, G. W., Crow, T. J., Fuxe, K., Olson, L., and Ungerstedt, U. 1970. *Brain Res.* **24**, 471–483.

Arbuthnott, G. W., Christie, J. E., Crow, T. J., Eccleston, D., and Walter, D. S. 1973. *Exper. Neurol.* **41**, 411–417.

Barchas, J. D., and Freedman, D. X. 1963. *Biochem. Pharmacol.* **12**, 1232–1235.

Bareggi, S. R., Markey, K., and Genovese, E. 1978a. *Eur. J. Pharmacol.* **50**, 301–306.

Bareggi, S. R., Markey, K., and Paoletti, R. 1978b. *Pharmacol. Res. Comm.* **10**, 65–73.

Bareggi, S. R., Genovese, E., and Markey, K. 1978c. *Eur. J. Pharmacol.* **50**, 301–306.

Bliss, E. L., Ailion, J., and Zwanziger, J. 1968. *J. Pharmacol. Exp. Ther.* **164**, 122–134.

Bowden, D. M., German, D. C., and Poynter, W. D. 1978. *Brain Res.* **145**, 257–276.

Braestrup, C. 1974. *J. Pharm. Pharmacol.* **26**, 139–141.

Bunney, B. S., Walters, J. R., Roth, R. H., and Aghajanian, G. K. 1973. *J. Pharmacol. Exp. Ther.* **185**, 560–571.

Bunney, B. S., Walters, J. R., Kuhar, M. J., Roth, R. H., and Aghajanian, G. K. 1975. *Psychopharmacol. Commun.* **1(2)**, 177–190.

Calderini, G., Morselli, P. L., and Garattini, S. 1975. *Eur. J. Pharmacol.* **34**, 345–351.

Cedarbaum, J. M., and Aghajanian, G. K. 1976. *Brain Res.* **112**, 413–419.

Cedarbaum, J. M., and Aghajanian, G. K. 1977. *Eur. J. Pharmacol.* **44**, 375–386.

Corrodi, H., Fuxe, K., and Hökfelt, T. 1968. *Life Sci.* **(I)7**, 107–112.

Crawley, J. N., Hattox, S. E., Maas, J. W., and Roth, R. H. 1978. *Brain Res.* **141**, 380–384.

Crawley, J. N., Laverty, R., and Roth, R. H. 1979a. *Eur. J. Pharmacol.* **57**, 247–250.

Crawley, J. N., Roth, R. H., and Maas, J. W. 1979b. *Brain Res.* **166**, 180–184.

Crawley, J. N., Maas, J. W., and Roth, R. H. 1980. *Life Sci.* **26**, 1373–1378.

Elsworth, J. D., Roth, R. H., Stogin, J. M., Leahy, D. J., Moore, R. R., and Redmond, D. E., Jr. 1980. *Neurosci. Abst.* **6**, 140 (#53.10).

Elsworth, J. D., Redmond, D. E., Jr., and Roth, R. H. 1981. *Brain Res.* **235**, 115–124.

Fujita, Y., and Tanaka, C. 1974. *Amine Fluorescence and Histochemistry* (M. Fujiwara and C. Tanaka, eds.) pp. 39–46. Igaku Shoin, Tokyo.

Garver, D. L., and Sladek, J. R., Jr. 1976. *Brain Res.* **103**, 176–182.

Gatter, K. C., and Powell, T. P. S. 1977. *Neuroscience* **2**, 441–445.

Hattox, S. E., and Crawley, J. N. 1979. *Catecholamines, Clinical and Basic Frontiers*, Vol. 1 (E. Usdin, I. Kopin, and T. Barchas, eds.), pp. 886–888. Pergamon Press, N.Y.

Jimerson, D. C., Ballenger, J. C., Lake, C. R., Post, R. M., Goodwin, F. K., and Kopin, I. J. 1981. *Psychopharmacol. Bull.* **17**, 86–87.

Karoum, F., Neff, N. H., and Wyatt, R. J. 1976. *J. Neurochem.* **27**, 33–35.

Karoum, F., Moyer-Schwing, J., Polkin, S. G., and Wyatt, R. J. 1977. *Brain Res.* **125,** 333–339.

Korf, J., Aghajanian, G. K., and Roth, R. H. 1973a. *Eur. J. Pharmacol.* **21,** 305–310.

Korf, J., Aghajanian, G. K., and Roth, R. H. 1973b. *Neuropharmacology* **12,** 933–938.

Korf, J., Roth, R. H., and Aghajanian, G. K. 1973c. *Eur. J. Pharmacol.* **26,** 276–282.

Korf, J., Bunney, B. S., and Aghajanian, G. K. 1974. *Eur. J. Pharmacol.* **25,** 165–169.

Lo Pachin, R. M., and Reigle, T. G. 1978. *J. Pharmacol. Exp. Ther.* **207,** 151–158.

Maas, J. W., Hattox, S. E., Landis, D. H., and Roth, R. H. 1976a. *Brain Res.* **118,** 167–173.

Maas, J. W., Landis, D. H., and Dekirmenjian, H. 1976b. *Psychopharmacol. Comm.* **2,** 403–410.

Maas, J. W., Hattox, S. E., Landis, D. H., and Roth, R. H. 1977. *Eur. J. Pharmacol.* **46,** 221–228.

Nielsen, M., and Braestrup, C. 1976. *J. Neurochem.* **27,** 1211–1217.

Nielsen, M., and Braestrup, C. 1977. *Naunyn–Schmiedeberg's Arch. Pharmacol.* **300,** 93–99.

Nowycky, M. C., and Roth, R. H. 1978. *Prog. Neuro-Psychopharmac.* **2,** 139–158.

Nyback, H. V., Walters, J. R., Aghajanian, G. K., and Roth, R. H. 1975. *Eur. J. Pharmacol.* **32,** 302–312.

Paulsen, E. C., and Hess, S. M. 1963. *J. Neurochem.* **10,** 453–459.

Redmond, D. E., Jr., Roth, R. H., Hattox, S. E., Stogin, J. M., and Baulu, J. 1979. *Neurosci. Abst.* **5,** 348.

Roffman, M., Reigle, T., Orsulak, P., and Schildkraut, J. J. 1975. *Res. Commun. Chem. Pathol. Pharmacol.* **10,** 403–417.

Roffman, M., Reigle, T., Orsulak, P., Cassens, G., and Schildkraut, J. J. 1979. *Neuropharmacology* **18,** 483–487.

Roth, R. H., Salzman, P. M., and Nowycky, M. C. 1978. *Psychopharmacology: A Generation of Progress* (M. A. Lipton, A. DiMascio, and K. F. Killam, eds.), pp. 185–198. Raven Press, New York.

Salzman, P. M., and Roth, R. H. 1979. *Prog. Neurobiol.* **13,** 1–60.

Schanberg, S. M., Schildkraut, J. J., Breese, G. R., and Kopin, I. J. 1968. *Biochem. Pharmacol.* **17,** 247–254.

Sjoqvist, B. 1975. *J. Neurochem.* **24,** 199–201.

Stone, E. A. 1975. *Life Sci.* **16,** 1725–1730.

Svensson, T. H., Bunney, B. S., and Aghajanian, G. K. 1975. *Brain Res.* **92,** 291–306.

Svensson, T. H., and Usdin, T. 1978. *Science* **202,** 1089–1091.

Tang, S. W., Helmeste, D. M., and Stancer, H. C. 1979. *Can. J. Physiol. Pharmacol.* **57(4),** 435–437.

Walter, D. S., and Eccleston, D. 1973. *J. Neurochem* **21,** 281–289.

3

Relationships between
Central Nervous System
Noradrenergic Function
and Plasma and Urinary MHPG
and Other Norepinephrine Metabolites*

JAMES W. MAAS†

JAMES F. LECKMAN
Yale University School of Medicine, New Haven

I. Introduction

Other chapters (Chapter 1 by Tabakoff and Jones; Chapter 2 by Roth and Chapter 5 by Hattox) review the evidence that indicates that MHPG is the major metabolite of the brain neurotransmitter norepinephrine (NE) and that changes in impulse flow in brain noradrenergic neurons

*Supported in part by Grant #MH 24393.
†Present address: The University of Texas Health Science Center at San Antonio, San Antonio, Texas.

MHPG: BASIC MECHANISMS
AND PSYCHOPATHOLOGY

are associated with corresponding changes in 3-methoxy-4-hy-droxyphenethyleneglycol (MHPG). Because the evidence indicates that the functional state of brain NE neuronal systems will be reflected in brain MHPG concentration, clinical investigators have focused on measures of urinary and, increasingly, plasma MHPG as potential indicators of the production of MHPG by brain, with the hope that inferences might thereby be made regarding the functional status of central nervous system (CNS) noradrenergic systems. In this chapter theoretical issues and empirical data dealing with the question of interrelationships between peripheral (i.e., plasma and urinary) measures of MHPG as well as other NE metabolites and CNS noradrenergic function will be reviewed.

II. Theoretical Issues: The Peripheral versus Central Model as Opposed to a Central–Peripheral Interactive Paradigm

Much investigative effort has been directed toward obtaining information as to how much MHPG found in urine or plasma originates in brain versus peripheral pools. Interest in obtaining an answer to this question turns on the implicit assumption that the determination of the fractional contribution to MHPG by brain in a body fluid will indicate whether or not a measure of MHPG in that body fluid can serve as an index of CNS NE metabolism. Furthermore, because there is a barrier to the movement of NE and normetanephrine (NM) out of brain (Maas and Landis, 1966, 1968; Weil-Mahlerbe et al., 1961), it has been assumed that NE and NM concentrations in plasma or urine are unrelated to CNS noradrenergic function. These assumptions are based on a paradigm, developed in the 1960s (Maas and Landis, 1966, 1968), that implicitly posits that CNS and peripheral noradrenergic systems function independently of each other. At the time this original conceptualization was formulated there was debate as to whether or not NE was a CNS neurotransmitter; the relationship between noradrenergic neuronal function and MHPG production was still to be demonstrated (Korf et al., 1973; Arbuthnott et al., 1973; Roth, Chapter 2, this volume), and knowledge of the existence of specific noradrenergic neurons and systems within brain was only beginning to emerge (Dahlstrom and Fuxe, 1964; 1965). Given the corpus of information that was then available, a paradigm based on the fractional contribution of brain MHPG to MHPG in peripheral body fluids seemed worthwhile and attractive. Furthermore, this original model has had heuristic value for the clinical investigator (Maas *et al.*, 1968; Maas *et al.*, 1972; Bond *et al.*, 1972; Jones *et al.*, 1973; Schildkraut *et al.*, 1973; Beckmann and Goodwin, 1975). However, as time has un- folded and newer data have emerged, this "peripheral versus central" formulation has come to have less theoretical appeal and excessive focus on it may obscure the fact that the correct interpretation of data ob- tained in clinical studies should be based on the more likely probability that CNS and peripheral adrenergic systems operate not as separate entities but in an interactive or linked fashion. The data supporting this suggestion come from neuroanatomical studies, the effects of manipula- tion of CNS NE neurons, correlational approaches, and investigations of the role of CNS mechanisms in the regulation of blood pressure. Some of these data are now reviewed.

The neuroanatomical findings will be considered first. The locii coe- ruleii (L.C.) are compact, pontine nucleii of NE neuronal cell bodies that, along with their projections, account for a large fraction of total brain NE. In addition to the well-known cephalad projections from these nucleii there are also, recently described, major projections to several areas of the spinal cord (Hancock and Fourgerousse, 1976; Nygren and Olson, 1977; Commissiong *et al.*, 1978). These caudal projections from the L.C. are probably of importance for the regulation of heart rate and blood pressure (Bolme *et al.*, 1974; Ward and Gunn, 1976), that is, in effect, functions that are controlled, in part, by the sympathetic nervous system. There are also catecholamine (CA) cell bodies (A_1–A_3) in the lower brain stem that, in addition to their cephalad tracts, send caudal projections into several regions of the spinal cord, among which are the lateral sympathetic columns (Carlsson *et al.*, 1964; Dahlstrom and Fuxe, 1964, 1965; Hokfelt *et al.*, 1974).

Jimmerson *et al.* (1979) reported that central stimulation of the sym- pathetic outflow of the pithed rat resulted in an increase in both plasma MHPG and DHPG levels. Stimulation of the L.C. produces not only an increase in MHPG cephalad in the cerebral cortex but also in the de- scending pathways of the spinal cord, and there is an accompanying two- to threefold increase in plasma MHPG concentrations after stimulation of the L.C. that is correlated with the increase in spinal cord MHPG levels ($r = 0.73$, $p < .01$) (Crawley *et al.*, 1978; Crawley *et al.*, 1979). Furthermore, the increase in plasma MHPG after L.C. stimulation is significantly reduced by treatment using the ganglionic blocking agent hexamethonium, which indicates that much of the increase in plasma MHPG after L.C. region stimulation is mediated by increased activity of the sympathetic nervous system (Crawley *et al.*, 1979). It has been re- ported that electrical stimulation of the coeruleus complex produces a large and abrupt increase in arterial pressure. The CNS anatomy underlying these effects of L.C. region stimulation is unclear. It could be due to the activation of terminals on the L.C. that arise from the medullary A_1 and A_2 group of CA cell bodies and that, as noted, also send projections of CA neurons down the spinal cord in the lateral sympathetic columns. Alternatively, it might be due to the activation via polysynaptic connections of descending CA neurons (Crawley et al., 1980).

In terms of the position being developed here, that an interactive rather than a peripheral versus central model is more appropriate for understanding relationships between plasma or urinary MHPG and CNS noradrenergic function, it should be noted that the magnitude of these plasma MHPG changes in rat that occur with central stimulation is far too large to be accounted for solely by changes in MHPG concentrations in either spinal cord and/or cortex (Crawley et al., 1978; Crawley et al., 1979). Furthermore, results from several different laboratories indicate that in rat the contribution by brain, per se, to total body production of MHPG is somewhere in the range of 0 to 30% (Breese et al., 1972; Bareggi et al., 1974; Karoum et al., 1974; Helmeste et al., 1979), and these findings are not supportive of the possibility that the noted changes in plasma MHPG after central stimulation were due to changes in CNS MHPG per se.

In human subjects it has been found that there is a strong correlation between CSF NE and plasma NE levels (Ziegler et al., 1980; Lake et al., 1981). Given the demonstrated barriers to the movement of NE from blood into brain (Weil-Mahlerbe et al., 1961) and from brain into blood (Maas and Landis, 1966), this finding is difficult to explain unless one posits some type of interaction or linkage between CNS and sympathetic nervous system NE neurons.

Lastly, data linking the functioning of CNS CA systems to the peripheral sympathetic nervous system reside in the compelling body of evidence that relates CNS adrenergic function to the regulation of blood pressure (B.P.) (Finch et al., 1972; Davies and Reid (eds), 1975; Scriabine et al., 1976). Changes in the activity of CNS NE systems produced by electrical stimulation or drugs can profoundly affect B.P. (Yamori et al., 1970; Nakamura et al., 1971; Chalmers and Wurtman, 1971; Finch et al., 1972). Several drugs that are useful in the treatment of essential hypertension in man affect the functional state of NE-containing neurons (Kobinger, 1967; Schmitt and Schmitt, 1969; Koch-Weser, 1973; Maas et al., 1979). Both urinary MHPG and plasma MHPG concentrations have been found to be significantly correlated with blood pressure (Leckman et al., 1981; Potter et al., Chapter 8, this volume).

Mechanisms by which events in peripheral adrenergic neurons can affect the activity of CNS CA neurons have received little attention, but intuitively it seems likely that, given the evidence for the regulation of peripheral adrenergic systems by central CA neurons, some mechanism for the converse is likely to exist. The actions of debrisoquin may be relevant to this point.

Debrisoquin is an antihypertensive agent that (a) possesses monoamine oxidase (MAO) inhibitory properties (Medina *et al.*, 1969), (b) does not penetrate brain (Medina *et al.*, 1969), and (c) produces a postganglionic blockade of adrenergic transmission (Moe *et al.*, 1964). When the drug was administered to monkeys, consistent with expectations given its peripheral MAO inhibitory action, it was found to lower plasma levels of homovanillic acid (HVA) but not to alter HVA production by brain. Unexpectedly, however, it was also found to decrease markedly MHPG production by brain (Maas *et al.*, 1979). The mechanism of this effect on brain MHPG is unknown, but it is possible that its effects on peripheral adrenergic systems, directly or indirectly, produce an alteration in the functioning of CNS noradrenergic systems via some type of feedback mechanism.

In the aggregate, the various lines of evidence previously reviewed: (1) suggest that there is an interaction or linkage between brain adrenergic systems and the functioning of peripheral CA neurons, particularly those in the sympathetic nervous system, and (2) argue against the possibility that CNS and peripheral adrenergic systems operate independently of each other. The likelihood that there are interactive links between central and peripheral adrenergic systems has important implications for investigators who utilize plasma or urinary measures of NE or its metabolites in their studies. For example, if CNS NE neuronal activity modulates outflow in the SNS one might find a relationship between urinary or plasma NE and NM and CNS noradrenergic function, even though there is a barrier to the movement of NE and NM out of brain (Weil-Mahlerbe *et al.*, 1961; Maas and Landis 1966 and 1968). Similarly, because of interactive links between the CNS and periphery, there may be a relationship between CNS noradrenergic activity and urinary VMA, even though the amount of VMA entering the periphery from brain is probably quite small.

III. Relationships between Brain, CSF, Plasma, and Urinary Concentrations of MHPG: The Empirical Data

A compilation of reported relationships between peripheral and central measures of adrenergic function in primates (given in Table I) will be described next. Recent studies with vervet monkeys indicate that

TABLE I

Relationships between Central and Peripheral Measures of Adrenergic
Function in Primates

1. MHPG levels in various brain regions of the monkey are significantly correlated with plasma MHPG concentrations (Elsworth *et al.*, in press).
2. MHPG in the CSF and plasma of monkeys is significantly correlated ($N = 67$, $r = .71$, and $p < .001$) (Elsworth *et al.*, in press).
3. Brain intraventricular injections of 6-OHDA in monkeys are associated with decreases in urinary MHPG levels (Maas *et al.*, 1972; Kraemer *et al.*, 1981).
4. Decreases in brain NE produced by 6-OHDA injections into the substania nigra of monkeys do not produce decreases in urinary MHPG levels (Kraemer *et al.*, 1981).
5. MHPG in the CSF and plasma of humans are significantly correlated. CSF MHPG versus plasma-free MHPG ($r = .74$, $p < .001$) and versus plasma-conjugated MHPG ($r = .66$, $p < .005$) (Jimmerson *et al.*, 1981).
6. CSF NE and plasma MHPG in humans are significantly correlated. CSF NE versus plasma-free MHPG, ($r = 0.43$, $p < .05$) and versus plasma conjugated MHPG ($r = .46$, $p < .05$) (Jimmerson *et al.*, 1981).
7. CSF NE and plasma NE in humans are significantly correlated (Ziegler *et al.*, 1980; Lake *et al.*, 1981).
8. Correlations between CSF MHPG and total urinary MHPG in humans. (a) Shaw *et al.* (1973), $N = 11$, no significant correlation. (b) Davis *et al.* (1981), $N = 14$ depressed men, $r = 0.77$, $p < .005$. (c) Maas *et al.* (1982), $N = 65$ depressed patients, females, $r = 0.61$, $p < .0001$; males, $r = 0.33$, $p < .001$. (d) Ågren, H. (1981), $N = 67$ depressed patients, $r = 0.531$, $p < .0001$.
9. Clonidine when given to human subjects in dosages where the action is primarily on CNS NE neurons produces significant decreases in plasma MHPG (Leckman *et al.*, 1980).

plasma-free MHPG is highly correlated with MHPG concentrations in most regions of brain studied, including amygdala, hippocampus, hypothalamus, and occipital cortex (Elsworth *et al.*, in press). In addition, these investigators also found that there were highly significant correlations between MHPG in plasma and CSF. Maas *et al.* (1973) and Kraemer *et al.* (1981) have reported that, following brain intraventricular injection of 6-hydroxydopamine (6-OHDA) in monkeys, there is a corresponding reduction in urinary MHPG excretion. The latter authors, however, found that after injection of 6-OHDA into the substantia nigra a decrease of brain NE was produced without there being a change in urinary MHPG levels. In terms of the earlier discussion of an interactive model versus a peripheral and central paradigm, the following should be noted regarding these findings using monkeys. Recent studies using a venoarterial difference method and the primate macacca arctoides have provided a direct measure of the rate of production of MHPG by whole brain in the awake animal (Maas, Hattox, & Landis,

1980), and these data indicate that it is unlikely that relationships between plasma or urinary MHPG and the monkey brain's production of MHPG occur only because of a central contribution to peripheral pools. Similarly, calculations using clearance rates of MHPG from brain (Maas *et al.*, 1977) and the concentration of MHPG in vervet brain (Elsworth *et al.*, in press) argue against the likelihood that the relationships noted between central and peripheral measures of MHPG can be explained solely in terms of the amount of MHPG that enters the periphery from brain.

In humans substantial correlations between CSF MHPG and free plasma MHPG and conjugated plasma MHPG have been reported (Jimmerson, *et al.*, 1981). Significant correlations between CSF NE and both plasma free and conjugated MHPG have also been found (Jimmerson *et al.*, 1981). CSF NE and plasma NE are also significantly correlated (Lake *et al.*, 1981; Ziegler *et al.*, 1980). As previously noted, the bidirectional barrier to the movement of NE between brain and blood makes the relationships among CSF NE, plasma NE, and MHPG difficult to explain unless one invokes the interactive model proposed in the preceding section.

Leckman *et al.* (1980) have reported that, following dosages of clonidine, where the action of the drug is primarily on CNS neurons, there is a significant decrease in plasma MHPG concentrations.

Four reports have dealt with the issue of correlations between CSF MHPG and urinary MHPG in human subjects. Shaw *et al.* (1973) did not find a significant correlation between MHPG in CSF and urine in a study in which CSF and urine specimens were obtained from 11 depressed patients (11 samples during depression and 6 samples during recovery). In contrast, Davis *et al.* (1981), Maas *et al.* (1982), and Agren (1981) in studies of 14, 65, and 64 depressed patients, respectively, found highly significant correlations between CSF and urinary MHPG concentrations (see Table I).

Some experimental issues relevant to the relationships among plasma, urinary, and CSF MHPG in human subjects should be noted before proceeding to a discussion of the implications of these correlations for the clinical investigator. Maas *et al.* (1979), using a venoarterial difference technique, have estimated that in humans approximately 60% of the total body production of MHPG has its origins in brain. However, the amount of MHPG that originates in brain and is then found in plasma or urine remains uncertain because the degree to which MHPG is metabolized to vanillylmandelic acid (VMA) in the periphery is not known. For example, Blombery *et al.* (1980) and Mårdh *et al.* (1981) found that over 40–50% of a bolus of deuterated MHPG administered iv was metabolized to VMA. Their findings are open to question, however, because of the extremely large, nonphysiological quantity of free MHPG administered. LaBrosse (1970) gave a tracer quantity of free [^{3}H]MHPG to a patient that had a neuroblastoma and found that 27% was converted to VMA. Maas *et al.* (unpublished observations) found that when a tracer quantity of [^{3}H]MHPG was slowly administered to monkeys only 4–6% was recovered as VMA. Although all studies agree that free MHPG is converted to VMA, further research is needed to determine the degree to which this conversion occurs under physiological conditions, as a function of species, and as a multiplicity of state and trait variables. Whatever the resolution of these questions, however, it should be emphasized that (a) significant correlations between central and peripheral concentrations of NE and MHPG do exist (see Table I) and (b) these correlations are consistent with the data reviewed earlier, which indicate that central and peripheral adrenergic neurons function as an interactive unit.

IV. Plasma and Urinary MHPG and Other NE Metabolites as Indices of Events in CNS NE Neurons

The data that support the likelihood that peripheral and central adrenergic systems function as a unit as well as the empirical findings summarized in Table I suggest that peripheral measures of NE metabolites may provide an index of CNS NE neuronal activity. Unfortunately, however, the resolving power of measures such as plasma or urinary MHPG as probes for central events is not known with any degree of exactness. Further research will be needed to deal with the crucially important issue of "how well" a given measure reflects CNS noradrenergic function. Some research strategies that should be pursued to obtain an answer to this question are as follows. In human studies of a given behavioral state or physiological response, for example, blood pressure, simultaneous measures of CSF NE and/or its metabolites and plasma or urinary NE or its metabolites, as well as a quantitative measure of the behavioral or physiological condition, should be obtained. From the appropriate analyses of relationships between the quantitated response or behavior under study and the CSF and peripheral measures of NE and its metabolites, one may obtain information as to how well a given peripheral measure is reflecting central events in the context of changes in the particular behavior or response being examined. Another approach would be to utilize statistical techniques that dampen the amount of "noise" or variance in the peripheral measure when they are used as markers for central events. Initial attempts in this direction are represented by Schildkraut's use of combinations of NE and metabolites in a discriminant function analysis or "D" score (Schildkraut, Chapter 7, this volume) and by the use of path analytic models (Gibbons *et al.*, unpublished observations).

In addition to these clinical approaches, further experiments using animals such as primates (which are more like man than rats in terms of NE metabolism), in which the functional state of CNS NE neurons is pharmacologically or physiologically manipulated while plasma or urinary measures of NE are obtained, should be pursued to clarify the degree to which a given peripheral measure reflects central events.

Finally, it should be emphasized that an exclusive focus on plasma or urinary MHPG as a measure of CNS NE metabolism is conceptually myopic. Given the data reviewed earlier, which indicate that CNS adrenergic neurons and the sympathetic nervous system function as an interactive unit, it is quite possible, even likely (see Table I), that plasma or urinary measures of NE, NM, or VMA may also reflect central adrenergic events, even though the direct contribution by brain to periphery of these substances is minimal.

V. Summary

The evidence we have seen suggests that there is an interaction or some sort of linkage between brain adrenergic systems and the functioning of peripheral CA neurons, particularly those in the sympathetic nervous system. Significant correlations among brain, CSF, plasma, and urinary concentrations of NE and MHPG have been observed by several different groups; and although these correlations may occur in part because of a direct contribution of brain MHPG to peripheral pools of MHPG, it is also likely that the mechanism underlying these relationships resides in an interactive linkage between central and peripheral adrenergic systems. The use of plasma and urinary MHPG as a probe for central adrenergic function has been discussed in relationship to these noted correlations and the central–peripheral interactive paradigm. The question of how well a peripheral adrenergic measure reflects CNS NE neuronal activity has also been discussed. Finally, the existence of interactions between central CA systems and the sympathetic nervous system has been found to broaden research strategies because it can no longer be assumed that measures of plasma or urinary NE, NM, or VMA do not reflect central events because the quantities of these substances entering the periphery from brain is quite small.

References

Ågren, H. 1981. *Biological Markers in Major Depressive Disorders.* Offsetcenter ab, Uppsala, Sweden.

Arbuthnott, G. W., Christie, J. E., Crow, T. J., Eccleston, D., and Walter, D. S. 1973. *Exp. Neurol.* **41,** 411–417.

Bareggi, S. R., Marc, V., and Marselli, P. L. 1974. *Brain Res.* **75,** 177–180.

Beckmann, H., and Goodwin, F. K. 1975. *Arch. Gen. Psychiatry* **32,** 17–21.

Blombery, P. A., Kopin, I. J., Gordon, E. K., Markey, S. P., and Ebert, M. H. 1980. *Arch. Gen. Psychiatry* **37,** 1095–1099.

Bolme, P., Fuxe, K., Nygren, L-G., Olson, L., and Sachs, C. H. 1974. *Dynamics of Degeneration and Growth of Neurons.* (K. Fuxe, L. Olson, and Y. Zotterman, eds.), pp. 597–602. Pergamon Press.

Bond, P. A., Jenner, F. A., and Sampson, G. A. 1972. *Psychol. Med.* **2,** 81–85.

Breese, G. R., Prange, A. J., Howard, M. A., Lipton, M. A., McKinney, W. P., Beaman, R. E., and Bushnell, P. 1972. *Nature New Biol.* **240,** 286–287.

Carlsson, A., Falck, B., Fuxe, K., and Hellarp, N. 1964. *Acta Physiol. Scand.* **60,** 112–119.

Chalmers, J. P., and Wurtman, R. J. 1971. *Circ. Res.* **28,** 480–491.

Commissiong, J. W., Hellstrom, S. O., and Neff, N. H. 1978. *Brain Res.* **148,** 207–213.

Crawley, J. N., Hattox, S. E., Maas, J. W., and Roth, R. H. 1978. *Brain Res.* **141,** 380–384.

Crawley, J. N., Roth, R. H., and Maas, J. W. 1979. *Brain Res.* **166,** 180–184.

Crawley, J. N., Maas, J. W., and Roth, R. H. 1980. *Brain Res.* **183,** 301–311.

Dahlstrom, A., and Fuxe, K. 1964. *Acta Physiol. Scand.* **64**(supple 232), 1–55.

Dahlstrom, A., and Fuxe, K. 1965. *Acta Physiol. Scand.* **64**(supple 274), 1–36.

Davies, D. S., and Reis, D. (eds). *Central Action of Drugs in Blood Pressure Regulation.* 1975. University Park Press, Baltimore.

Elsworth, J. D., Redmond, D. E., and Roth, R. H. 1982. *Brain Res.* **235,** 115–124.

Finch, L., Haeusler, H., and Thoenen, H. 1972. *Br. J. Pharmacol.* **44,** 356P.

Hancock, M. B., and Fourgerousse, C. L. 1976. *Brain Res. Bull.* **1,** 229–234.

Helmeste, D. M., Stancer, H. G., Coscina, D. V., Takahashi, S., and Warsh, J. J. 1979. *Life Sci.* **25,** 601–606.

Hokfelt, T., Fuxe, K., Goldstein, M., and Johansson, O. 1974. *Brain Res.* **66,** 235–251.

Jimmerson, D. C., Sun, C. L., Yamaguchi, I., and Kopin, I. J. 1979. *Catecholamines-Basic and Clinical Frontiers* (Udin, Kopin, Barchas, eds.) Pergamen Press, New York.

Jimmerson, D. C., Ballenger, J. C., Lake, C. R., *et al.* 1981. *Psychopharmacol. Bull.* **17,** 86–87.

Jones, F., Maas, J. W., Dekirmenjian, H., and Fawcett, J. A. 1973. *Science* **179,** 300–302.

Karoum, F., Wyatt, R., and Costa, E. 1974. *Neuropharmacol.* **13,** 165–176.

Kobinger, W. 1967. *Naunyn–Schmiedeberg's Arch. Pharmacol. Exp. Pathol.* **258,** 48–58.

Koch-Weser, J. 1973. *N. Eng. J. Med.* **288,** 627–629.

Korf, J., Aghajanian, G. K., and Roth, R. H. 1973. *Eur. J. Pharmacol.* **21**, 305–310.
Kraemer, G. W., Breese, G. R., Prange, A. J., Moran, E. C., Lewis, J. K., Kemnitz, J. W., Bushell, P. J., Howard, J. L., and McKinney, W. P. 1981. *Psychopharmacol.* **73**, 1–11.
LaBrosse, E. H. 1970. *J. Clin. Endocr.* **30**, 580–589.
Lake, C. R., Gullner, H. G., Polinsky, R. J., Ebert, M. H., Ziegler, M. G., and Barterr, F. C. 1981. *Science* **211**, 955–957.
Leckman, J. F., Maas, J. W., Redmond, Jr., D. E., and Heninger, G. R. 1980. *Life Sci.* **26**, 2179–2185.
Leckman, J. F., Maas, J. W., and Heninger, G. R. 1981. *Eur. J. Pharmacol.* **70**, 111–120.
Maas, J. W., and Landis, D. H. 1966. *Psychosom. Med.* **28**, 247–256.
Maas, J. W., and Landis, D. H. 1968. *J. Pharmacol. Exp. Ther.* **163**, 147–162.
Maas, J. W., Fawcett, J. A., and Dekirmenjian, H. 1968. *Arch. Gen. Psychiatry* **19**, 129–134.
Maas, J. W., Fawcett, J. A., and Dekirmenjian, H. 1972. *Arch. Gen. Psychiatry* **26**, 252–262.
Maas, J. W., Dekirmenjian, H., Garver, D., Redmond, Jr., D. E., and Landis, D. H. 1973. *Eur. J. Pharmacol.* **23**, 121–130.
Maas, J. W., Hattox, S. E., Landis, D. H., and Roth, R. H. 1977. *Eur. J. Pharmacol.* **46**, 221–228.
Maas, J. W., Hattox, S. E., Greene, N. M., and Landis, D. H. 1979. *Science* **205(#4410)**, 1025–1027.
Maas, J. W., Hattox, S. E., and Landis, D. H. 1979. *Biochem. Pharmacol.* **28**, 3153–3156.
Maas, J. W., Hattox, S. E., and Landis, D. H. 1980. *Life Sci.* **26**, 929–934.
Maas, J. W., Koslow, S., Davis, J., Katz, M., Mendels, J., Robins, E., Stokes, P., and Bowden, C. 1980. *Psychol. Med.* **10**, 759–776.
Maas, J. W., Kocsis, J. H., Bowden, C. L., Danis, J. M., Redmond, D. E., Hanin, I., and Robins, E. 1982. *Psychol. Med.* **12**, 37–43.
Mårdh, G., Sjoquist, B., Neimchem, J., and Anggard, E. 1981. *J. Neurochem.* **38**, 1181–1185.
Medina, M. A., Giachetti, A., and Shore, P. A. 1969. *Biochem. Pharmacol.* **18**, 891–901.
Moe, R. A., Bates, H. M., Palkoski, Z. M., and Banziger, R. 1964. *Curr. Ther. Res.* **6**, 299–318.
Nakamura, K., Gerold, M., and Thoenen, H. 1971. *Naunyn–Schmiedeberg's Arch. Pharmacol.* **268**, 125–139.
Nygren, L., and Olson, L. 1977. *Brain Res.* **132**, 85–93.
Schildkraut, J. J., Keeler, B. A., Grab, E. L., *et al.* 1973. *Lancet* **1**, 1251–1252.
Schmitt, H., and Schmitt, H. 1969. *Eur. J. Pharmacol.* **6**, 8–12.
Scriabine, A., Clineschmidt, B. V., and Sweet, C. S. 1976. *Ann. Rev. Pharmacol. Toxicol.* **16**, 113–123.
Shaw, D. M., O'Keeffee, R., MacSweeney, D. A., and Brooksbank, B. W. L., *et al.* 1973. *Psychol. Med.* **3**, 333–336.
Ward, D. G., and Gunn, C. G. 1976. *Brain Res.* **107**, 401–406.
Weil-Mahlerbe, H., Whitby, L. G., and Axelrod, J. 1961. *J. Neurochem.* **8**, 55–64.
Yamori, Y., Lovenberg, W., and Sjoerdsma, S. 1970. *Science* **170**, 544–546.
Ziegler, M., Lake, C., Wood, J., and Brooks, B. 1980. *Clin. Exp. Hyperten.* **2(6)**, 995–1008.

4

Effects of Pharmacological Agents on MHPG

J. I. JAVAID

JOAN RUBINSTEIN

JOHN M. DAVIS

Illinois State Psychiatric Institute, Chicago

I. Introduction

Over the last 15 years much has been learned about the synthesis, storage, release, and metabolism of biogenic amines. This progress resulted from both the availability of labeled precursors and amines of high specific activity and the development of specific and sensitive methods for the measurement of these amines and their metabolites. The

MHPG: BASIC MECHANISMS
AND PSYCHOPATHOLOGY

methods used for the study of norepinephrine (NE) turnover have generally employed tracer amounts of radiolabeled tyrosine, the precursor of NE, or the amine itself while blocking the synthesis of endogenous NE by inhibiting the synthetic enzymes (Schildkraut et al., 1969; Schubert et al., 1970). It is assumed that the radiolabeled compound equilibrates with the endogenous pools rapidly and uniformly and that the inhibition of amine synthesis does not otherwise alter the activity of the neuronal system involved. Although the radioautographic studies do show that the radiolabeled amines distribute rapidly in respective neuronal areas, there is some evidence that these assumptions may not be completely valid (Weiner, 1974).

As an alternative, Meek and Neff (1973) have suggested that neurogenic amine turnover may best be studied by measuring the predominant central nervous system (CNS) metabolite of the amine. In the case of NE this predominant metabolite has been identified as 3-methoxy-4-hydroxyphenethyleneglycol (MHPG) in a number of mammalian species including man (Maas and Landis, 1968; Maas et al., 1968; Maas et al., 1979; Mannarino et al., 1963; Rutledge and Jonason, 1967). In rats most of the MHPG is converted to its sulfate conjugate (Schanberge et al., 1968). Therefore, studies of the effects of drugs on MHPG and MHPG-SO_4 excretion should provide useful information as to the effects of these drugs on NE metabolism in vivo.

In this chapter we shall review the literature concerning the effects of different pharmacological agents on central noradrenergic systems. We shall focus on how changes in MHPG levels relate to the effects of these drugs on NE turnover. An attempt will be made to explain the mechanism by which the drugs may be causing these effects. Lastly, correlations between drug effects on NE turnover and on adrenergic receptor activity will be explored.

Of all the drug classes, the effect of antidepressants on MHPG has been the most widely studied because their major mode of action is thought to be mediated through an alteration of noradrenergic, as well as serotonergic, functions. However, it is interesting to note that neuroleptics and stimulants (thought to act primarily through dopaminergic systems) and narcotics (which act via endorphin systems) also have significant effects on MHPG levels. Therefore, in the following we shall cover the effects of all the preceding drug classes on MHPG as well as those of electroconvulsive therapy (ECT) and some direct-acting adrenergic agents.

II. Effect of Antidepressants

The observation that psychoactive drugs that alter affective states in humans also have profound effects on catecholamine disposition and metabolism in animal brains prompted a hypothesis about the pathophysiology of affective disorders. The catecholamine hypothesis of affective disorders (Bunney and Davis, 1965; Schildkraut, 1965) proposed that depression is related to a functional deficiency of neurotransmitters at central adrenergic receptor sites, whereas mania is associated with a functional excess. It was clearly recognized, however, that abnormalities in catecholamine metabolism alone could not account for all the diverse clinical and biological phenomena present in the affective disorders. Schildkraut noted as early as 1965 that the hypothesized absolute or relative functional deficiency of norepinephrine at receptors could occur as a result of a number of different biochemical mechanisms including: a decrease in NE biosynthesis, impairment of NE binding and storage, increased intracellular release and deamination of NE, and a decrease in receptor sensitivity to NE. In addition, these biochemical differences might be related to differences in the clinical phenomenology or to subtypes of depressive disorders.

Subsequent studies have shown that certain subgroups of patients having affective disorders excrete decreased amounts of urinary MHPG during episodes of depression and increased amounts during mania (Bond *et al.,* 1972; DeLeon-Jones *et al.,* 1973; Maas *et al.,* 1968; Schildkraut, 1974; Schildkraut *et al.,* Chapter 7, in this volume). Also, urinary MHPG has been used to predict response to dextroamphetamine (Fawcett and Siomopoulos, 1971) and different tricyclic antidepressants (TCAs). Hence, there is a substantial body of evidence showing that abnormalities in NE metabolism occur in some depressive disorders and that biochemical measures related to NE metabolism, such as MHPG levels, might help to differentiate subtypes of depression and predict responses to different antidepressants (van Kammen, Chapter 9, in this volume).

In this section we shall look at the effects of different antidepressant drugs on MHPG levels in animals and humans. The data from animal studies are divided into acute and chronic treatments because there are interesting differences in response depending on the duration of drug administration.

A. Acute Drug Treatment

Nielsen and Braestrup (1977a,b) studied the effects of acute administration of antidepressants on the formation of MHPG. They found that total brain MHPG levels decreased in rats treated with 10 mg/kg desmethylimipramine (DMI), but amitriptyline (AT) and maprotiline had no effect. Similarly, Tang *et al.* (1978) found that a single dose or four daily injections of DMI in rats decreased total brain MHPG levels, whereas AT did not cause any significant changes. It has also been reported that acute treatment of rats with DMI (Roffman *et al.*, 1977b; Schildkraut *et al.*, 1976; Tang *et al.*, 1978) or imipramine (IMI) (Roffman *et al.*, 1977a,b) decreases brain MHPG-SO_4 levels, whereas AT has no appreciable effect on MHPG-SO_4 levels 4 or 6 h after acute administration (Roffman *et al.*, 1977b). Bareggi *et al.* (1978a) studied the effect of DMI on MHPG-SO_4 formation after electrical stimulation of the locus coeruleus. They found that electrical stimulation of the locus coeruleus increased the formation of MHPG-SO_4 by increasing the neuronal activity. Treatment with DMI (10 mg/kg) 30 min before stimulation did not affect this increase in MHPG-SO_4 levels. However, DMI treatment alone reduced the levels of MHPG-SO_4 in the cortex-hippocampus. Also, studies in which radiolabeled precursors were used *in vivo* have shown reduced NE uptake in rat brain (Nyback *et al.*, 1968; Schildkraut *et al.*, 1969; Schubert *et al.*, 1970) and reduced metabolite formation after acute treatment with DMI.

The decreased formation of MHPG after acute administration of DMI can be explained by the inhibitory effect of DMI on NE reuptake at the presynaptic neuronal membrane (Glowinski and Axelrod, 1964; Hertting *et al.*, 1961; Javaid *et al.*, 1979; Ross and Renyi, 1975). Because NE released into the synaptic cleft cannot reenter the neurons, it will not be deaminated by the intraneuronal monoamine oxidase (MAO); hence, there is a reduced formation of MHPG. This is supported by the finding that acute treatment with DMI increased the formation of [^{3}H]normetanephrine (NM) from intraventricularly administered [^{3}H]NE (Schildkraut *et al.*, 1969; Nielsen, 1975). This increase in NM is expected because NE can be O-methylated extraneuronally by catechol O-methyltransferase (COMT).

An alternative explanation is that the inhibition of NE reuptake increases the NE concentration in the synaptic cleft causing increased stimulation of α-adrenergic receptors. This then decreases the activity of the presynaptic neurons by a negative feedback mechanism (Langer,

1977). This hypothesis is supported by the fact that pretreatment of rats with phenoxybenzamine, an α-adrenergic receptor blocker, reversed the effect of DMI on the levels of brain MHPG-SO$_4$ (Bareggi et al., 1978a). Further support comes from studies with the nontricyclic antidepressant mianserine, which is a weak inhibitor of NE uptake but a potent blocker of α-adrenergic receptors (Baumann and Maitre, 1977). Tang et al. (1979b) and Przegalinski et al. (1981) reported that mianserin increased the total brain MHPG levels in rats after both acute and chronic treatment. This is the predicted response of a blockade on the receptors mediating the negative feedback.

B. Chronic Drug Treatment

The effects of TCAs on the levels of MHPG in rat brain vary with the duration of drug treatment. Although all the previously mentioned studies reported a decrease in brain MHPG levels after acute treatment with DMI, the results of chronic drug treatment are not in complete agreement. Roffman et al. (1977b) investigated the effects of chronic administration of TCAs. The drugs were administered twice daily (10 mg/kg) for 2 weeks, and the animals were sacrificed 6 h after the last injection. They found that under these experimental conditions there was a significant increase in brain MHPG-SO$_4$ levels in the animals treated with DMI or IMI. Also, AT or nortriptyline (NT) treatment caused only a slight and nonsignificant increase in brain MHPG-SO$_4$ levels. Similarly, Tang et al. (1978) found that chronic treatment with DMI (20 mg/kg per day for 21 days) caused significant increase in total brain MHPG levels, but AT treatment, whether acute or chronic, had no effect. However, Bareggi et al. (1978a) reported that, in rats, probenacid-induced accumulation of MHPG-SO$_4$ decreased after a single dose of DMI (10 mg/kg) but was not effected after multiple doses (10 mg/kg, twice a day for 3 days).

Schildkraut et al. (1970) have previously shown that acute administration of DMI and IMI decreased the rate of disappearance of intracisternally administered [^{3}H]NE from rat brain, whereas chronic treatment with these drugs accelerated the rate of [^{3}H]NE disappearance. An increase in NE turnover after chronic administration of DMI, IMI, or protriptyline (PT) in rats has also been reported by measuring NE disappearance after synthesis is blocked by α-methyl paratyrosine (Neff and Costa, 1967; Rosloff and Davis, 1974). The results are compatible with the observation that chronic treatment with DMI or IMI increased rat brain MHPG levels.

Not all studies agree, however, Nielson and Braestrup (1977a) treated rats with DMI (10 mg/kg per day) for 4 to 20 days. They reported that after 4 and 10 days total MHPG levels were decreased whereas after 20 days there was no change. These findings suggest that treatment with DMI for 4 or 10 days caused the same qualitative changes in NE metabolism as acute treatment, namely a decrease in turnover, and are at variance with the preceding reports. Likewise, the fact that Nielsen and Braestrup did not find any changes in total MHPG levels after 20 days is at variance with the results of Roffman *et al.* (1977b) and Tang *et al.* (1978) who reported increased MHPG levels after similar treatment duration.

A possible explanation for the difference between the acute and chronic effects of TCAs on MHPG levels is that, through complex adaptive changes, the receptors mediating the negative feedback become subsensitive in response to the chronic overstimulation by increased NE levels in the synapse. Crews and Smith (1978) have reported such a decreased α-adrenergic receptor sensitivity by measuring physiologic parameters in rat heart following 3 weeks of DMI treatment.

Przegalinski *et al.* (1981) reported that some of the new atypical antidepressant drugs (mianserin, trazodone, damitracen, and pizotifen) increased brain MHPG-SO$_4$ levels in rats after chronic but not acute treatment. The only exception was mianserine, which, as noted previously, also increased MHPG-SO$_4$ levels after acute treatment. They proposed that the serotonin receptor-blocking action of these drugs facilitates noradrenergic activity. However, this hypothesis would not explain the failure of AT (a TCA with serotonin receptor-blocking activity) to affect MHPG levels.

C. Human Studies

The literature on the effect of TCA treatment on MHPG levels in humans shows variable results. There are a number of factors that make it difficult to compare different studies. The first problem is the heterogeneity of the patient population and the differences in the type and duration of antidepressant treatment. Second, the biological fluid used for MHPG measurement may vary. Thus, TCA treatment may have a different effect on urinary MHPG than on cerebrospinal fluid (CSF) or plasma MHPG. Also, the time of fluid sampling during treatment is not always consistent. Other factors such as diet, physical activity, and choice of method for MHPG determination may add additional variability to the results.

It has been shown that patients who respond to amphetamine, IMI, or DMI with a mood elevation have a modest increase or no change in urinary MHPG levels during treatment, whereas patients who do not respond to these drugs have decreased MHPG excretion (Maas, 1975). DeLeon-Jones et al. (1974) have reported that depressed patients who did not respond to IMI treatment had significantly decreased urinary MHPG levels during the treatment. Cobbin et al. (1979) used pretreatment urinary MHPG levels in depressed patients as an index for drug selection. They reported that the patient group with low pretreatment MHPG levels showed an increase during drug treatment. Conversely, the high pretreatment MHPG level group had decreased levels during the antidepressant administration. It should be noted, however, that not all patients received the same drug. Another study (Beckmann and Goodwin, 1975) found that both responders and nonresponders to IMI had decreased MHPG excretion; however, the decrement was considerably smaller in responders. On the other hand, Modai et al. (1979) have reported that urinary MHPG levels in bipolar depressed patients increased significantly during AT treatment in both responders and nonresponders.

As noted in the preceding discussion, numerous methodological factors may contribute to varying results in human studies. However, there appears to be a trend toward increased MHPG levels in TCA responders and decreased levels in nonresponders. TCAs affect all known aspects of adrenergic action-synthesis, release, metabolism, and receptor function. Therefore, a plausible explanation for these findings would be that, in responders, the net effect of TCAs is to maintain or increase NE turnover resulting in normal or increased MHPG excretion. Conversely, in nonresponders, the net effect would be to decrease turnover thus reducing MHPG levels.

Thoren et al. (1980) found that, in a group of patients with severe obsessive–compulsive disorders, the MHPG levels in CSF were significantly reduced during clorimipramine (CMI) or NT treatment. Roccatagliata et al. (1981) reported that, in patients with endogenous depression, treatment with IMI did not affect the CSF MHPG levels in the group as a whole. However, considering the responders only, a significant decrease was observed.

There is substantial evidence that the inhibitors of the enzyme MAO are effective antidepressants. The inhibition of MAO would result in decreased catabolism of the biogenic amines thus increasing their effective concentration at the monoaminergic receptors. Although the effects of MAO inhibitors on MHPG levels in animals have not been studied, one would certainly expect a decrease in both central and peripheral MHPG formation, both acutely and chronically. Beckmann and Murphy (1977) have studied the effects of the MAO inhibitor phenelzine on the urinary excretion of MHPG in humans. As expected, they found that urinary MHPG levels were significantly reduced during phenelzine treatment. They did not find any relationship between pretreatment urinary MHPG and clinical response to phenelzine.

III. Effect of ECT

In addition to pharmacologic agents, ECT is commonly used in treating depressive illness. The possibility that ECT might influence the turnover of NE has been investigated by the technique of injecting [^{3}H]NE into the brain ventricles and monitoring its decline following ECT. ECT was found to increase the rate of discharge of [^{3}H]NE within the brain in both acute studies (Schildkraut et al., 1967; Schildkraut, 1974) and chronic studies (Schildkraut and Draskoczy, 1974; Ladisich et al., 1969; Kety et al., 1967). Schildkraut and Draskoczy (1974) studied the formation of radioactive metabolites in rats that received an injection of [^{3}H]NE 20 min before ECT. Their results show a significant increase in deaminated, O-methylated metabolites—MHPG + vanillylmandelic acid (VMA)—in ECT-treated rats.

The effect of ECT on the activity of biosynthetic enzymes was investigated by Musacchio et al. (1968), who reported that a series of ECT (2/day for 7 days) increased the activity of tyrosine hydroxylase, the rate-limiting enzyme in NE synthesis. Pryor et al. (1972) reported that a series of ECT increased the activity of MAO; this effect persisted for 6 weeks. However, Spilman and Badal (1960) reported no change in MAO activity following a series of 12 ECT (1/day).

These studies suggest that ECT increases NE turnover in rats. However, in humans, Harnryd et al. (1979) reported that, after a series of ECT in schizophrenic women, MHPG levels in CSF decreased significantly. Because of the limited amount of data, an attempt to explain the inconsistency between the effects of ECT in animals and in humans seems premature. Further research is needed concerning the mechanism of action of ECT in general and specifically its effect on NE turnover.

IV. Effect of Lithium

Lithium (Li) is commonly used for the treatment of acute mania as well as for prophylaxis in affective disorders. The biochemical mechanisms by which Li mediates its clinical effects are not known. Greenspan *et al.* (1970) reported that, out of a small group of patients, urinary MHPG levels in two hypomanic patients decreased during Li treatment. However, the differences were not statistically significant. Similarly, Beckmann *et al.* (1975) did not find any consistent changes in urinary MHPG levels in 10 depressed patients during Li treatment, when considering the group as a whole. However, they did find that during the third and fourth week of Li treatment, MHPG excretion increased in the responders but showed no change or a decrease in nonresponders. Wilk *et al.* (1972) did not find any consistent changes in CSF MHPG levels during Li treatment.

V. Effect of Neuroleptics

Neuroleptic drugs, such as the phenothiazines and butyrophenones, are a class of pharmacologic agents effectively used for the treatment of schizophrenia. Although the antischizophrenic effects of neuroleptics are thought to be mediated through the dopaminergic system, it has been suggested that drug-induced extrapyramidal side effects in humans may be mediated through the noradrenergic system. Thus, potent cataleptogenic neuroleptics like haloperidol (HLD) have been shown to increase the turnover of both dopamine (DA) and NE (Anden *et al.*, 1970; Burki *et al.*, 1975), whereas pimozide (PMZ) has a minimal effect on NE turnover and produces limited extrapyramidal side effects in humans (Pinder *et al.*, 1976).

The effect of acute administration of neuroleptics on rat brain MHPG levels has been studied by a number of investigators. Keller *et al.* (1973) found that all the drugs studied increased brain MHPG levels in a dose-dependent manner. The potency of this effect decreased in the following order: methiothepin, HLD, clozapine (CLP), thioridazine, chlorpromazine (CPZ), PMZ. These authors suggested that the sedative action of these neuroleptics may be related to their potency to increase levels of MHPG. Berridge and Sharman (1974) also reported that HLD and CLP increased levels of rat brain $MHPG-SO_4$. Similarly, Burki *et al.* (1975)

found that HLD, perlapine, and CLP increased NE turnover in the brain stem of rats. Alfredsson *et al.* (1977) reported that, following high doses of CPZ (30 mg/kg), there was an increase in the brain levels of MHPG-SO$_4$ in rats. They did not, however, find any significant changes at a lower dosage (7.5 mg/kg).

Ader *et al.* (1980) have reported the effects of single as well as repeated administration of neuroleptics. In accordance with other reports, they found that, after single doses of CLP (15 mg/kg), HLD (1 mg/kg), or CPZ (2 mg/kg), there was a marked increase in brain MHPG levels. However, after 2 weeks' administration of CLP or HLD, the MHPG levels were reduced to the control level.

Neuroleptics have been shown to block DA receptors (Snyder *et al.*, 1974), which via a feedback mechanism probably accounts for the increased DA turnover mentioned in the first paragraph of this section. Similarly, the neuroleptic-induced increase in MHPG levels is probably due to increased NE turnover caused by feedback activation of noradrenergic neurons as a result of adrenergic receptor blockade by neuroleptics. Peroutka and Snyder (1980) have shown that CPZ and HLD are approximately equipotent blockers of α-adrenergic receptors as compared with DA receptors. After repeated administration, it is presumed that the adrenergic receptors would become supersensitive in response to their chronic blockade. This would compensate for the effect of the blockade and explain the lack of change of MHPG levels after chronic drug treatment.

VI.   Effect of Stimulants

CNS stimulants like amphetamine (AMP) and cocaine are believed to produce their effects by increasing the concentrations of catecholamines at postsynaptic receptors through the release of amines from presynaptic nerve terminals or by blocking their reuptake. Both cocaine and AMP have been shown to affect NE turnover, although different studies have yielded variable results depending on the method used. Thus, NE turnover in rat brain was found to be increased by AMP as determined by the rate of disappearance of intracerebrally administered [^{3}H]NE (Cook and Schanberg, 1970; Schildkraut, 1970). On the other hand, NE turnover appears to be decreased or unchanged when the accumulation of NE from labeled precursors is determined (Costa *et al.*, 1972; Bralet and Lallemant, 1975).

Bareggi et al. (1975, 1978b) reported that acute administration of d-AMP (5 mg/kg) produced a significant increase in levels of rat brain MHPG-SO$_4$. Similarly, Roffman et al. (1978) found that acute administration of d-AMP increased MHPG-SO$_4$ levels in whole rat brain in a dose-related manner at 2.5 and 5.0 mg/kg. However, increasing the dose further to 10 mg/kg attenuated this increase. On the other hand, Calderini et al. (1975) found an increase in brain MHPG-SO$_4$ levels after 15 mg/kg of d-AMP but not after lower doses. Roffman et al. (1978) also found that d-AMP was two to four times more potent than l-AMP in increasing the levels of MHPG-SO$_4$ in whole rat brain. These findings are in agreement with the report that d-AMP is five times more potent than l-AMP in maintaining amphetamine self-administration in monkeys (Balster and Schuster, 1973).

Cassens et al. (1979) studied the effects of chronic administration of and withdrawal from AMP on brain levels of MHPG-SO$_4$ in the rat. In contrast to acute treatment, brain MHPG-SO$_4$ levels in rats after chronic administration did not differ from control animals. During the withdrawal phase the authors found a significant decrease in brain MHPG-SO$_4$ levels.

The increase in MHPG levels after acute d-AMP treatment is most likely due to the increase in NE release. After chronic treatment, however, excessive stimulation of adrenergic receptors would reduce NE release via feedback inhibition, thus reducing the MHPG levels to normal. At this point NE release is dependent on d-AMP. During withdrawal, because the releasing effect of AMP would be absent, there would be a further decrease in NE turnover.

Schildkraut et al. (1971) have reported an increase in urinary excretion of MHPG in humans during AMP administration and a rapid decrease on withdrawal. Similarly, Fawcett et al. (1972) reported that d-AMP administration increased urinary MHPG levels in depressed patients who had a euphoric response to the drug. However, the nonresponders showed a modest decrease. Based on these observations, the investigators suggested that one can predict TCA response in depressed patients.

In contrast, Beckmann et al. (1976) reported a decrease in MHPG levels after d-AMP administration. When Angrist et al. (1972) administered dl-AMP to a group of drug abusers, no consistent changes in urinary MHPG levels were observed. Shekim et al. (1979) studied the effect of d-AMP treatment on urinary MHPG levels in hyperactive boys. They reported that d-AMP administration decreased MHPG excretion in the responders but had no effect on MHPG levels in nonresponders.

Cocaine has been shown to decrease NE turnover in rats as determined by a decrease in [³H]NE synthesis from [³H]tyrosine after pre-treatment with the drug (Scheel-Kruger, 1972). Similarly, Crews and Smith (1981) reported that, when rat brain slices labeled with [³H]NE were incubated with 10^{-4} M cocaine, markedly less [³H]MHPG was formed than in control slices. This decrease in MHPG formation is most likely due to the inhibitory effect of cocaine on NE reuptake. Javaid *et al.* (1977) did not find any significant changes in urinary MHPG levels in humans after cocaine administration.

VII. Effect of Narcotics

Early work by Vogt (1954) and by Maynert and Klingman (1962) provided evidence that narcotics may affect noradrenergic systems. In particular, they showed that narcotics produce a decrease in brain NE concentrations. Later, several workers, using methods such as the incor-poration of [³H]tyrosine into NE, found that the acute administration of morphine increases NE synthesis in rats and mice (Gold *et al.*, 1979; Lipman and Spencer, 1978; Sparber and Meyer, 1978). Vetulani and Bednarczyk (1977) studied NE synthesis by measuring the accumulation of 3,4-dihydroxyphenylalanine (DOPA) in rats treated with an inhibitor of L-aromatic amino acid decarboxylase. They found that acute admin-istration of morphine increased DOPA formation in NE predominant parts of the brain. In contrast, naloxone, an opiate antagonist, decreased DOPA formation in DA areas but not in NE predominant areas. Similar-ly, it has been found that acute narcotic administration increases the concentration of MHPG in rat brain (LoPachin and Reigle, 1978; Roff-man *et al.*, 1979). This drug-induced increase in MHPG levels was at-tenuated by a narcotic antagonist.

Studies on the effect of chronic morphine treatment on NE synthesis have been inconsistent. For example, Smith *et al.* (1972) and Lipman and Spencer (1978) found that tolerance developed to the narcotic-induced increase in NE synthesis, whereas Clouet and Ratner (1970) and Sparber and Meyer (1978) did not. Furthermore, NE synthesis decreased 18–54 h following morphine withdrawal (Gold and Redmond, 1977). Similarly, when rats were chronically maintained on morphine, a decrease in MHPG levels was observed 16 h after the last does (Roffman *et al.*, 1979).

Few studies of the effects of narcotics on NE and its metabolites have been done on humans and only two include MHPG. Meyer *et al.* (1978) studied the effect of 10 days of heroin administration on levels of urinary MHPG. No statistically significant change in MHPG levels was found. A few subjects showed an increase in MHPG levels the day before heroin was begun, which persisted throughout the 10 days. This may have been a nonspecific stress effect, although it is possible that a subgroup of patients respond with an increase in MHPG levels. DeLeon-Jones et al. (1982) studied the effects of methadone administration and "cold-turkey" withdrawal on levels of urinary MHPG in a group of volunteer addicts. Results were compared with MHPG levels in normal controls. Based on the data from chronic animal studies, it was hypothesized that among humans one would also observe essentially no change in NE turnover during stable methadone administration. Moreover, if any change occurred in NE turnover, it would be during withdrawal when abstinence symptoms are most pronounced. The results show that, as anticipated, no changes in MHPG excretion occurred during stable methadone maintenance. However, levels of MHPG during withdrawal were identical to levels obtained during treatment. This contrasts with the animal studies, which show a decrease in NE turnover during withdrawal.

It has been shown that clonidine blocks withdrawal symptoms in morphine-dependent rats (Vetulani and Bednarczyk, 1977) and man (Gold et al., 1979). This raises the question as to what adrenergic mechanisms may be implicated in opiate addiction and withdrawal. As will be discussed in more detail in Section XI, clonidine stimulates α_2-adrenergic receptors, thus lowering NE turnover via a negative feedback mechanism. This suggests that alterations in adrenergic receptor sensitivity may be implicated in opiate addiction. This is further suggested because chronic morphine administration increases the number of α_2- as well as β-adrenergic receptors in rat cortex and brainstem (Hamburg and Tallman, 1981).

VIII. Effect of 6-Hydroxydopamine (6-OHDA)

Intraventricular administration of 6-OHDA is used to produce experimental sympathotectomy in animals. Maas et al. (1972, 1973) reported that 6-OHDA treatment of monkeys decreased excretion of total MHPG in urine. From these results they suggested that urinary MHPG could be used as an estimate of NE changes in the brain. Bareggi et al. (1974) found that, although levels of brain MHPG-SO$_4$ were decreased after intraventricular injection of 6-OHDA in rats, there was no change in levels of urinary MHPG-SO$_4$. Similarly, Helmeste *et al.* (1979) found a substantial reduction in brain MHPG levels after 6-OHDA treatment in rats but there was no change in plasma MHPG levels. Kraemer *et al.* (1981) reported decreased levels of urinary MHPG in rhesus monkeys after high doses of 6-OHDA.

IX.   Effect of L-DOPA

L-DOPA is a precursor of NE and is commonly used for the treatment of Parkinson's Disease. Wilk and Mones (1971) did not find any changes in MHPG levels in CSF after large doses of L-DOPA.

X.   Effect of Adrenergic Agonists and Antagonists

Propranolol, a β-adrenergic blocking agent commonly used in treating hypertension, has been shown to have therapeutic potential for the treatment of acutely psychotic patients. Atsmon *et al.* (1972) found that pretreatment levels of MHPG were correlated with the clinical outcome of the treatment. Acutely psychotic patients who showed high excretion of MHPG improved with propranolol treatment. However, propranolol reduced urinary MHPG levels in all psychotic patients. Speiser and Weinstock (1976) reported that, in rats, prolonged isolation caused hyperactivity and a significant increase in urinary MHPG levels. Pretreatment of isolated rats with propranolol abolished hyperactivity and reduced urinary MHPG levels. The effect of propranolol on MHPG levels is most likely related to its ability to decrease excessive NE release rather than its blockade of β-adrenergic receptors. This is supported by the fact that *d*-propranolol, which is a much weaker β-adrenergic antagonist than is *l*-propranolol, also attenuated the stress-induced increase in MHPG levels. Hollister *et al.* (1980) have reported that asthmatic patients treated with β-adrenergic stimulant drugs had higher than normal levels of urinary MHPG.

Clonidine is an α$_2$-adrenergic receptor agonist and is used for the treatment of hypertension. Several studies indicate that acute clonidine treatment decreases brain MHPG concentration (Braestrup and Nielsen, 1976; Maas *et al.,* 1976; Tang *et al.,* 1979a,b). Tang *et al.* (1979a) reported that the decrease in rat brain MHPG levels persisted even after chronic treatment for 21 days. The cessation of clonidine administration after chronic treatment resulted in an increase in brain MHPG levels. The clonidine-induced decrease in MHPG levels is presumably mediated through a decrease in NE release via feedback inhibition due to stimulation of α_2-receptors. This hypothesis is supported by results reported by Braestrup and Nielsen (1976) who found that clonidine treatment decreased the levels of brain MHPG in rats, whereas the α-adrenergic antagonists phenoxybenzamine and acepron induced an increase. Similarly, Maas *et al.* (1976) have shown in monkeys that acute treatment with clonidine decreased total brain MHPG levels, whereas piperoxane, an α_2-adrenergic antagonist, increased brain MHPG levels.

XI. Relationship between NE Turnover and Adrenergic Receptors

In the preceding sections we have seen that many drugs have differing effects on MHPG levels when given acutely versus chronically and that these differences may be explained by adrenergic receptor adaptation and feedback inhibition mediated by these receptors. Because much interest has been focused on drug effects on neurotransmitter receptors during the last few years, we shall now explore the correlation between MHPG levels and receptor changes in more depth.

In addition to the effects on α-adrenergic receptors, numerous investigators have also studied the effects of psychoactive drugs on the β-adrenergic receptors. The literature consistently reports that chronic treatment with antidepressant drugs causes a decrease in β-adrenergic receptor density as determined by [^{3}H]dihydroalprenolol (DHA) binding. Classical TCAs—IMI (Pandey *et al.,* 1979b), DMI, doxepin (Banerjee *et al.,* 1977), AT, NT, and chlorimipramine (CMI) (Sellinger-Barnette *et al.,* 1980)—as well as newer non-MAO-inhibitor antidepressants— trazodone (Clements-Jewery, 1978), bupropion (Pandey *et al.,* 1979b; Sellinger-Barnette *et al.,* 1980), and iprindole (Banerjee *et al.,* 1977; Sellinger-Barnette *et al.* 1980)—all show this effect. Similarly, ECT (Bergstrom and Kellar, 1979; Pandey, *et al.,* 1979a), Li (Treiser and Kellar, 1979; Pandey *et al.,* 1979b), and the MAO inhibitors—phenelzine (Pandey *et al.,* 1979b), pargyline (Peroutka and Snyder, 1980), nialamide, and tranylcypromine (Sellinger-Barnette *et al.*, 1980)—also decrease β-adrenergic receptor density. In contrast to this chronic effect, Sarai *et al.* (1978) have shown that acute treatment with antidepressant drugs has no pronounced effect on β-adrenergic receptor density.

There are contradictory reports on the effects of stimulants on β-adrenergic receptor density. Banerjee *et al.* (1979) found increased β-adrenergic receptor density in rats treated for 6 weeks with AMP (10 mg/kg) or cocaine. At lower doses of AMP (5 mg/kg), however, they reported a decrease in β-adrenergic receptor density. On the other hand, Sellinger-Barnette *et al.* (1980) did not find any statistically significant change after 16-day administration of AMP (10 mg/kg) or cocaine.

Hamburg and Tallman (1981) have reported that chronic morphine administration increases the density of β-adrenergic receptors. Similarly, chronic propranolol treatment has been shown to increase β-adrenergic receptor density (Wolfe *et al.*, 1978), whereas L-DOPA has no effect (Sellinger-Barnette *et al.*, 1980). Chronic treatment with either the α_1-adrenergic antagonist prazosin or the α_2-adrenergic antagonists piperoxane and yohimbine, was shown to decrease DHA binding (Swann *et al.*, 1981). Neuroleptics such as CPZ and HLD had no effect (Pandey *et al.*, 1979b; Sellinger-Barnette *et al.*, 1980).

The mechanism by which receptor subsensitivity or supersensitivity is produced is an important question. One possible mechanism has been related to the overexposure and underexposure of β-adrenergic receptor sites to agonists and antagonists. It is generally believed that underexposure to agonists or overexposure to antagonists causes supersensitivity, whereas overexposure to agonists causes subsensitivity of receptors. For example, because of their effects on the reuptake, release, and metabolism of biogenic amines, it is believed that treatment with most antidepressants results in increased levels of NE in the synapse. Continuous exposure of the β-adrenergic receptors to these increased NE levels produces subsensitivity of these receptors. Conversely, chronic treatment with propranolol overexposes the receptors to an antagonist and results in supersensitivity.

The literature cited throughout the chapter suggests that in animal studies MHPG levels correlate with NE turnover, which in turn appears to be controlled by α-adrenergic receptors via a feedback mechanism. Likewise, β-adrenergic receptor density appears to correlate with the resulting NE concentration at the synapse. This is supported by the observation that chronic treatment with many antidepressants (e.g., IMI, DMI, mianserin, and trazodone) increases MHPG levels and also produces subsensitivity of β-adrenergic receptors. Thus, direct receptor binding assays and the measurement of MHPG levels provide complementary techniques for studying adrenergic activity. However, further work needs to be done to explain the fact that chronic treatment with AT and NT produces subsensitivity of β-adrenergic receptors without affecting MHPG levels.

XII. Conclusion

The data presented in this chapter show how the changes in MHPG levels produced by psychoactive drugs can be used to reflect NE turnover and that these changes are related to other drug effects on the adrenergic system. It should be emphasized that MHPG measurements offer an additional method for studying drug effects on noradrenergic neuronal activity and are not a substitute for other methods of determining activity of noradrenergic systems. For example, animal studies on the effects of TCAs on the firing rate of brain noradrenergic neurons, as measured by a single cell recording, are in good agreement with studies of the effects of TCAs on NE reuptake. Secondary amine antidepressants, DMI and NT, are more potent in decreasing cell firing than the tertiary amine antidepressants, IMI and AT. Similarly, DMI and NT are more potent inhibitors of NE reuptake than are IMI or AT. However, only DMI affects brain MHPG levels, NT and PT do not.

A summary of the effects of pharmacological agents on MHPG is presented in Table I. Although for many of the drugs contradictory reports have been presented, certain trends do emerge. DMI and some other non-MAO-inhibitor antidepressants decrease MHPG formation acutely but increase it chronically. MAO inhibitors decrease MHPG levels both acutely and chronically. Many neuroleptics have been shown to increase MHPG levels when given acutely but not chronically. Acute administration of d-AMP increases MHPG levels, whereas cocaine decreases MHPG levels. Although both these drugs are stimulants, AMP acts primarily by releasing NE, whereas cocaine acts through reuptake inhibition. Hence, MHPG formation may be a good way to determine whether a drug affects release or reuptake of NE. Chronic treatment with morphine attenuates the increase in MHPG levels seen with acute treatment. Many drugs have this seemingly contradictory effect on MHPG formation after chronic versus acute administration. These differences are most likely due to adaptive changes in the adrenergic receptors mediating NE turnover via feedback inhibition. Thus, MHPG levels may provide a useful measure for these adaptive changes in adrenergic receptors.

TABLE I
Effect of Different Drugs on the Formation of MHPG

Drug	Treatment duration	Reference	Source	Effect
Antidepressant				
Desmethylimi-pramine (DMI)	Acute	Schildkraut, 1976	Rat brain	Decrease
			Rat brain	Decrease
		Nielsen, 1977a,b	Rat brain	Decrease
		Roffman, 1977b	Rat brain	Decrease
		Tang, 1978 Bareggi, 1978a	Rat brain	Decrease
	Short-term re-peated doses	Tang, 1978	Rat brain	Decrease
		Bareggi, 1978a	Rat brain	No effect
	Chronic	Roffman, 1977b	Rat brain	Increase
		Nielsen, 1977a	Rat brain	Decrease after 10 days; no effect after 20 days
		Tang, 1978	Rat brain	Increase
	Therapeutic treatment	Maas, 1975	Human urine	Decrease in non-responders; no change or Increase in responders
Imipramine (IMI)	Acute	Roffman, 1977a,b	Rat brain	Decrease
	Chronic	Roffman, 1977b	Rat brain	Increase
		Nielsen, 1977a	Rat brain	No effect
	Therapeutic treatment	Beckman, 1975	Human urine	Decrease in both responders and nonre-sponders
		Maas, 1975	Human urine	Decrease in non-responders; no change in responders
		Roccatagliata, 1981	Human CSF	Decrease in responders
Amitriptyline (AT)	Acute	Nielsen, 1977a,b	Rat brain	No effect
		Roffman, 1977b	Rat brain	No effect
		Tang, 1978	Rat brain	No effect
	Chronic	Roffman, 1977b	Rat brain	No effect
		Tang, 1978	Rat brain	No effect
	Therapeutic treatment	Modai, 1979	Human urine	Increase
Nortriptyline (NT)	Chronic	Roffman, 1977b	Rat brain	No effect

TABLE I (*Continued*)

Drug	Treatment duration	Reference	Source	Effect
	Therapeutic treatment	Thoren, 1980	Human CSF	Decrease
Mianserine	Acute and chronic	Tang, 1979b	Rat brain	Increase
		Przegalinski, 1981		Increase
Trazodone	Acute	Przegalinski, 1981	Rat brain	No effect
	Chronic	Przegalinski, 1981	Rat brain	Increase
Phenelzine	Therapeutic treatment	Beckman, 1977	Human urine	Decrease
ECT	Therapeutic treatment	Harnryd, 1979	Human CSF	Decrease
Neuroleptics				
Chlor- promazine (CPZ)	Acute	Kellar, 1973	Rat brain	Increase
		Alfredsson, 1977	Rat brain	Increase
		Ader, 1980	Rat brain	Increase
Haloperidol (HLD)	Acute	Keller, 1973	Rat brain	Increase
		Berridge, 1977	Rat brain	Increase
		Ader, 1980	Rat brain	Increase
	Chronic	Ader, 1980	Rat brain	No effect
Clozapine (CLP)	Acute	Keller, 1973	Rat brain	Increase
		Berridge, 1977	Rat brain	Increase
		Ader, 1980	Rat brain	Increase
	Chronic	Ader, 1980	Rat brain	No effect
Stimulants				
Amphetamine (AMP)	Acute	Bareggi, 1975; 1978b	Rat brain	Increase
			Rat brain	Increase
		Calderini, 1975 Roffman, 1978	Rat brain	Increase
	Chronic	Cassens, 1979	Rat brain	No effect
	Withdrawal	Cassens, 1979	Rat brain	Decrease
	Single dose	Schildkraut, 1971	Human urine	Increase
		Fawcett, 1972	Human urine	Increase in re- sponders; De- crease in non- responders
		Beckman, 1976	Human urine	Decrease in re- sponders; no effect in non- responders
		Shekim, 1979	Children's urine	
		Angrist, 1972	Human urine	No consistent changes

Table I continues

TABLE I   *(Continued)*

Drug	Treatment duration	Reference	Source	Effect
Cocaine	*in vitro*	Crews, 1981	Rat brain	Decrease
	Single dose	Javaid, 1977	Human urine	No effect
Narcotics				
Morphine	Acute	LoPachin, 1978	Rat brain	Increase
		Roffman, 1979	Rat brain	Increase
	Chronic	Roffman, 1979	Rat brain	Decrease
Methadone	Acute	LoPachin, 1978	Rat brain	Increase
	Maintenance	Meyer, 1978	Human urine	No effect
		DeLeon-Jones, 1980	Human urine	No effect
Pentazocine	Acute	LoPachin, 1978	Rat brain	Increase
Cyclazocine	Acute	LoPachin, 1978	Rat brain	Increase
Adrenergic drugs				
Propranol	Acute	Speiser, 1976	Rat brain	Decrease
	Therapeutic treatment	Atsmon, 1972	Human urine	Decrease
Clonidine	Acute	Braestrup, 1976	Rat brain	Decrease
		Tang, 1979a,b	Rat brain	Decrease
		Maas, 1976	Monkey urine	Decrease
	Chronic	Tang, 1979a	Rat brain	Decrease

References

Ader, J. P., Sebens, J. B., and Korf, J. 1980. *Psychopharmacol.* **70,** 239–245.
Alfredsson, G., Wiesel, F.-A., and Skett, P. 1977. *Psychopharmacol.* **53,** 13–18.
Anden, N. E., Butcher, S. G., Corrodi, H., Fuxe, K., and Ungerstedt, U. 1970. *Eur. J. Pharmacol.* **11,** 303–314.
Angrist, B. M., Shopsin, B., Gershon, S., and Wilk, S. 1972. *Psychopharmacologia* **26,** 1–9.
Atsmon, A., Blum, I., Steiner, M., Lotz, A., and Wijsenbeck, H. 1972. *Psychopharmacol.* **27,** 249–254.
Balster, R. L., and Schuster, C. R. 1973. *Pharmacol. Biochem. Behav.* **1,** 67–77.
Banerjee, S. P., Kung, L. S., Riggi, S. J., and Chanda, S. K. 1977. *Nature* **286,** 455–456.
Banerjee, S. P., Sharma, V. K., Kung-Cheung, L. S., Chanda, S. K., and Riggi, S. J. 1979. *Brain Res.* **175,** 119–130.
Bareggi, S. R., Marc, V., and Morselli, P. L. 1974. *Brain Res.* **75,** 177–180.
Bareggi, S. R., Stabenau, J. R., Norige, K., and Shaskin, E. 1975. *Trans. Am. Soc. Neurochem.* **6,** 253.
Bareggi, S. R., Markley, K., and Genovese, E. 1978a. *Eur. J. Pharmacol.* **50,** 301–306.
Bareggi, S. R., Markey, K., and Paoletti, R. 1978b. *Pharmacol. Res. Comm.* **10,** 65–73.
Baumann, P. A., and Maitre, L. 1977. *Naunyn-Schmiedeberg's Arch. Pharmacol.* **300,** 31–37.

Beckmann, H., and Goodwin, F. K. 1975. *Arch. Gen. Psychiatry* **32,** 17–21.
Beckmann, H., St.-Laurent, J., and Goodwin, F. K. 1975. *Psychopharmacologia* **42,** 277–282.
Beckmann, H., van Kammen, D. P., Goodwin, F. K., and Murphy, D. L. 1976. *Biol. Psychiatry* **11,** 377–387.
Beckmann, H., and Murphy, D. L. 1977. *Neuropsychobiol.* **3,** 49–55.
Bergstrom, D. A., and Kellar, K. J. 1979. *J. Pharmacol. Exp. Ther.* **209,** 256–261.
Berridge, T. L., and Sharman, D. F. 1974. *Br. J. Pharmacol.* **50,** 156–158.
Bond, P. A., Jenner, F. A., and Sampson, G. A. 1972. *Psychol. Med.* **2,** 81–85.
Braestrup, C., and Nielsen, M. 1976. *J. Pharmacol. Exp. Ther.* **198,** 596–608.
Bralet, J., and Lallemant, A. M. 1975. *Arch. Int. Pharmacodynamic Ther.* **217,** 332–341.
Bunney, Jr., W. E., and Davis, J. M. 1965. *Arch. Gen. Psychiatry* **13,** 483–494.
Burki, H. R., Ruch, W., and Asper, H. 1975. *Psychopharmacologia* **41,** 27–33.
Calderini, G., Morselli, P. L., and Garattini, S. 1975. *Eur. J. Pharmacol.* **34,** 345–350.
Cassens, G., Kuruc, A., Orsulak, P. J., and Schildkraut, J. J. 1979. *Comm. Psychopharmacol.* **3,** 217–223.
Clements-Jewery, S. 1978. *Neuropharmacol.* **17,** 779–781.
Clouet, D. H., and Ratner, M. 1970. *Science* **168,** 854–856.
Cobbin, D. M., Requin-Blow, B., Williams, L. R., and Williams, W. O. 1979. *Arch. Gen. Psychiatry* **36,** 1111–1115.
Cook, J. D., and Schanberg, S. M. 1970. *Biochem. Pharmacol.* **19,** 1165–1179.
Costa, E., Groppeti, A., and Naimzada, M. K. 1972. *Br. J. Pharmacol.* **44,** 742–751.
Crews, F. T., and Smith, C. B. 1978. *Science* **202,** 322–324.
Crews, F. T., and Smith, C. B. 1981. *Neuropharmacol.* **20,** 363–369.
DeLeon-Jones, F., Maas, J. W., Dekirmenjian, H., and Fawcett, J. A. 1973. *Science* **179,** 200–202.
DeLeon-Jones, F., Davis, J. M., Maas, J. W., Dekirmenjian, H., and Garver, D. L. 1974. *Sci. Proc. Am. Psych. Assoc.* **127,** 42–43.
DeLeon-Jones, F., Davis, J. M., Inwang, E. E., and Dekirmenjian, H., 1982. Submitted for publication.
Fawcett, J., and Siomopoulos, V. 1971. *Arch. Gen. Psychiatry* **25,** 247–255.
Fawcett, J., Maas, J. W., and Dekirmenjian, H. 1972. *Arch. Gen. Psychiatry* **26,** 246–251.
Glowinski, J., and Axelrod, J. 1964. *Nature* **204,** 1318–1319.
Gold, M. S., and Redmond, Jr., D. E. 1977. *Neurosci. Abst.* **3,** 250.
Gold, M. S., Redmond, Jr., D. E., and Kleber, H. D. 1979. *Am. J. Psychiatry* **136,** 100–102.
Greenspan, K., Schildkraut, J. J., Gordan, E. K., Baer, L., Aronoff, M. S., and Durell, J. 1970. *J. Psychiatry Res.* **7,** 171–183.
Hamburg, M., and Tallman, J. F. 1981. *Nature* **291,** 493–495.
Harnryd, C., Bjerkenstedt, L., Grimm, V. E., and Sedvall, G. 1979. *Psychopharmacol.* **64,** 131–134.
Helmeste, D. M., Stancer, H. C., Coscina, D. V., Takahashi, S., and Warsh, J. J. 1979. *Life Sci.* **25,** 601–606.
Hertting, G., Axelrod, J., and Whitby, L. G. 1961. *J. Pharmacol. Exp. Ther.* **134,** 146–153.
Hollister, L. E., Prusmack, J. J., Knopes, K., and Kanaske, K. 1980. *Commun. Psychopharmacol.* **4,** 135–140.
Javaid, J. I., Dekirmenjian, H., and Davis, J. M. 1977. *Cocaine and Other Stimulants* (E. H. Ellinwood, Jr., and M. M. Kilbey, eds.), pp. 665–673. Plenum Press, New York.
Javaid, J. I., Perel, J. M., and Davis, J. M. 1979. *Life Sci.* **24,** 21–28.
Keller, H. H., Bartholini, G., and Pletscher, A. 1973. *Eur. J. Pharmacol.* **23,** 183–186.
Kety, S., Javoy, F., Thierry, A. M., Julou, L., and Glowinski, J. 1967. *Proc. Nat. Acad. Sci.* **58,** 1249–1254.

66 J. I. Javaid, J. Rubinstein, and J. M. Davis

Kraemer, G. W., Breese, G. R., Prange, A. J., Moran, E. C., Lewis, J. K., Kemnitz, J. W., Bushnell, P. J., Howard, J. L., and McKinney, W. T. 1981. *Psychopharmacol.* **73**, 1–11.
Ladisich, W., Steinhauff, N., and Matussek, N. 1969. *Psychopharmacologia* **15**, 296–304.
Langer, S. Z. 1977. *Br. J. Pharmacol.* **60**, 481–497.
Lipman, J. J., and Spencer, P. S. J. 1978. *Lancet* **2**, 521.
LoPachin, R. M., and Reigle, T. G. 1978. *J. Pharmacol. Exp. Ther.* **207**, 151–158.
Maas, J. W. 1975. *Arch. Gen. Psychiatry* **32**, 1357–1361.
Maas, J. W., Fawcett, J., and Dekirmenjian, H. 1968. *Arch. Gen. Psychiatry* **19**, 129–134.
Maas, J. W., and Landis, D. H. 1968. *J. Pharmacol. Exp. Ther.* **163**, 147–162.
Maas, J. W., Dekirmenjian, H., Garver, D., Redmond, Jr., D. E., and Landis, D. H. 1972. *Brain Res.* **41**, 507–511.
Maas, J. W., Dekirmenjian, H., Garver, D., Redmond, Jr., D. E., and Landis, D. H. 1973. *Eur. J. Pharmacol.* **23**, 121–130.
Maas, J. W., Hattox, S. E., Landis, P. H., and Roth, R. H. 1976. *Brain Res.* **118**, 167–173.
Maas, J. W., Hattox, S. E., Greene, N. M., and Landis, D. H. 1979. *Science* **205**, 1025–1027.
Mannarino, E., Kirshner, N., and Nashold, B. S. 1963. *J. Neurochem.* **10**, 373–379.
Maynert, E. W., and Klingman, G. E. 1962. *J. Pharmacol. Exp. Ther.* **135**, 285–295.
Meek, J. L., and Neff, N. H. 1973. *J. Pharmacol. Exp. Ther.* **184**, 570–575.
Meyer, R. E., Schildkraut, J. J., Mirin, S. M., Orsulak, P. J., Randall, M., McDougle, M., Platz, P. A., Grab, E., and Barbor, T. 1978. *Psychopharmacol.* **56**, 327–333.
Modai, I., Apter, A., Golomb, M., and Wijsenbeek, H. 1979. *Neuropsychobiol.* **5**, 181–184.
Musacchio, J., Julou, L., Kety, S., and Glowinski, J. 1968. *Proc. Natl. Acad. Sci.* **63**, 1117–1119.
Neff, N. H., and Costa, E. 1967. *Antidepressant Drugs* (S. Garattini and M. H. G. Dukes, eds.), pp. 28–34, Int. Congr. Ser. 122. Amsterdam, Excerpta. Medica Foundation.
Nielsen, M. 1975. *J. Pharm. Pharmacol.* **27**, 206–209.
Nielsen, M., and Braestrup, C. 1977a. *Naunyn-Schmiedeberg's Arch. Pharmacol.* **300**, 87–92.
Nielsen, M., and Braestrup, C. 1977b. *Naunyn-Schmiedeberg's Arch. Pharmacol.* **300**, 93–99.
Nyback, H., Borzecki, F., and Sedvall, G. 1968. *Eur. J. Pharmacol.* **4**, 395–403.
Pandey, G. N., Heinze, W. J., Brown, B. D., and Davis, J. M. 1979a. *Nature* **280**, 234–235.
Pandey, G. N., Heinze, W. B., Brown, B. D., and Davis, J. M. 1979b. *Fed. Proc.* **38**, 592.
Peroutka, S. J., and Snyder, S. H. 1980. *Science* **210**, 88–90.
Pinder, R. M., Brogden, R. N., Sawyer, P. R., Speight, T. M., Spencer, R., and Avery, G. S. 1976. *Drugs* **12**, 1–40.
Pryor, G. T., Scott, M. K., and Peache, S. 1972. *J. Neurochem.* **19**, 891–893.
Przegalinski, E., Kordecka-Magiera, A., Mogilnicka, E., and Maj, J. 1981. *Psychopharmacol.* **74**, 187–190.
Roccatagliata, G., Albano, C., and Abbruzzese, G. 1981. *Neuropsychobiol.* **7**, 169–171.
Roffman, M., Cassens, G., and Schildkraut, J. J. 1977a. *Biochem. Pharmacol.* **26**, 2355–2358.
Roffman, M., Kling, M. A., and Cassen, G. 1977b. *Comm. Psychopharmacol.* **1**, 195–206.
Roffman, M., Cassens, G., and Schildkraut, J. J. 1978. *Biochem. Pharmacol.* **27**, 1774–1777.
Roffman, M., Reigle, T., Orsulak, P., Cassens, G., and Schildkraut, J. J. 1979. *Neuropharmacol.* **18**, 483–487.
Rosloff, B. N., and Davis, J. M. 1974. *Psychopharmacologia* **40**, 53–64.
Ross, S. B., and Renyi, A. L. 1975. *Acta Pharmacol. Toxicol.* **35**, 382–394.
Rutledge, C. O., and Jonason, J. J. 1967. *J. Pharmacol. Exp. Ther.* **157**, 493–502.
Sarai, K., Frazer, A., Brunswick, D., and Mendels, J. 1978. *Biochem. Pharmacol.* **27**, 2179–2181.
Schanberge, S. M., Schildkraut, J. J., Breese, G. R., and Kopin, I. J. 1968. *Biochem. Pharmacol.* **17**, 247–254.

Scheel-Kruger, J. 1972. *Eur. J. Pharmacol.* **18**, 63–73.
Schildkraut, J. J. 1965. *Am. J. Psychiatry* **122**, 509–522.
Schildkraut, J. J. 1970. *Am. J. Psychiatry* **126**, 925–931.
Schildkraut, J. J. 1974. *J. Nerv. Ment. Dis.* **158**, 348–360.
Schildkraut, J. J., Schanberg, S. M., Breese, G. R., and Kopin, I. J. 1967. *Am. J. Psychiatry* **124**, 600–608.
Schildkraut, J. J., Dodge, G. A., and Logue, M. A. 1969. *J. Psychiatry Res.* **7**, 29–34.
Schildkraut, J. J., Winokur, A., and Applegate, C. W. 1970. *Science* **168**, 867–869.
Schildkraut, J. J., Watson, R., Draskoczy, P. R., and Hartmann, E. 1971. *Lancet* **2**, 485–486.
Schildkraut, J. J., and Draskoczy, P. R. 1974. *Biology of Convulsive Therapy* (M. Fink, S. Kety, J. McGaugh, and T. A. Williams, eds.), pp. 143–170. Wiley, New York.
Schildkraut, J. J., Koffman, M., Orsulak, P. J., Schatzberg, A. F., Kling, M. A., and Reigle, T. G. 1976. *Pharmakopsychiatr. Neuropsychopharmakol.* **9**, 193–202.
Schubert, J., Nybeck, H., and Sedvall, G. 1970. *J. Pharm. Pharmacol.* **22**, 136–138.
Sellinger-Barnette, M. M., Mendels, J., and Frazer, A. 1980. *Neuropharmacol.* **19**, 447–454.
Shekim, W. O., Dekirmenjian, H., Chapel, J. L., Javaid, J. I., and Davis, J. M. 1979. *J. Ped.* **95**, 389–394.
Smith, C. B., Villarreal, J. E., Bednarczyk, J. H., and Sheldon, M. I. 1972. *Science* **170**, 1106–1107.
Snyder, S. H., Banerjee, S. P., Yamamura, H. I., and Greenberg, D. 1974. *Science* **184**, 1243–1253.
Sparber, S. B., and Meyer, D. R. 1978. *Pharmacol. Biochem. Behav.* **9**, 319–325.
Speiser, Z., and Weinstock, M. 1976. *Pharmacol. Biochem. Behav.* **4**, 531–534.
Spilman, E. L., and Badal, D. W. 1960. *Arch. Gen. Psychiatry* **2**, 545–547.
Swann, A. C., Grant, S. J., Hattox, S. E., and Maas, J. W. 1981. *Eur. J. Pharmacol.* **73**, 301–305.
Tang, S. W., Helmeste, D. M., and Stencer, H. C. 1978. *Naunyn-Schmiedeberg's Arch. Pharmacol.* **305**, 207–211.
Tang, S. W., Helmeste, D. M., and Stencer, H. C. 1979a. *Psychopharmacol.* **61**, 11–12.
Tang, S. W., Helmeste, D. M., and Stencer, H. C. 1979b. *Can. J. Physiol. Pharmacol.* **57**, 435–437.
Thoren, P., Asberg, M., Bertilsson, L., Mellstrom, B., Sjoqvist, F., and Traskman, L. 1980. *Arch. Gen. Psychiatry* **37**, 1289–1294.
Treiser, S., and Kellar, K. J. 1979. *Eur. J. Pharmacol.* **58**, 85–86.
Vetulani, J., and Bednarczyk, B. 1977. *J. Pharmacol.* **29**, 567–569.
Vogt, M. 1954. *J. Physiol.* (London) **123**, 451–481.
Weiner, N. 1974. *Neuropsychopharmacology of Monoamines and Their Regulatory Enzymes* (E. Usdin, ed.), pp. 143–159. Raven Press, New York.
Wilk, S., and Mones, R. 1971. *J. Neurochem.* **18**, 1771–1773.
Wilk, S., Shopsin, B., Gershon, S., and Suhl, M. 1972. *Nature* **235**, 440–441.
Wolfe, B. B., Harden, T. K., Sporn, J. R., and Molinoff, P. B. 1978. *J. Pharmacol. Exp. Ther.* **207**, 446–457.

5

Methods for Determining MHPG in Plasma, CSF, and Urine

SUSAN E. HATTOX

Departments of Psychiatry and Pharmacology
Yale University School of Medicine, New Haven

I. Introduction

The development of a scientific hypothesis forms a framework for experimental paradigms designed to prove or disprove that hypothesis. Answers to critical questions, however, must be based on facts elucidated

69

MHPG: BASIC MECHANISMS
AND PSYCHOPATHOLOGY

from data collected by accurate and precise methods. Much of our understanding of the use of MHPG as a marker of noradrenergic activity has been made possible by the development in the 1960s and 1970s of the methods that are described in this chapter.

The majority of published methods for the measurement of MHPG levels in CSF, plasma, and urine are based on initial isolation by solvent extraction or column chromatography, further isolation by gas or liquid chromatography, and detection by electron capture, mass spectrometry, or amperometry. Table I summarizes the characteristics of methods

TABLE I

Characteristics of Methods for Measurement of MHPG in CSF

Detection	Reference standard	Isolation	Derivatization (liquid GC phase)	Recovery (%) [N][a]	Precision [N][a]	Reference
ecGC	Internal MHPG	AG × 4 Cl⁻	TFA (6% QF-1-0065)	80–90	—[b]	Schanberg et al., 1968
	Internal MHPG	Ethyl acetate extraction	TFA (3% OV-17)	28.9 ± 2.9	—	Gordon and Oliver, 1971
	Internal MHPG	Ethyl acetate extraction	PFP (6% QF-1)	—	—	Karoum et al., 1971
	External MHPG	Ethyl acetate extraction	TFA (3% OV-17)	—	—	Wilk et al., 1971a
	Internal MHPG	AG 1 × 4 Cl⁻ Dichloromethane extraction	Acetyl TFA (4% OV-1)	—	—	Bond, 1972
	Internal aldrin	Ethyl acetate extraction, tlc of 4′ acetyl derivative	Acetyl HFB (3% OV-1)	40.4 ± 1.4 [61]	Mean ± proportionate SD [35] 8.39 ± 7.98%	O'Keeffe and Brooksbank, 1973
	Internal γ-benzene hexachloride	Ethyl acetate extraction 4′ acetyl formation Dichloromethane extraction	Acetyl TFA (2.5% E 301)	—	—	Davidson et al., 1977
GC–MS	[²H₂]MHPG (V)	Ethyl acetate extraction	TFA (3% XE60)	—	7% coefficient of variation	Bertilsson, 1973
	[²H₃]MHPG (VI)	Alumina Ethyl acetate extraction	TFA (3% OV-17)	—	—	Gordon et al., 1974
	[²H₃]MHPG (VII)	Ethyl acetate extraction	PFP (3% SE-54)	—	—	Karoum et al., 1975
	[²H₃]MHPG (VIII)	Ethyl acetate extraction	TFA (1% SE-30) (3% OV-17)	100 ± 5.1 [7]	8.2 [16] coefficient of variation	Sjöquist et al., 1975
	[²H₃]MHPG (VI)	Diethyl ether extraction pH 2.0	PFP (OV-17)	106 ± 1		Swahn et al., 1976
	[²H₂]MHPG (V)	Ethyl acetate extraction	TFA (3% OV-17)	—	—	Murray et al., 1977
	[²H₅]MHPG (IX)	Ethyl acetate extraction pH 6.5 + 10	PFP (3% OV-1)	—	—	Muskiet et al., 1978

TABLE I   (Continued)

Detection	Reference standard	Isolation	Derivatization (liquid GC phase)	Recovery (%) [N][a]	Precision [N][a]	Reference
	[²H₃]MHPG (VII)	Ethyl acetate extraction	PFP (3% OV-17)	79 as compared with external standard		Faull et al., 1979
HPLC	External MHPG	C₁₈ Reverse-phase citrate–acetate buffer, pH 5.15 Ethyl acetate extraction, pH 1		95	7.3 coefficient of varition	Anderson et al., 1981
	External MHPG	C₁₈ Reverse-phase potassium phosphate methanol / H₂O, pH 2.5		96.5 extraction	1.1% SD	Krstulovic et al., 1981
Fluorimetry	External MHPG Internal MHPG sulphate	Sephadex G-10 DEAE Sephadex A-25	Ethylenediamine Heat in acid Heat with Ethylene-diamine	85 from G-10 —	— —	Korf et al., 1971 Extein et al., 1973

[a]The number in square brackets indicates the sample size.
[b]The dash indicates that data were not available.

developed for the analysis of MHPG in CSF in terms of the detector, reference standard, isolation procedure, derivative, and gas chromatographic phase employed as well as the recovery and precision of the method. Tables II and III summarize the characteristics of those methods that have been developed for analysis of MHPG in plasma and urine, respectively. A comparison of the concentration of MHPG measured in CSF, plasma, and urine employing the various methods may be found in Tables V, VI, and VIII, respectively.

TABLE II
Characteristics of Methods for Measurement of MHPG in Plasma

Detection	Reference standard	Isolation	Derivatization (liquid GC phase)	Recovery (%) [N][a]	Precision [N][a]	Reference
ecGC	External MHPG	Hexane wash Ethyl acetate extraction KHCO₃ wash	TFA (3% OV-17)	65 ± 1.6 [27]	10% [6]	Dekirmenjian and Maas, 1974
	Internal MHPG	Ethyl acetate extraction	PFP (3% SE-30)	70–80	30.1% coefficient of variation	Markianos and Beckmann, 1976
	Internal or External MHPG	Ethyl acetate extraction	PFP (3% SE-30)	68–89	—[b]	Halaris et al., 1977

Table II continues

TABLE II (*Continued*)

Detection	Reference standard	Isolation	Derivatization (liquid GC phase)	Recovery (%) [N][a]	Precision [N][a]	Reference
GC–MS	[²H₃]MHPG (**VIII**)	Ethyl acetate extraction	TFA (1% SE-30) (3% OV-17)	MHPG 100 + 5.1 MHPG-S 101 ± 7.2	5.4 [18] coefficient of variation	Sjöquist *et al.*, 1975
	[²H₂]MHPG (**V**)	Hexane wash Ethyl acetate extraction KHCO₃ wash	TFA (3% OV-17)	5 ng 107 ± .3 [10] 70% as compared to external standard	3.5 [30] coefficient of variation	Maas *et al.*, 1976
	[²H₃]MHPG (**VII**)	Ethyl acetate extraction	PFP (3% SE-54)			Karoum *et al.*, 1977a,b
	[²H₃]MHPG (**VII**)	Perchlorate precipitation acetylation isopropyl extraction	Acetyl-TFA (3% OV-17)	10 ng 101.5 ± 3.2 [7] 20 ng 99.5 ± 3.4 [9] 10 ng 55.2[c] [8] 20 ng 55.6[c] [8]	7.7 [10] coefficient of variation	Takahashi *et al.*, 1977
	[²H₅]MHPG (**IX**)	NaCl precipitation Ethyl acetate extraction pH 1:0	PFP (SE 54)	—	—	Muskiet *et al.*, 1980

[a]The number in square brackets indicate the sample size.
[b]The dash indicates that data were not available.
[c]As compared with external standard.

TABLE III
Characteristics of Methods for Measurement of MHPG in Urine

Detection	Reference standard	Isolation	Derivatization (liquid GC phase)	Recovery (%) [N][a]	Precision [N][a]	Reference
Spectrophotometry 360 nm	Internal MHPG	BaCl₂ precipitation CG-50 Ethyl acetate extraction, pH 6.2, K₂CO₃ back-extraction	Oxidation to vanillin, toluene extraction, K₂CO₃ back-extraction	12.3 [18]	±9.5% maximum difference from mean	Ruthven and Sandler, 1965
360 nm	Internal MHPG	Ethyl acetate extraction, pH 6.2	Oxidation to vanillin, toluene extraction, K₂CO₃ wash	70.4 ± 23.3 [9]	—[b]	Sapira, 1968
360 nm	Internal MHPG External MHPG	BaCl₂ precipitation, Ethyl acetate extraction, pH 6.8–7.0	Oxidation to vanillin, toluene extraction, K₂CO₃ wash	54.9 [23]	±4.13% maximum difference from mean	Nicholas *et al.*, 1969

TABLE III   (*Continued*)

Detection	Reference standard	Isolation	Derivatization (liquid GC phase)	Recovery (%) [N][a]	Precision [N][a]	Reference
348 nm	Internal MHPG	BaCl₂ precipitation, Na₂WO₄ precipitation, HC10₄ precipitation, ethyl acetate extraction, pH 6.5	Oxidation to vanillin, toluene extraction, NH₄OH back-extraction	85.7 ± 8.3 [10]	5.3% difference from mean	Bigelow et al., 1971
Fluorimetry	Internal MHPG	Ethyl acetate wash, pH 1.0, AG 1 × 4, ethyl acetate extraction, pH 6.0.	Oxidation with FeCl₃ reagent	59 ± 4 [24]		Antun et al., 1971
		Ethyl acetate extraction, pH 1.0, phosphate wash, pH 7.6, silica gel TLC	Heat in acid, heat with ethylene-diamine	53 ± 4		Zawad and Brown, 1976
Densitometry	External MHPG	BaCl₂ precipitation, ethyl acetate extraction, cellulose TLC	Diazotized sulphanilic acid	70 ± 6 [5]		Breebaart et al., 1972
Gas Chromatography ecGC	Internal MHPG	Ethyl acetate extraction, acidic AG 1 × 4, ethyl acetate extraction	TFA (6% QF-1-0065)	55.4	6.3% [16]	Wilk et al., 1967
ecGC	Internal MHPG	Dichloro-methane or ethyl acetate extraction, pH 8.0	(1) TMS (10% SE-52) (2) PFP (6% QF-1)			(1) Karoum et al., 1969 (2) Karoum et al., 1971
ecGC	External MHPG	Ethyl acetate extraction, pH 6.0, KHCO₃ wash	TFA (6% QF-1)	92.7 ± 10.3		Dekirmenjian and Maas, 1970

Table III continues

TABLE III (*Continued*)

Detection	Reference standard	Isolation	Derivatization (liquid GC phase)	Recovery (%) [N][a]	Precision [N][a]	Reference
FID	Internal phenan-threne	Acetone pre-cipitation, ethyl acetate extraction, pH 1.0, Na$_2$CO$_3$ ex-traction, ethyl acetate ex-traction, pH 6.0, K$_2$CO$_3$ extraction	Oxidation to va-nillin chlo-roform extraction Methoxime TMS	91.5 (free) 97.5 (total)	—	Kahane *et al.*, 1970
ecGC	Internal MHPG	AG 1 × 4 Dichloro-methane ex-traction	Acetyl TFA (4% OV-1)	— —	5.9% SD [3] —	Bond, 1972 Bond and Howlett, 1974
FID	Internal dotria-contane	Benzene wash, pH 1.0, acetone pre-cipitation, ethyl acetate extraction, Na$_2$CO$_3$ ex-traction, dichloro-methane extraction	Acetyl (3% QF-1)	80	—	Kahane *et al.*, 1972
ecGC	External MHPG	Ethyl acetate wash, pH 1.5, ethyl acetate extraction, pH 6.0	TFA	—	—	Martin *et al.*, 1972
ecGC	Internal aldrin	Ethyl acetate extraction,. silica gel TLC	Acetyl HFB (3% OV-1)	40.4 ± 1.4 [16]	6.88 ± 6.60% Mean ± SD of % difference between duplicates	O'Keefe and Brooksbank, 1973
ecGC	Internal α-lindane, MHPG	AG 1 × 4	PFP (5% OV-210)	62 ± 2.5 SD	—	Fellows *et al.*, 1975
FID	Internal phenan-threne	Ethyl acetate extraction, pH 1.0, dichloro-methane ex-traction	Acetyl boronate (3% OV-101)	52.1 ± 4.1 [40]	8.15 ± 7.43% [20] as above	Biondi *et al.*, 1977 Biondi *et al.*, 1979
FID	Internal propyl-gallate	Ethyl acetate extraction, pH 6.2	TMS (3% OV-1; OV-225)	80.8 ± 13.6	—	Muskiet *et al.*, 1977
ecGC	External MHPG	BaCl$_2$ precipita-tion, ethyl acetate ex-traction, pH 5.5	HFB (3% OV-17)	78.5 ± 12.7	—	Sharpless, 1977
ecGC		Ethyl acetate extraction, pH 7.0	HFB (1% OV-1)	—	—	Mathieu *et al.*, 1980

TABLE III (*Continued*)

Detection	Reference standard	Isolation	Derivatization (liquid GC phase)	Recovery (%) [N][a]	Precision [N][a]	Reference
GC–MS	Internal MHPG	Ether extraction, pH 6.0	PFP (5% OV-210 + 1% SE-52)	—	—	Karoum et al., 1973
	[²H₃]MHPG (VI)	Alumina, ethyl acetate extraction	TFA (3% OV-17)	—	—	Gordon et al., 1974
	[²H₃]MHPG (VIII)	BaCl₂ precipitation, ethyl acetate extraction	TFA (1% SE-30; 3% OV-17)	100 ± 5.1	2.8% coefficient of variation	Sjöquist et al., 1975
	[²H₃]MHPG-SO₄ (X)	XAD-2 LH-20	TFA (3% OV-17)	—	—	Murray et al., 1977
	Internal MHPG	Ethyl acetate extraction, pH 6.0, KHCO₃ wash	PFP (3% OV-1; 3% QF-1; 3% SP-2250)	—	—	Edwards et al., 1979
HPLC Electrochemical		Solvent extraction C₁₈ reverse phase, acetate/perchlorate/methanol, pH 2.9, alumina C₁₈ reverse phase acetate/methanol/1-heptane sulfonic acid	Oxidation to vanillin	— —	— —	Kissinger et al., 1977; Mitchell and Coscia, 1978
	Internal isovanillyl alcohol MHPG	Toluene extraction, K₂CO₃ wash, ethyl acetate extraction C₁₈ reverse phase acetate/methanol, pH 4.7, ethyl acetate extraction, pH 1.0 C₁₈ reverse phase KH₂PO₄, pH 2.5, acetonitrile/water gradient	Oxidation to vanillin, reduction to vanillyl alcohol	— 95–99	— —	Buchanan et al., 1979; Krstulovic et al., 1980
Fluorimetric		Ethyl acetate extraction, pH 6.0, KHCO₃ wash, basic extraction		72.6 [3]	8.2% coefficient of variation	Taylor et al., 1981

[a]The number in square brackets indicates the sample size.
[b]The dash indicates that data were not available.

II.   Measurement of MHPG in CSF

A.   Electron Capture Gas Chromatography (ecGC)

1. Initial Isolation. Shown to be a major metabolite of norepinephrine in brain of various species (Axelrod *et al.,* 1959; Mannarino *et al.,* 1963; Rutledge and Jonason, 1967), MHPG was originally identified and quantitated in CSF by Schanberg *et al.* (1968), who adapted the procedure of Wilk *et al.* (1967) from urine to CSF. Initial isolation was by anion-exchange chromatography, a step also employed later by Bond (1972). All other procedures developed for ecGC analysis employ initial ethyl acetate extraction of the CSF sample, which may also contain ascorbic acid and/or ethylenediaminetetraacetic acid (EDTA) to retard oxidation (see Table I).

2. Derivatization and Chromatography. The second isolation step, gas chromatography, requires that the volatility of MHPG be increased to allow gas phase analysis. In addition, electron capturing groups must be introduced into the molecule for detection. Both requirements are accomplished by forming a chemical derivative of MHPG. This procedure substitutes labile hydroxyl and phenolic hydrogen atoms with nonpolar halogen-containing functional groups, thus reducing hydrogen bonding and increasing volatility.

A variety of derivatives have been employed for both electron capture and mass spectrometric detection of MHPG in CSF. Schanberg *et al.* (1968), Gordon and Oliver (1971), Gordon *et al.* (1974), Wilk *et al.* (1971a), Bertilsson (1973), Sjöquist *et al.* (1975), and Murray *et al.* (1977a) prepared the tris(trifluoro)acetyl (TFA) derivative (**I**) of MHPG by reacting the dried residue from the initial isolation step with trifluoroacetic anhydride in ethyl acetate at room temperature for 15–90 min. Studies in this laboratory have shown maximum derivatization under these conditions at 1 h (S. E. Hattox, unpublished observations).

I

Karoum *et al.* (1971, 1975), Swahn *et al.* (1976), Muskiet *et al.* (1978), and Faull *et al.* (1979) prepared the tris(pentafluoro)propionyl (PFP) derivative (II) of MHPG by heating the residue 5–30 min at 60–75°C with pentafluoropropionic anhydride. In some cases the reagent is a mixture of pentafluoropropanol and pentafluoropropionic anhydride (4:1 v/v) when the sample is being prepared for simultaneous analysis of MHPG and acidic compounds (Swahn et al., 1976; Faull et al., 1979). The structure of the MHPG derivative (II), however, remains the same.

$$CF_3CF_2\underset{\underset{O}{\|}}{C}O \!-\!\!\!\overset{CH_3O}{\diagdown}\!\!\!\underset{}{\bigcirc}\!\!\!-\!\!\underset{\underset{O\underset{\|}{C}CF_2CF_3}{|}}{C}HCH_2O\underset{\overset{\|}{O}}{C}CF_2CF_3 \qquad \textbf{II}$$

Bond (1972) and Davidson et al. (1977) prepared the 4'-acetyl-bis(trifluoro)acetyl derivative (III) of MHPG. Acetic anhydride is added to CSF or the effluent from an anion exchange column, and the reaction is carried out in a basic aqueous solution. After further isolation of the 4'-acetyl derivative by extraction into dichloromethane, the TFA derivative is formed as described above.

$$CH_3\underset{\underset{O}{\|}}{C}O \!-\!\!\!\overset{CH_3O}{\diagdown}\!\!\!\underset{}{\bigcirc}\!\!\!-\!\!\underset{\underset{O\underset{\|}{C}CF_3}{|}}{C}HCH_2O\underset{\overset{\|}{O}}{C}CCF_3 \qquad \textbf{III}$$

O'Keeffe and Brooksbank (1973) prepared the 4'-acetylbis(hepta-fluoro)butyl derivative (IV) of MHPG to increase the response of the electron-capture detector and to increase sensitivity. In this method the 4'-acetyl derivative is further isolated by thin-layer chromatography, dissolved in tetrahydrofuran, and reacted with heptafluorobutyric anhydride for 5 min.

$$CH_3\underset{\underset{O}{\|}}{C}O \!-\!\!\!\overset{CH_3O}{\diagdown}\!\!\!\underset{}{\bigcirc}\!\!\!-\!\!\underset{\underset{O\underset{\|}{C}CF_2CF_2CF_3}{|}}{C}HCH_2O\underset{\overset{\|}{O}}{C}CF_2CF_2CF_3 \qquad \textbf{IV}$$

Änggård and Sedvall (1969) investigated in detail the properties of a variety of derivatives for ecGC determination of MHPG. They found the PFP derivative to be more stable and to give a higher electron-capture response than the TFA derivative.

A prerequisite for derivatization in high yield is that the residue from the initial isolation be completely dry. This is usually accomplished by initial removal of water from the organic phase with Na_2SO_4, evaporation *in vacuo*, or by sequential evaporations from ethyl acetate, methanol, and benzene. All derivatization procedures require as a final step the careful evaporation of reagents under a stream of dry air or nitrogen. Any remaining reagents will poison the gas chromatographic column. This procedure must be performed carefully because the derivatized MHPG may be lost if evaporation continues after removal of the reagents (S. E. Hattox, unpublished observations). Samples are dissolved in ethyl acetate for gas chromatographic analysis. Chromatography has been successfully employed by using a wide variety of liquid phases (as shown in Table I). For highest precision, all solvents should be freshly redistilled or of nanograde quality and all glassware should be acid washed (S. E. Hattox, unpublished observations).

3. The Use of Standard References. The basis for all quantitative methods is that the concentration of the compound to be measured is proportional to the detector response to that compound, in this case MHPG. The detector response to an unknown sample is compared to the detector response to a sample containing a known amount of MHPG. Ideally, detector response will be linearly proportional to MHPG concentration, and a calibration curve of response versus MHPG concentration can be constructed. Calibration curves may be prepared using either internal or external standards. In the former, known amounts of standard are added to replicates of the unknown sample and carried through the entire procedure to correct for incomplete recovery. In the latter, the standard samples of known concentration are prepared separately from the unknown samples. Standards may be compounds that are similar in structure to MHPG or MHPG itself may be used. The ideal standard will be chemically identical to MHPG so that its recovery from each step in the isolation procedure will be the same as MHPG, but will differ in a manner that will allow the detector to differentiate between MHPG and the standard. This situation is most closely approximated when MHPG is added in known amounts to replicate samples as an internal standard or when stable isotope-labeled MHPG is added as an internal standard for mass spectrometric analysis.

4. Recovery and Precision. Using their methods, Gordon and Oliver (1971) and O'Keeffe and Brooksbank (1973) report the recovery of MHPG as 28.9 and 40.4%, respectively. One of the major losses of MHPG may be due to inefficient extraction into ethyl acetate.

Although extraction of MHPG from urine and plasma have been high (Dekirmenjian and Maas, 1970 and 1974; Karoum et al., 1969; Wilk et al., 1967), these fluids are highly ionized and recovery of MHPG from CSF may be improved by extraction from NaCl-saturated samples.

Values for the precision of most of the ecGC methods for measuring MHPG in CSF are not available, with the exception of O'Keeffe and Brooksbank (1973). They report the mean ± the standard deviation of the percentage difference between duplicate estimations as 8.39 ± 7.98%.

5. *Summary.* A variety of approaches have been taken concerning the use of reference standards for ecGC measurement of MHPG in CSF (as shown in Table I). Authentic MHPG has been used both as internal and external standard, and aldrin (O'Keeffe and Brooksbank, 1973) and γ-benzene hexachloride (Davidson et al., 1977) have been employed as internal standards. Both peak height and peak area have been used to measure detector response. An examination of the levels of MHPG measured in CSF using these various methods (as shown in Table V) indicates that free MHPG in human lumbar CSF measured by the method of Karoum and co-workers (1971) gave values comparable to those obtained by the more specific GC–MS techniques. All other ecGC methods were used to measure only total (free plus conjugated) MHPG after enzymatic hydrolysis, as described in Section IV. The range of values found by ecGC techniques was 10–26.5 ng/ml human lumbar CSF, with those methods that used internal standards not related in structure to MHPG giving the lower results. All results using ecGC detection were, however, within the range of values for free and total MHPG reported using GC–MS techniques, suggesting that ecGC methods can give satisfactory results and that either internal or external standards may be used.

B. Gas Chromatography–Mass Spectrometry (GC–MS)

Electron-capture GC methods have the advantages of sensitivity, simplicity, and low cost. On the debit side, the technique suffers from lack of specificity and the necessity of indirect measurement of recovery. The use of the mass spectrometric technique of selected ion monitoring (Sweeley et al., 1966), on the other hand, is sensitive, specific, and rectifies the problem of variable recovery by using as internal standards MHPG molecules in which two or more hydrogen atoms have been replaced by the heavy stable isotope of hydrogen, deuterium. Section VI describes the synthesis of a number of stable isotope-labeled internal standards for MHPG. The assumption is made that the internal standard and endogenous MHPG will be chemically identical, recovered to the same extent, but detected as different compounds by the mass spectrometer on the basis of the differences in their masses due to the presence of heavy isotopes. However, mass spectrometers are costly, complicated, and specialized knowledge is necessary for their use.

The isolation and derivatization procedures that were originally developed for use with electron-capture detection have been adapted for use with mass spectrometric detection. The two most prevalent derivatives prepared are the tris(trifluoro)acetyl (Bertilsson 1973; Gordon *et al.*, 1974; Murray *et al.*, 1977a; Sjöquist *et al.*, 1975) and the tris(pentafluoro)propionyl compounds (Faull *et al.*, 1979; Karoum *et al.*, 1975; Muskiet *et al.*, 1978; Swahn *et al.*, 1976), prepared by the methods described in Section II,A,2.

Deuterium-labeled standards are invariably processed as internal standards. The amount of endogenous MHPG present is calculated by measurement of the ratio of peak heights or areas of ions derived from endogenous MHPG and deuterium-labeled MHPG, respectively, and interpolation from a calibration curve of peak height ratios measured from known amounts of unlabeled and labeled MHPG. This procedure is described in greater detail in Section III,C. Calibration curves may be prepared in artificial CSF and carried through the entire procedure or prepared by direct derivatization of known combinations of unlabeled and labeled MHPG. Sjöquist *et al.* (1975) and Murray *et al.* (1977a) found no differences in results obtained using the two types of curves.

The ions that are chosen for monitoring depend on the derivative prepared and the number and location of deuterium atoms in the internal standard. Table IV lists the ions monitored in the various GC–MS methods developed for MHPG measurement. The specificity of GC–MS techniques allow high accuracy and precision of measurement. This specificity, however, should be validated by monitoring two ions derived from endogenous MHPG as well as one from the internal standard. The ratio of the two ions from MHPG will remain constant if no interfering substances are present. The intensity of a given ion in the mass spectrometer varies with the electron voltage (eV), and instruments with quadrupole mass analyzers are particularly sensitive to this effect. Figure 1 shows the relationship between ion intensity (which determines sensitivity) and eV in a quadrupole instrument, suggesting that eV should be optimized in each method.

Because the internal standard will be degraded at the same rate as the

TABLE IV
Fragment Ions Monitored in GC–MS Analysis of MHPG

Derivative	m/z	Fragment ion
Tris(trifluoro)acetyl	472	M^+
	358	$M^+ - CF_3COOH$
	345	$M^+ - CF_3COOCH_2$
Pentafluoropropionyl	622	M^+
	458	$M^+ - C_2F_5COOH$
	445	$M^+ - C_2F_5COOCH_2$
4'-Acetylbis(trifluoro)acetyl	376	$M^+ - COCH_2$
	249	$M^+ - COCH_2CF_3COOCH_2$

endogenous MHPG, their ratio will remain constant over time. This allows storage of derivatized samples for several days at $-70°C$ in the derivatizing reagent (Swahn *et al.*, 1976; S. E. Hattox, unpublished observations) or after evaporation (Faull *et al.*, 1979), giving flexibility to the assay as compared with ecGC methods.

The precision of the GC–MS methods, expressed as the coefficient of

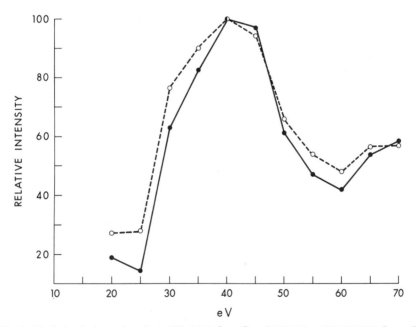

Fig. 1. Variation in intensity of m/z 472 (M^+) O- - -O and 358 ($M - CF_3COOH$) ●——● with electron voltage in a Finnigan 3200 quadrupole mass spectrometer.

variation, ranges from 7.0 (Bertilsson, 1973) to 8.2% (Sjöquist *et al.*, 1975), lower variation than the ecGC methods. Sjöquist and co-workers (1975) and Swahn *et al.* (1976) have confirmed recoveries of added MHPG of 100 and 106%, respectively. Faull *et al.* (1979) reported an extraction recovery of 79% by comparing peak heights of extracted MHPG with directly derivatized MHPG.

A comparison of CSF levels of free and conjugated or total MHPG measured by the various GC–MS methods (Table V) shows comparable values, indicating the reliability of the technique, regardless of the derivative formed. Human lumbar and ventricular CSF levels indicate that no gradient is present. Values determined in CSF from controls as well as a variety of neurological and psychiatric patients range from 7.0–16.7 ng/ml free MHPG and 7.4–24.3 ng/ml total MHPG. Although an early study by Karoum *et al.* (1971) using an ecGC method indicated that MHPG in CSF was mainly conjugated, later studies using GC–MS techniques have shown that MHPG in human CSF is mainly unconjugated as shown in Table V.

C. High Performance Liquid Chromatography (HPLC)

Methods for the measurement of MHPG levels in CSF without time consuming derivatization steps have been developed, utilizing reverse phase HPLC (Anderson *et al.*, 1981; Krstulovic *et al.*, 1981). Unprocessed CSF or the residue of an ethyl acetate extract of acidified CSF is separated on a C_{18} reverse-phase column; MHPG is detected electrochemically. Values for free MHPG measured by these methods are in the same range as those found by the more specific GC–MS techniques. Although too recently developed to have been evaluated in multiple laboratories, these methods appear to be fast, relatively inexpensive, and an accurate means for measuring MHPG levels in CSF and should find rapid acceptance.

D. Fluorimetry

Korf *et al.* (1971) developed a fluorimetric method for the measurement of MHPG, HVA, and 5-HIAA in a single sample of CSF. The biogenic amine metabolites are initially separated from each other by Sephadex G10 chromatography and the fluorophore of MHPG is developed by reaction with ethylenediamine and $K_3Fe(CN)_6$. Fluorescence at

500 nm is proportional to the concentration of MHPG in standard solutions, and CSF concentrations are calculated by comparison with an external standard curve. It is unclear whether unconjugated MHPG as well as MHPG sulfate is measured by this method, because free MHPG has been reported (Ruthven and Sandler, 1965; Wilk, 1967) to be destroyed under strongly acidic conditions such as those employed here. Extein et al. (1973) adapted the method of Meek and Neff (1972) for analysis of MHPG sulfate in rabbit CSF. Initial isolation is carried out on DEAE Sephadex A-25, followed by fluorophore formation by heating in acid and reacting with ethylenediamine. Fluorescence is measured at 465 nm and results are calculated from an internal standard curve. Internal standards are added after the initial isolation step. Human CSF MHPG values obtained using the method of Korf et al. (1971) (see Table V) are higher than those obtained later using more specific methods, and whereas the method of Extein et al. (1973) gives similar high values for rabbit CSF, no other measurements of rabbit CSF using other methods have been published for comparison. The high values may be due to high blanks or to the interference of related compounds (e.g., normetanephrine, metanephrine, and epinephrine described by Korf et al., 1971).

TABLE V
Concentration of MHPG in CSF of Various Species

Species, method	Reference	MHPG (ng/ml) + SD [N]				$\frac{Free}{Total} \times 100$
		Free	Total	Sulfate	Glucuronide	
Human (lumbar)						
Flourimetry	Korf et al., 1971[b]	29 ± 15[a] [21]				
ecGC	Saran et al., 1978	34 ± 11 [8]				
	Gordon and Oliver, 1971		15.1 ± 7.7			
	Chase et al., 1973[d]	10 ± 1[a] [22]	14 ± 1.4 [7]			
	Post et al., 1973		12.2 ± 1.3 [22]			
	Gordon et al., 1973[a,d]	11 [7]		4.7 [7]		
	Karoum et al., 1971	11 [2]	26.5 [2]			36
	Wilk et al., 1971a					
	Wilk and Mones, 1971b		16 [19]			

Table V continues

TABLE V (*Continued*)

Species, method	Reference	MHPG (ng/ml) + SD [N]				$\dfrac{\text{Free}}{\text{Total}} \times 100$
		Free	Total	Sulfate	Glucuronide	
	O'Keeffe and Brooksbank, 1973		9.8 [2]			
	Shaw et al., 1973[d]		10.8 ± 2.8 [13]			
	Davidson et al., 1977[d]		10 ± 5 [11]			
GC–MS						
	Bertilsson, 1973[c]		13.4 ± 3.5 [14]			89
	Bertilsson et al., 1974[e]		9.7 ± 5.3 [7]			
			12.1 ± 3.6 [11]			
	Bertilsson et al., 1977[c]		13.6 [7]			
			9.3 [4]			
	Karoum et al., 1975[f]	10.6 ± 0.8[a] [17]	14.2 ± 0.9[a] [17]			
	Sjöquist et al., 1975[b,d]		13.4 ± 1.1 [16]			
	Swahn et al., 1976[d]	7.0 ± 0.8 [15]	7.4 ± 2 [5]			95
	Sedvall et al., 1978[b]		7.5 ± 0.5 [49]			
	Belmaker et al., 1979[f]		8.8 ± 0.9 [10]			
	Murray et al., 1977[b,d]	11.4 [43]	14 [43]			84
	Karoum et al., 1977a[d]	11.0 ± 1.2[a] [5]		1.7 ± 0.5[a] [5]	0.2 ± .03[a] [5]	86
	Muskiet et al., 1978[d,f]	16.7 ± 12.9 [5]				
	Faull et al., 1979	8.9 ± 0.5[a] [23]	9.7 ± 0.6[a] [22]			
HPLC	Krstulovic et al., 1981	5.1 ± 4.7 [20]		0.2 ± 0.2 [12]		94
Human (ventricular)						
ecGC	Gordon and Oliver, 1971		12.5 ± 3.2 [4]			
	O'Keeffe and Brooksbank, 1973[d]		8.8 [1]			
GC–MS	Karoum et al., 1975[d]	11.7 ± 1 [8]	16.3 ± 1.3 [8]			72
Monkey (ventricular)						
GC–MS	Gordon et al., 1974		19.1 ± 10.6 [5]			
Rabbit (cisternal)						
Fluorimetry	Extein et al., 1973			27 ± 6 [11]		

[a]Standard error of the mean.
[b]Patients with heterogeneous psychiatric disorders.
[c]Depressed patients.
[d]Patients with heterogeneous neurological disorders.
[e]Hypertensive patients.
[f]Probenecid treated.

III.   Measurement of MHPG in Plasma

Plasma is a more complex matrix than cerebrospinal fluid, containing a much larger number of compounds that can potentially interfere with the analysis of MHPG. The methods that have been used are adaptations of those applied to CSF and both ecGC and GC–MS techniques. Table II summarizes the characteristics of these methods.

A.   Electron Capture Gas Chromatography

Dekirmenjian and Maas (1974) were the first to measure free and total plasma MHPG levels in a number of species by modifying methods originally applied to urine (Dekirmenjian and Maas, 1970) and cerebrospinal fluid (Gordon and Oliver, 1971; Wilk et al., 1971a). An initial wash of the plasma to remove fatty acids was added prior to extraction and the MHPG containing ethyl acetate was washed with a $KHCO_3$ solution to back-extract amphoteric compounds. Finally, the TFA derivative of the residual MHPG was formed. This method was reported to result in a recovery of 65% and replicate samples gave values within 10% of each other. Dekirmenjian and Maas (1974) and Halaris et al. (1977) found that 72–75% of blood MHPG is present in the plasma fraction and 25–28% in the particulate fraction.

Markianos and Beckmann (1976) and Halaris et al. (1977) used simple ethyl acetate extraction and PFP derivatization to recover 68–89% of MHPG. Markianos and Beckmann (1976) report a coefficient of variation of 30%, the low precision of the method probably being due to interfering substances. The values obtained using these methods are shown in Table V. Human and monkey plasma values are in good agreement with later GC–MS data, but ecGC values for total MHPG in rat plasma are unreliably high, reflecting the lack of specificity of ecGC techniques.

B.   Gas Chromatography–Mass Spectrometry

The increased specificity of GC–MS makes it ideal for analysis of very low levels of MHPG in an extremely complex fluid such as plasma. Sjöquist et al. (1975), Karoum et al. (1977a,b), and Muskiet et al. (1980) have combined initial ethyl acetate extraction with trifluoroacetyl or pentafluorpropionyl formation, whereas Maas et al. (1976) adapted the

isolation procedure of Dekirmenjian and Maas (1974) involving a hexane wash and back-extraction of ethyl acetate with $KHCO_3$ followed by
trifluoroacetylation. This latter method, which is described in detail in
Section III,C, gives values consistently slightly lower than other GC–MS
methods (see Table VI), perhaps due to removal of additional interfering substances. The method of Takahashi and co-workers (1977) includes perchlorate precipitation of protein followed by acetylation, extraction of the 4'-acetyl MHPG into isopropylacetate, and trifluoroacetylation. All GC–MS methods reported have high precision with coefficients of variation ranging from 3.5 (Hattox, see Section III,C) to 7.7%
(Takahashi *et al.*, 1977). Accuracy, calculated by measurement of known
amounts of added MHPG in the 5–20-ng range, is also excellent. Recoveries of 100, 99.5–101.5, and 107% occur with the methods of Sjöquist *et
al.* (1975), Takahashi *et al.* (1977), and Maas *et al.* (1976; S. E. Hattox
unpublished observations), respectively.

TABLE VI
Concentration of MHPG in Plasma of Various Species

| Species, method | Reference | MHPG (ng/ml) + *SD* [N] | | | | $\frac{Free}{Total} \times 100$ |
		Free	Total	Sulfate	Glucuronide	
Human						
ecGC	Dekirmenjian and Maas, 1974	5.4 ± 1.5 [4]	15.7 ± 2.0 [5]			32
	Markianos and Beck-mann, 1976		10.9 ± 3.4 [11]			
	Halaris *et al.*, 1977		7.9 ± 3.9 [6]			
GC–MS	Sjöquist *et al.*, 1975		10.3 ± 0.6 [18]			
	Mass *et al.*, 1976, see Section III, C					
	Maas *et al.*, 1979	3.9 ± 1.0[a] [10]				
	Swann *et al.*, 1980	3.5 ± 0.5[a]				
	Sweeney *et al.*, 1980[b]	2.8 ± 0.1[a] [10]	7.2 ± 0.9 [5]			49
	Leckman *et al.*, 1980	3.50 ± 0.2[a] [3]				
	Karoum *et al.*, 1977a,b	5.8 ± 0.6[a] [10]		8.3 ± 0.6[a] [10]	7.9 ± 0.5[a] [10]	26
	Takahashi *et al.*, 1977	4.6 ± 1.0 [10]	16.5 ± 4.4 [10]			29

TABLE VI   (*Continued*)

Species, method	Reference	MHPG (ng/ml) + *SD* [N]				$\dfrac{\text{Free}}{\text{Total}} \times 100$
		Free	Total	Sulfate	Glucuronide	
Monkey						
ecGC	Dekirmenjian and Mass, 1974					
Macaca speciosa			20.4 ± 1.0 [13]			
Rhesus		19.0 ± 0.8 [2]	42.6 ± 4.9 [6]			45
Rhesus	Halaris *et al.*, 1977		36.5 ± 15.7 [3]			
GC–MS	Maas *et al.*, 1976, see Section III,C					
Macaca speciosa		12.3 [7]				
Macaca arctoides	Maas *et al.*, 1977	11.0 [13]				
Rat						
ecGC	Dekirmenjian and Maas, 1974		43.2 ± 2.6 [8]			
	Halaris *et al.*, 1977		51.6 ± 22.7 [3]			
GC–MS	Mass *et al.*, 1976					
	Crawley *et al.*, 1978		10.6 ± 1.4[a] [4]			
	Takahashi *et al.*, 1977	2.5 ± 0.8 [10]	14.6 ± 4.6 [10]			18
	Helmeste *et al.*, 1979		15.2 ± 1.5[a] [10]			

[a]Standard error of the mean.
[b]Patients with heterogeneous psychiatric disorders.
[c]Depressed patients.

MHPG in human plasma has been found to be mainly conjugated as shown in Table V, with sulfate and glucuronide conjugates being equally predominant (Karoum, 1977). Sweeney *et al.* (1980), however, found no correlation between free and total MHPG in a given individual. It should be kept in mind when comparing values that subject populations varied with respect to activity, diet, and clinical diagnosis in the studies, all factors that could influence CSF and plasma MHPG concentration. In addition, plasma MHPG in humans shows a circadian rhythm, with higher levels being observed during midday as compared with morning, evening, and night. The work of Markianos *et al.* (1976) indicates that the diurual variation of total MHPG levels are not significant, whereas later studies (Swann *et al.*, 1980; Sweeney *et al.*, 1980) suggest that significant differences occur between noon and morning or afternoon levels of free MHPG but not for levels of conjugated MHPG. Values for plasma-free MHPG in controls and depressed patients ranged from 3.5 to 5.8 ng/ml and for conjugated MHPG from 6.3 to 22 ng/ml as shown in Table V. The extent of conjugation in monkey plasma is not known with certainty because the more specific GC–MS methods have not measured both free and total MHPG. Dekirmenjian and Maas (1974), however, found 45% of Rhesus monkey plasma in the free form. Free MHPG in monkey plasma is reported to range from 9.3 to 19 ng/ml and conjugated MHPG from 20.4 to 42.6 ng/ml. Rat plasma MHPG is mainly conjugated with total levels having been reported as 10.7–14.6 ng/ml.

C. Effects of Sample Storage on the Precision and Accuracy of Plasma MHPG Measurement by GC–MS

The development of rapid, sensitive, and specific methods for the measurement of MHPG in complex fluids has made possible the design of large-scale clinical and basic science studies requiring analysis of multiple samples collected from large numbers of individuals over long periods of time. In these cases, it is essential to know how long samples can be stored without significant deterioration; whether samples should be stored with or without internal standard; and whether calibration curves can be prepared, dried, and stored with samples when there are significant differences between preparations of internal standard.

1. Experimental Design. Our laboratory developed the experimental design shown in Fig. 2 to answer these questions (S. E. Hattox, D. H. Landis, and J. W. Maas, unpublished observations). A pool of human plasma was divided into two portions, one that was stored at $-70°C$ with 200 ng/ml deuterated internal standard (V), (see Fig. 5) and one that was stored without internal standard. Deuterated standard was added to this portion after storage but before the individual samples were aliquoted. Five 2-ml aliquots of plasma stored with and without deuterated internal standard were injected after work-up four times each to allow calculation of variance (SD^2) due to sample and its preparation, variance due to instrumental factors and the sum, or total variance. A series of calibration curves was pipetted, evaporated under dry N_2, and stored at $-70°C$ for calculation of the MHPG levels in samples stored with $[^2H_2]MHPG$. At each specified time point a second calibration curve was constructed using the same solution of internal standard that had been added to the thawed plasma. This curve was employed for calculation of the MHPG

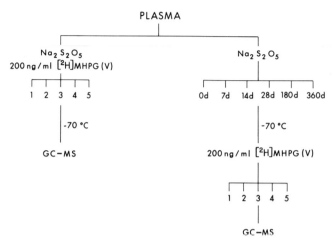

Fig. 2. Experimental design for determining changes in precision and accuracy of MHPG measurement with sample storage.

levels in samples stored without internal standard. Changes in accuracy were calculated by comparing ng MHPG/ml plasma in samples stored with and without internal standard. All samples were stored with 0.5 mg/ml sodium metabisulfite to reduce oxidation, and groups were analyzed after 0, 7, 14, and 28 days and after 6 and 12 months.

2. Method. After storage the samples were thawed and 1 ml 0.3M sodium acetate buffer was added. They were washed twice with 10 ml hexane to remove fatty acids, and extracted with 10 ml nanograde ethyl acetate. The ethyl acetate layer was back-extracted with 1 ml 1 M $KHCO_3$ to remove interfering amphoteric compounds and the ethyl acetate layer was evaporated *in vacuo.* Two 1-ml aliquots of ethyl acetate were used to transfer the residue to 0.5-dram vials and the samples were trifluoroacetylated by reacting them with 0.1 ml trifluoroacetic anhydride at room temperature for 1 h. The samples were carefully evaporated and reconstituted in 50–100 μl ethyl acetate for GC–MS analysis of free MHPG. All solvents were of nanograde quality and all containers were acid-washed glassware.

Samples were analyzed on a Finnigan Corp. (Sunnyvale, California) Model 3200 quadrupole, electron-impact ionization mass spectrometer equipped with gas chromatographic inlet system and programmable multiple ion monitor (PROMIM). Gas chromatographic separation was accomplished on a 1.5 m × 2 mm ID glass column packed with 3% OV-17 on 100/120 Mesh Gas Chrom Q. Analog output was measured by hand. The ratio of peak heights of ions at m/z 358:360, derived by expulsion of CF_3COO from the α carbon plus the β hydrogen from endogenous MHPG and [$^2H_2$]MHPG, respectively, was measured. Results were calculated by interpolation from a standard curve prepared by direct derivatization of known amounts of authentic unlabeled MHPG and 200 ng [$^2H_2$]MHPG, as shown in Fig. 3. Identical results were obtained when 200 and 40 ng [$^2H_2$]MHPG were employed. Sample analysis time after work-up was 2.5 min, the coefficient of variation was 3.5% ($N = 30$) and the signal to noise ratio was 50:1 with 40 pg injected. An example of the analysis of samples stored 6 months with [$^2H_2$]MHPG is shown in Fig. 4.

3. Results. The effect of sample storage on precision and accuracy of measurement of levels of MHPG is shown in Table VII. No significant change in precision was observed with samples stored with or without standard as compared with fresh samples. There was a significant difference in the MHPG levels measured in samples stored as little as 1

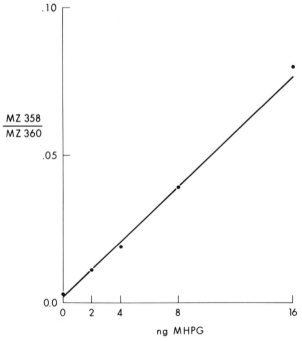

Fig. 3. Standard calibration curve of peak height ratios of m/z 358:360 derived from known amounts of authentic MHPG and 200 ng [$^2H_2$]MHPG (**V**), respectively.

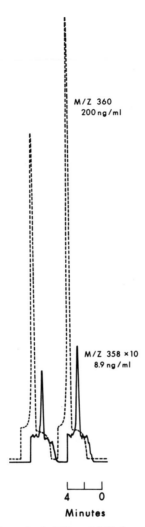

M/Z 360
200 ng/ml

M/Z 358 ×10
8.9 ng/ml

4 0

Minutes

Fig. 4. Selected ion recording of m/z 358 and 360 from a plasma sample stored with [^{2}H$_2$]MHPG (**V**) and Na$_2$S$_2$O$_5$ at $-70°$C for 6 months.

month without internal standard, but no significant difference was found between values measured in fresh samples and samples stored up to 1 year with internal standard. These data show the absolute necessity of adding internal standard to plasma samples before storage if accurate values for plasma MHPG are to be obtained. Calibration curves stored in dried form were stable for at least 6 months.

TABLE VII

Change in Precision and Accuracy in Quantitation of MHPG in Plasma During Storage at −70°C

Storage (day)	Total variance	Coefficient of variation (%)	MHPG (ng/ml)
Internal standard added before storage			
0	.03737	3.3	3.75
7	.05333	6.5	3.6
14	.02589	3.0	3.8
28	.02779	2.1	3.9
180	.01516	1.4	3.8
360	.00606	2.1	3.7
Internal standard added after storage			
7	.03854	3.3	3.4
14	.04261	2.9	3.8
28	.07945	2.9	4.9
180	.01958	1.6	4.4
360	.01394	3.9	3.0

IV. Measurement of MHPG in Urine

A far greater variety and number of methods have been published for the determination of MHPG levels in urine than in other body fluids and tissues. There are three separate steps involved in the majority of these. A cursory examination of Table III indicates that a relatively small number of methods for (1) isolation of MHPG from the urinary matrix have been combined with several (2) chemical modification schemes to allow (3) detection by a limited number of techniques. These three steps, many of which have been described in detail in Sections II and III, have been combined in numerous different ways and can be adapted to suit individual requirements and facilities.

A. Isolation

Two main approaches to the isolation of MHPG from other potentially interfering urinary components have been employed: extraction and chromatography. Extraction schemes have utilized partitioning between ethyl acetate, ether, or dichloromethane and buffered urine at neutral or acidic pH. Karoum et al. (1969) examined the relative recovery of MHPG from 10 ml NaCl-saturated water at varying pH when extracted with 30 ml ethyl acetate or ether. Ninety-nine percent of the MHPG was extracted by ethyl acetate from a solution of pH 1.0. Many acidic compounds were also extracted at pH 1.0, however, and a more selective extraction, although at lower efficiency, was found at pH 6.0 (Karoum *et al.*, 1969). Biondi *et al.* (1977, 1979), Bond (1972), Kahane *et al.* (1972), and O'Keeffe and Brooksbank (1973) formed the 4'-acetyl derivative of MHPG directly in urine or chromatographic eluant and subsequently extracted the derivative into dichloromethane. Ion-exchange chromatography (AG-1, CG-50) has been used in conjunction with other isolation procedures to separate MHPG from interfering compounds (Antun *et al.*, 1971; Bond, 1972; Fellows *et al.*, 1975; Ruthven and Sandler, 1965). Thin-layer chromatographic procedures have also been successfully employed (Breebaart *et al.*, 1972; O'Keeffe and Brooksbank, 1973; Zawad and Brown, 1976). A final chromatographic step is often employed as a means not only for further purification of the sample but also as a means of introducing it into the detector (see Table III). Thus, gas chromatography serves as an introduction system for electron-capture, flame ionization, and mass spectrometric detectors; and C_{18} reverse-phase ion pair high-performance liquid chromatography can introduce the sample into electrochemical and fluorimetric detectors. A more thorough treatment of GC conditions, originally worked out for analysis of urinary MHPG and later applied to other body fluids, may be found in Section II.

B. Derivatization

In many cases, the original MHPG molecule must be chemically altered or derivatized to increase detection sensitivity or to increase sample volatility allowing detection in the gaseous phase. MHPG may be oxidized with sodium periodate to form vanillin, which is subsequently measured (Bigelow *et al.*, 1971; Buchanan *et al.*, 1979; Kissinger *et al.*, 1977; Nicholas *et al.*, 1969; Ruthven and Sandler, 1965; Sapira, 1968). In addition, derivatization is an absolute requirement when gas chromatography is to be used for isolation. The two most frequently employed derivatives are the tris(trifluoro)acetyl (TFA) and tris(pentafluoro)propionyl (PFP) compounds followed by the 4'-acetylbis(trifluoro)acetyl and 4'-acetylbis(heptafluoro)butyryl compounds. The syntheses of these derivatives are discussed in Section II,A,2. In addition, the trimethylsilyl (TMS) derivative has been employed by Karoum *et al.* (1969) and Muskiet *et al.* (1977), the acetyl by Kahane *et al.*

(1972), and the acetyl boronate by Biondi *et al.* (1977, 1979). An important consideration in the choice of derivative is the formation of a single rather than multiple derivatives for maximum sensitivity and specificity.

C. Detection

Early efforts to quantitate MHPG in urine were based on its oxidation by metaperiodate to vanillin, which was then isolated and measured spectrophotometrically by absorbance at 340–380 nm (Bigelow *et al.*, 1971; Nicholas *et al.*, 1969; Ruthven and Sandler, 1965; Sapira, 1968). The majority of published methods, however, employ either electron-capture (ec) or flame ionization detection (FID) of MHPG (see Table III) or vanillin (Kahane *et al.*, 1970) in a gas chromatographic effluent. The higher amounts of MHPG present in urine as compared with CSF and plasma overcome to some extent the lack of specificity (ec and FID) and sensitivity (FID) of GC techniques relative to GC–MS, which make the latter preferable for analysis of CSF and plasma. Mass spectrometry in addition to ec and FID however, has also been used as a specific and sensitive detector for the GC effluent (Edwards *et al.*, 1979; Gordon *et al.*, 1974; Karoum *et al.*, 1973; Murray *et al.*, 1979; Sjöquist *et al.*, 1975). If available, this technique combines rapid sample processing with high sensitivity and specificity. Finally, both electrochemical and fluorimetric detection of HPLC effluents have been utilized with success. (Buchanan *et al.*, 1979; Kissinger *et al.*, 1977; Krstulovic *et al.*, 1980; Mitchell and Coscia, 1978; Taylor *et al.*, 1981).

D. Use of Reference Standards

Both internal and external standards as described in Section II have been employed, although by far the greatest majority of laboratories have chosen to use an internal MHPG standard. Other internal standards include phenanthrene (Biondi *et al.*, 1977; Kahane *et al.*, 1970), dotriacontane (Kahane *et al.*, 1972), aldrin (O'Keeffe and Brooksbank, 1973), α-lindane (Fellows *et al.*, 1975), and propylgallate (Muskiet *et al.*, 1977). In those cases where values are reported, the use of internal standards other than MHPG, on the one hand, gave inaccurate results as compared with those reported using the more specific GC–MS techniques (see Table VIII) and should be considered undesirable. The use of an external MHPG standard, on the other hand, appeared to give

TABLE VIII
Concentration of MHPG in Human Urine

Method	Reference	MHPG (ng/ml) $\pm$ SD [N]				$\dfrac{\text{Free}}{\text{Total}} \times 100$
		Free	Total	Sulfate	Glucuronide	
Spectrophotometry	Ruthven and Sandler, 1965		3.0 $\pm$ 0.8 [18]			
	Sapira, 1968	0.9 $\pm$ 0.69[a]				
	Nicholas et al., 1969		1.87 $\pm$ 0.6 [23] 1.45 $\pm$ 0.3[a] [23]			
	Bigelow et al., 1971		2.42 $\pm$ 0.57 [10] 1.23 $\pm$ 0.38[a] [10]			
Fluorimetry	Antun et al., 1971				0.756 $\pm$ 0.459 [12] (conjugated)	
	Zawad and Brown, 1976		Male 1.56 $\pm$ 0.18 [6] 0.96 $\pm$ 0.14[a] [6] Female 1.21 $\pm$ 0.32 [5] 0.58 $\pm$ 0.17[a] [5]			
Densitometry	Breebaart et al., 1972		3.128 [10] 17[b] [10]			
Gas Chromatography	Wilk et al., 1967		0.86[a] [35]			
	Karoum et al., 1969		2.4 $\pm$ 0.8			
	Karoum et al., 1971		1.58 [3]			
	Dekirmenjian and Maas, 1970		Male 1.6 $\pm$ 0.38 [5] 0.95 $\pm$ 0.12[a] [5] Female 1.32 $\pm$ 0.36 [6] 1.09 $\pm$ 0.29[a] [6]			
	Kahane et al., 1970	0.174[a]	2.11[a]			
	Bond, 1972		Male 1.83 1.09[a]			
	Bond and Howlett, 1974	Male .15 $\pm$ .06 [7] .096 $\pm$ .025[a] [7] Female .19 $\pm$ .11 [6] .15 $\pm$ .09[a] [6]	2.41 $\pm$ .50 [7] 1.55 $\pm$ .59[a] [7] 2.45 $\pm$ .82 [6] 1.51 $\pm$ .57[a] [6]	1.36 $\pm$ .44 [7] .85 $\pm$ .34[a] [7] 1.26 $\pm$ .46 [6] .98 $\pm$ .37[a] [6]	.91 $\pm$ .13 [7] .64 $\pm$ .23[a] [7] 1.0 $\pm$ .28 [6] .78 $\pm$ .25[a] [6]	
	Martin et al., 1972		2.17 [3]	1.19 [3]	.905 [3]	
	O'Keeffe and Brooksbank, 1973		1.05[a] [7]			

Table VIII continues

TABLE VIII (*Continued*)

Method	Reference	MHPG (ng/ml) ± SD [N]				$\dfrac{\text{Free}}{\text{Total}} \times 100$
		Free	Total	Sulfate	Glucuronide	
	Sharpless, 1977		Male 2.105 ± .624 [6] Female 1.618 ± .476 [5]			
GC–MS	Karoum et al., 1973	.049 ± .007 [9] .027 ± .003[a] [9]	1.863 ± .113 [9] 1.273 ± .111[a] [9]	.845 ± .074 [9] .583 ± .058[a] [9]	.979 ± .084 [9] .685 ± .065[a] [9]	5
	Sjöquist et al., 1975		7.4[c] [20]			
	Murray et al., 1977	.08 ± .03 [10] .05 ± .02[a] [10]	2.43 ± .84 [10] 1.56 ± .39[a] [10]	1.05 ± .38 [10] .67 ± .18[a] [10]		3
	Edwards et al., 1979		1.4 [3]			
HPLC	Buchanan et al., 1979	.16–.47	2.69–3.60	.60–1.01	1.42–1.52	
	Krstulovic et al., 1980	.06[a] [20]			.69[a] [20] (conjugated)	

[a] μg/mg creatinine.
[b] μmole/24 h.
[c] nmole/ml.

values comparable with those obtained using an internal MHPG standard.

E.   Recovery, Precision, and Accuracy

Recovery of MHPG from urine in methods using isolation by extraction, subsequent conversion to vanillin, and spectrophotometric detection was in the range of 54.9–85.7%, as shown in Table III. Addition of an ion-exchange chromatography step decreased the recovery drastically to 12.3% (Ruthven and Sandler, 1965). The precision of these methods is good, but the values recorded are, in most cases high, perhaps due to interfering compounds. Recovery of MHPG by methods featuring ethyl acetate extraction and ec or FID analysis of a GC effluent ranges from 78.5 to 92.7%. Again, ion-exchange chromatography decreased recovery as did formation of the 4′-acetyl derivative in aqueous solution with subsequent extraction with dichloromethane. Precision is high (5.9–8.1%), but with the exception of the methods of Bond (1972), Bond and Howlett (1974), and Martin (1972), urinary MHPG values reported using ecGC and FID are lower than those recorded with GC–MS techniques and stable isotope-labeled internal standards. This inaccuracy may be due to partial rather than complete recovery of the MHPG from urine.

Humans are estimated by these methods to excrete 1.3–3.1 mg MHPG per 24 h or 0.9–2.1 μg MHPG per μg creatinine, 90–99% conjugated as sulfuric or glucuronic acid esters (see Table VIII). Whereas Sweeney *et al.* (1978) and Tang *et al.* (1981) were unable to detect a significant diurnal variation in urinary MHPG, Hollister *et al.* (1978) found a slight but descernible pattern, which peaked at 4–6 P.M. Excercise does not appear to have an effect on urinary MHPG exretion (Goode *et al.*, 1973; Sweeney *et al.*, 1978; Tang *et al.*, 1981), but Sweeney *et al.* (1978) showed a significant correlation between anxiety and urinary MHPG levels.

V. Hydrolysis of Conjugated MHPG

Methods for the quantitation of the sulfate and glucuronide conjugates of MHPG were developed simultaneously with methods for the measurement of the unconjugated compound. Although rats, rabbits, monkeys, and humans are known to conjugate MHPG, the proportion of conjugated to free metabolite varies with species as does the extent of conjugation found in various tissues and fluids.

Ruthven and Sandler (1965) and Wilk *et al.* (1967) demonstrated that MHPG was unstable when heated or stored in acid, and subsequent efforts were directed toward enzymatic hydrolysis of the conjugates in CSF and plasma. Initial experiments to determine the effects of pH, enzyme concentration, incubation time and temperature, and buffer concentrations were carried out in urine. The methodology developed was transferred largely intact to the analysis of CSF and plasma. The far lower quantities of MHPG found in these fluids, however, required an increase in sensitivity of detection resulting in increased interference from other compounds present.

Two approaches to measurement of free and conjugated metabolite have been taken. Free MHPG can be removed from the acidified sample by exhaustive extraction with ethyl acetate and/or diethyl ether, after which the pH is raised and the sulfate and glucuronic acid groups are enzymatically cleaved to release free MHPG. This free MHPG is then quantitated by one of the methods previously described (Sections II, III, and IV). Two disadvantages have been ascribed to this procedure: (a) that MHPG conjugates are unstable in acidified samples and (b) that traces of free MHPG might remain in the sample, giving falsely high values for the conjugates. Traces of organic solvent remaining in the sample may inhibit enzymatic activity although all methods removing free MHPG before hydrolysis call for heating the samples for a few minutes to remove dissolved organic solvent. In rebuttal to these disadvantages, Martin *et al.* (1972) found no loss of the sulfate conjugate from urine during the acidified extraction, and Karoum *et al.* (1977a) carried an aliquot of acid-extracted sample through the incubation procedure without enzyme for correction of traces of free MHPG not extracted.

The earliest methods were developed using glusulase, an enzyme preparation containing both arylsulfatase and β-glucuronidase activity, which is reportedly inhibited by inorganic phosphate and sulfate (La-Brosse *et al.*, 1961). Dekirmenjian and Maas (1970) defined optimal parameters for the hydrolysis of MHPG conjugates in urine. MHPG was found to be unstable over a 24-h incubation period at 37°C at a pH of 5.5 or less, whereas maximum hydrolysis occurred at pH 6.0–7.0. Because the pH of the incubation medium decreased as hydrolysis proceeded, a 0.1 M buffer was found to increase reproducibility. Release of MHPG continued for the first 18 h after which no change in MHPG level was observed. It was found that the presence of ascorbate decreased measured metabolite levels and reproducibility, whereas EDTA and sodium metabisulfite increased reproducibility. Halaris *et al.* (1977) and Markianos and Beckmann (1976), using electron-capture gas chromatographic methods, reported that hydrolysis of plasma conjugates by glusulase was complete in two h. Clearly, it is important for each laboratory to confirm the time of hydrolysis for the specific parameters chosen. Gordon *et al.* (1971) found added [^{3}H]MHPG-SO$_4$ was completely hydrolyzed by glusulase.

A major disadvantage with the use of glusulase is the presence of relatively large quantities of MHPG (16 ng/0.1 ml) in occasional lots of the enzyme (Maas, personal communication; S. E. Hattox, unpublished observations) prohibiting its use in CSF and plasma, which contain low levels of total MHPG. Similar contamination of an arylsulfatase-β-glucuronidase preparation from a different source has been reported (Sjöquist *et al.*, 1974) indicating that all enzyme preparations must be analyzed under conditions of incubation before use, and enzyme blanks are essential. Many laboratories have removed inhibiting sulfate and phosphate ions by precipitation with BaCl$_2$.

Martin and co-workers (1972) compared the activity of glusulase and arylsulfatase Type H-1 in the release of MHPG from its conjugates in urine. They confirmed the original finding of Dekirmenjian and Maas (1970) of 18 h as maximal hydrolysis time for glusulase, but found the H-1 sulfatase optimum release in 4–8 h. This preparation has a temperature optimum at 41°C and a sharp pH optimum at 6.0. Swahn *et al.* (1976) and Sjöquist *et al.* (1975) have reported 96 and 101% hydrolysis, respectively, of added MHPG-SO$_4$ employing this enzyme, whereas Bertilsson (1973) reported 81% efficiency of hydrolysis, possibly due to traces of ethyl acetate remaining in the sample after extraction of free metabolite. A recent study by Faull *et al.* (1979) found Type H-1 sulfatase to have completed maximum hydrolysis within 1 h using a rat brain perfusate of artificial CSF. Karoum *et al.* (1980) compared pure (Limpet) with crude (Helix Pomatia) sulfatase, finding a threefold increase in hydrolysis of MHPG-SO$_4$ with the latter enzyme. These authors recommend either a 1 h incubation at 40°C or overnight incubation at −10°C. Martin and co-workers (1972) also found enhanced rate of hydrolysis at 41°C with sulfatase H-1. Considering the lack of agreement about incubation times and hydrolysis efficiencies, it is clear that a definitive study using the most specific techniques and stable isotope-labeled internal standards for the glucuronide and sulfate conjugates as well as free MHPG is greatly needed.

Bond and Howlett (1974) extensively compared the hydrolysis of urinary MHPG conjugates by enzyme preparations containing arylsulfatase activity, β-glucuronidase activity, or both activities from a number of sources. These authors concluded that combined aryl sulfatase-β-glucuronidase preparations from Sigma (Type H-2) and Industrie Biologique Française were comparable, whereas Type II β-glucuronidase (*E. coli*, Sigma) was preferable to Type B-10 (bovine liver) because an excess of the latter or excessive incubation times led to decreased values and reproducibility. These authors (Bond and Howlett, 1974) assume that because the sum of glucuronide and sulfate conjugates measured by glucuronidase or sulfatase enzymes is greater than the total conjugates measured using combined aryl sulfatase-β-glucuronidase enzymes, the glucuronidase in the combined preparation is not giving complete hydrolysis and results, therefore, will be low. A number of other enzymes, e.g., β-glucuronidase Type I (Bertilsson, 1973; Swahn *et al.*, 1976), a preparation from *Patella vulgata* viscera (O'Keeffe and Brooksbank, 1973), and Helicase (Davidson *et al.*, 1977) have also been used to hydrolyze MHPG conjugates.

Murray and co-workers (1977b) have developed a nonenzymatic procedure for the hydrolysis of MHPG sulfate in human urine. This method involves two isolation steps: initial extraction on Amberlite XAD-2 and subsequent column chromatography on Sephadex LH-20. Cleavage of the sulfate occurs during tristrifluoroacetylation, eliminating the need for enzymatic hydrolysis. Although not yet applied to CSF or plasma, this method may circumvent the problems of high blanks and long incubation times inherent in the enzymatic methods.

VI. Synthesis of Stable Isotope-Labeled MHPG

A major advantage to the use of GC–MS techniques is the possibility of using as an internal standard a compound that differs from the compound one wishes to analyze only by the substitution of two or more atoms of hydrogen, carbon-12, nitrogen-14, oxygen-16, etc. with their respective stable isotopes. Each deuterium, carbon-13, and nitrogen-15 atom substituted in a molecule will increase its molecular weight by 1 atomic mass unit (amu), whereas each oxygen-18 atom will increase the molecular weight by 2 amu. Stable isotope-labeled compounds are ideal internal standards because chemically they are nearly identical to their unlabeled analogs and so will behave similarly with respect to chemical processes affecting recovery, e.g., degradation, extraction efficiency, derivatization yield, detector response, and adsorption onto glass and metal surfaces and gas chromatographic liquid phases. The mass spectrometer, however, analyzes according to mass rather than chemical properties and will distinguish between two compounds that differ only in mass.

As a synthesis of 1-(3-methoxy-4-hydroxyphenyl)-2-[2,2-^{2}H]glycol (**V**) (see Fig. 5), Bertilsson (1973) reduced 3-methoxy-4-hydroxymandelic acid (VMA) with lithium aluminum deuteride in ethylene glycol dimethyl ether for 18 h at 20°C. After decomposition of the product with D_2O followed by 2 M HCl (to pH 5.0), the deuterium-labeled product was extracted into ethyl acetate. After drying with anhydrous sodium sulfate, the ethyl acetate was evaporated, leaving a red oil. The product was taken up in 10% aqueous acetone at a concentration of 1 μg/ml and stored at −20°C. In the product the ratio of MHPG/[^{2}H$_2$]MHPG was 0.14. Murray et al. (1977) modified this procedure by carrying out the reaction for 12 days and purifying the labeled MHPG by TLC. The yield was 13%. This method was further modified by Maas et al. (1976) to include the formation of the piperazine salt of the deuterium-labeled MHPG. The red oil was taken up in ethanol and added to benzene

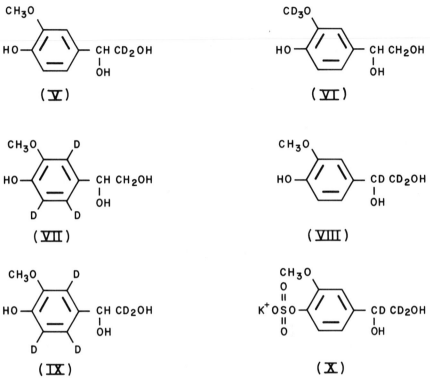

Fig. 5. Structures of MHPG labeled with deuterium in various positions for use as internal standards.

according to the method of Benigni and Verbiscar (1963). Piperazine in benzene (5%) was added and the resulting precipitate was recrystallized from benzene–hexane. The yield of this method was 20%, the maximum deuterium incorporation was 98.75%, and the ratio of MHPG/[²H₂]MHPG was 0.002.

1-(3-[*Methoxy*-²H₃]-4-hydroxyphenyl)-2-glycol (**VI**) is shown in Fig. 5. Gordon *et al.* (1974) enzymatically methylated 3,4-dihydroxyphenyl glycol in the 3 position of the ring using S-adenosyl-L-[*meth-yl*-²H₃]methionine and catechol O-methyltransferase prepared from rat liver. The deuterated product was purified by paper chromatography and found to contain 5% unlabeled MHPG. Markey *et al.* (1980) chemically synthesized (**VI**) by methylation of catechol with deuteromethyl iodide and formation of 3-[*methoxy*-²H₃]-4-hydroxymandelic acid by reaction with sodium glyoxylate. The acid was then reduced to (**VI**) with diborane.

1-([2,5,6-^{2}H]-3-Methoxy-4-hydroxyphenyl)-2-glycol (**VII**) (see Fig. 5 and Karoum *et al.*, 1975) was prepared from 3-methoxy-4-hydroxylmandelic acid, the ring positions were labeled with deuterium by acid exchange using D_2O, DCl, and CD_3COOD. The labeled acid was subsequently reduced with borane methyl sulfide to form [$^2H_3$]MHPG containing 1% unlabeled MHPG.

For a synthesis of 1-(3-methoxy-4-hydroxyphenyl)-2-[1,2,2-^{2}H]glycol (**VIII**) (see Fig. 5.), Sjöquist *et al.* (1975) prepared MHPG labeled in all three side chain positions by initially exchanging the benzylic hydrogen of VMA in NaOD and D_2O according to Lindstrom *et al.* (1974), and subsequently reducing the acid with lithium aluminum deuteride by the method of Bertilsson described above. The product was found to contain 0.8% unlabeled MHPG and could be stored at $-20°C$ in distilled H_2O.

Synthesis of 1-([2,5,6-^{2}H]-3-methoxy-4-hydroxyphenyl)-2-[2,2-^{2}H]-glycol (**IX**) (see Fig. 5) was accomplished by Muskiet *et al.* (1978, 1980) by reduction according to the method of Bertilsson (1973) of [$^2H_3$] VMA prepared by the method of Karoum *et al.* (1975).

As a synthesis of 1-(3-methoxy-4-sulfoxyphenyl)-2-[1,2,2-^{2}H]glycol (**X**) (see Fig. 5), Murray *et al.* (1977b) prepared MHPG sulfate completely labeled in the side chain from 3-methoxy-4-benzyloxybromoacetophenone by reduction with sodium borodeuteride and decomposition with NaOD in D_2O. The labeled glycol was extracted into diethyl ether, dried with sodium sulfate, and evaporated to an oil. The diacetate of the glycol was formed by reaction with acetic anhydride in pyridine, and the product was again extracted into diethyl ether that was dried and evaporated. The protecting benzyl group was deacetylated and sulfated in the 4'-position by reacting in anhydrous dimethylformamide with dicyclohexylcarbodiimide and concentrated sulfuric acid. The potassium salt was formed by addition of a potassium hydroxide solution. Subsequent isolation by Sephadex LH-20 yielded a solid material of which 10% corresponded to labeled MHPG sulfate.

In addition, deuterium-labeled MHPG may be purchased from Merck, Sharp and Dohme, Ltd., Montreal Canada (**VIII**), and Productkontroll AB, Stockholm, Sweden (**VI**), see Fig. 5.

VII. Summary

During the 1970s, increasingly sophisticated techniques of very high sensitivity, accuracy, and reproducibility have contributed to the accumulation of data essential to the elucidation of the function of noradrenergic systems in man and animals. The future holds the promise of even more sensitive techniques (e.g., negative ion GC–MS) that will more finely tune our insight into the biochemical actions and interactions of the neuroregulator, norepinephrine.

References

Anderson, G. M., Young, J. G., Cohen, D. J., Shaywitz, B. A., and Batter, D. K. 1981. *J. Chromatogr.* **222,** 112–115.

Änggård, E. and Sedvall, G. 1969. *Anal. Chem.* **41,** 1250–1256.

Änggård, E., Sjöquist, B., and Sjöström, R. 1970. *J. Chromatogr.* **50,** 251–259.

Antun, F. T., Pullar, I. A., Eccleston, D., and Sharman, D. F. 1971. *Clin. Chim. Acta* **34,** 387–392.

Axelrod, J., Kopin, I. J., and Mann, J. D. 1959. *Biochim. Biophys. Acta,* **36,** 576–577.

Belmaker, R. H., Ebstein, R. P., Dasberg, H., Levy, A., Sedvall, G., and van Praag, H. M. 1979. *Psychopharmacology* **63,** 293–296.

Benigni, J. D. and Verbiscar, A. J. 1963. *J. Med. Chem.* **6,** 607–608.

Bertilsson, L. 1973. *J. Chromatogr.* **87,** 147–153.

Bertilsson, L., Åsberg, and Thorén, P. 1974. *Eur. J. Clin. Pharmacol.* **7,** 365–368.

Bertilsson, L., Haglund, K., Östman, J., Rawlins, M. D., Ringberger, V. -A., and Sjöquist, F. 1977. *Eur. J. Clin. Pharmacol.* **11,** 125–128.

Bigelow, L. B., Neal, S., and Weil-Malherbe, H. 1971. *J. Lab. Clin. Med.* **77,** 677–683.

Biondi, P. A., Cagnasso, M., and Secchi, C. 1977. *J. Chromatogr.* **143,** 513–518.

Biondi, P. A., Fedele, G., Motta, A., and Secchi, C. 1979. *Clin. Chim. Acta* **94,** 155–161.

Bond, P. A. 1972. *Biochem. Med.* **6,** 36–45.

Bond, P. A., and Howlett, D. R. 1974. *Biochem. Med.* **10,** 219–228.

Breebaart, K., Haan, A. M. F. H., and Wadman, S. K. 1972. *Clin. Chim. Acta* **37,** 157–164.

Buchanan, D. N., Fucek, F. R., and Domino, E. F. 1979. *J. Chromatogr.* **162,** 394–400.

Chase, T. N., Gordon, E. K., and Ng, L. K. Y. 1973. *J. Neurochem.* **21,** 581–587.

Crawley, J. N., Hattox, S. E., Maas, J. W., and Roth, R. H. 1978. *Brain Res.* **141,** 380–384.

Davidson, D., Pullar, I. A., Mawdsley, C., Kinloch, N., and Yates, C. M. 1977. *J. Neurol. Neurosurg. Psychiatry* **40,** 741–745.

Dekirmenjian, H., and Maas, J. W. 1970. *Anal. Biochem.* **35,** 113–122.

Dekirmenjian, H., and Maas, J. W. 1974. *Clin. Chim. Acta* **52,** 203–210.

Edwards, D. J., Rizk, M., and Neil, J. 1979. *J. Chromatogr.* **164,** 407–416.

Extein, I., Korf, J., Roth, R. H., and Bowers, M. B., Jr. 1973. *Brain Res.* **54,** 403–407.

Faull, K. F., Anderson, P. J., Barchas, J. D., and Berger, P. A. 1979. *J. Chromatogr.* **163,** 337–349.

Fellows, L., Riederer, P., and Sandler, M. 1975. *Clin. Chim. Acta* **59,** 255–257.

Goode, D. J., Dekirmenjian, H., Meltzer, H. Y., and Maas, J. W. 1973. *Arch. Gen. Psychiatry* **29,** 391–396.

Gordon, E. K., and Oliver, J. 1971. *Clin. Chim. Acta* **35,** 145–150.

Gordon, E. K., Oliver, J., Goodwin, F. K., Chase, T. N., and Post, R. M. 1973. *Neuropharmacol.* **12,** 391–396.

Gordon, E. K., Oliver, J., Black, K., and Kopin, I. J. 1974. *Biochem. Med.* **11,** 32–40.

Halaris, G. E., DeMet, E. M., and Halari, M. E. 1977. *Clin. Chim. Acta* **78**, 285–294.

Helmeste, D. M., Stancer, H. C., Coscina, D. V., Takahashi, S., and Warsh, J. J. 1979. *Life Sci,* **25**, 601–606.

Hollister, L. E., Davis, K. L., Overall, J. E., and Anderson, T. 1978. *Arch. Gen. Psychiatry* **35**, 1410–1415.

Kahane, Z., Ebbighansen, W., and Vestergaard, P. 1972. *Clin. Chim. Acta* **33**, 413–417.

Kahane, Z., Mowat, J. H., and Vestergaard, P. 1970. *Clin. Chim. Acta* **30**, 683–687.

Karoum, F., Anah, C. O., Ruthven, C. R. J., and Sandler, M. 1969. *Clin. Chim. Acta* **24**, 341–343.

Karoum, F., LeFèvre, H., Bigelow, L. B., and Costa, E. 1973. *Clin. Chim. Acta* **43**, 127–137.

Karoum, F., Ruthven, C. R. J., and Sandler, M. 1971. *Biochem. Med.* **5**, 505–514.

Karoum, F., Gillin, J. C., Wyatt, R. J., and Costa E. 1975. *Biomed. Mass Spectrom.* **2**, 183–189.

Karoum, F., Moyer-Schwing, J., Potkin, S. G., and Wyatt, R. J. 1977a. *Brain Res.* **125**, 333–339.

Karoum, F., Moyer-Schwing, J., Potkin, S. G., and Wyatt, R. J. 1977b. *Commun. Psychopharmacol.* **1**, 343–352.

Karoum, F., Chuang, L. -W., and Wyatt, R. J. 1980. *Biochem. Med.* **24**, 314–320.

Kissinger, P. T., Bruntlett, C. S., Davis, G. C., Felice, L. J., Riggin, R. M., and Shoup, R. E. 1977. *Clin. Chem.* **23**, 1449–1455.

Korf, J., van Praag, H. M., and Sebens, J. B. 1971. *Biochem. Pharmacol.* **20**, 659–668.

Krstulovic, A. M., Bertani-Dziedzic, L., Dziedzic, S. W., and Gitlow, S. E. 1981. *J. Chromatogr.* **223**, 305–314.

Krstulovic, A., Matzura, C. T., Bertani-Dziedzic, L., Cerqueira, S., and Gitlow, S. E. 1980. *Clin. Chim. Acta* **103**, 109–116.

LaBrosse, E. H., Mann, J. D., and Kety, S. S. 1961. *J. Psychiat. Res.* **1**, 68–75.

Leckman, J. F., Maas, J. W., Redmond, D. E., and Heninger, G. R. 1980. *Life Sci.* **26**, 2179–2185.

Lindström, B., Sjöquist, B., and Änggård, E. 1974. *J. Labelled Compounds* **10**, 187–194.

Maas, J. W., Hattox, S. E., Landis, D. H., and Roth, R. H. 1976. *Brain Res.* **118**, 167–173.

Maas, J. W., Hattox, S. E., Landis, D. H., and Roth, R. H. 1977. *Eur. J. Pharmacol.* **46**, 221–228.

Maas, J. W., Hattox, S. E., Greene, N. M., and Landis, D. H. 1979. *Science* **205**, 1025–1027.

Mannarino, E., Kirshner, N., and Nashold, B. S., Jr. 1963. *J. Neurochem.* **10**, 373–379.

Markey, S. P., Powers, K., Dubinsky, D., and Kopin, I. J. 1980. *J. Labelled Compounds Radiopharmacol.* **17**, 103–114.

Markianos, E., and Beckmann, H. 1976. *J. Neural Transm.* **39**, 79–93.

Martin, B. R., Timmons, M. C., and Prange, A. J. 1972. *Clin. Chim. Acta* **38**, 271–275.

Mathieu, P., Greffe, J., Pharaboz, M. -O., Deruaz, D. and Guilluef, R. 1980. *Clin. Chim. Acta* **103**, 297–304.

Meek, J. L., and Neff, N. H. 1972. *Br. J. Pharmacol.* **45**, 435–441.

Mitchell, J., and Coscia, C. J. 1978. *J. Chromatogr.* **145**, 295–301.

Murray, S., Jones, D. H., Davies, D. S., Dollery, C. T., and Reid, J. L. 1977a. *Clin. Chim. Acta* **79**, 63–68.

Murray, S., Baillie, T. A., and Davies, D. A. 1977b. *J. Chromatogr.* **143**, 541–551.

Muskiet, F. A. J., Fremouw - Ottevangers, D. C., Walthers, B. G., and deVries, J. A. 1977. *Clin. Chem.* **23**, 863–866.

Muskiet, F. A. J., Jeuring, H. J., Adèr, J. -P., and Wolthers, B. G. 1978. *J. Neurochem.* **30**, 1495–1499.

Muskiet, F. A. J., Nagel, G. T., and Wolthers, B. G. 1980. *Anal. Biochem.,* **109**, 130–136.

Nicholas, J. L., Brown H., and Swander, A. M. 1969. *Clin. Chem.* **15**, 884–890
O'Keeffe, R., and Brooksbank, B. W. L. 1973. *Clin. Chem.* **19**, 1031–1035.
Post, R. M., Goodwin, F. K., Gordon, E., and Watkin, D. M. (1973). *Science* **179**, 897–899.
Ruthven, C. R. J., and Sandler, M. 1965. *Clin. Chim. Acta* **12**, 318–324.
Rutledge, C. O., and Jonason, J. 1967. *J. Pharmacol. Exp. Ther.* **157**, 493–502.
Sapira, J. D. 1968. *Clin. Chim. Acta* **20**, 139–145.
Saran, R. K., Sahuja, R. C., Gupta, N. N., Hasan, M., Bhargava, K. P., Shanker, K., and Kishor, K. 1978. *Science* **200**, 317–318.
Schanberg, S. M., Breese, G. R., Schildkraut, J. J., Gordon, E. K., and Kopin, I. J. 1968. *Biochem. Pharmacol.* **17**, 2006–2008.
Sedvall, G., Bjerkenstedt, L., Lindström, L., and Wode-Helgodt, B. 1978. *Life Sci.* **23**, 425–430.
Sharpless, N. S. 1977. *Res. Commun. Chem. Path. Pharmacol.* **18**, 257–271.
Shaw, D. M., O'Keeffe, R., MacSweeney, D. A., Brooksbank, B. W. L., Noguera, R., and Coppen, A. 1973. *Psycholog. Med.* **3**, 333–336.
Sjöquist, B., and Änggard E. 1974 *J. Neurochem.* **22**, 1161.
Sjöquist, B., Lindstrom, B., and Änggård, E. 1975. *J. Chromatogr.* **105**, 309–316.
Swahn, C. -G., Sandgärde, B., Wiesel, F. -A., and Sedvall, G. 1976. *Psychopharmacology* **48**, 147–152.
Swann, A. C., Maas, J. W., Hattox, S. E., and Landis, D. H. 1980. *Life Sci.* **27**, 1857–1862.
Sweeley, C. C., Elliott, W. H., Fries, I., and Ryhage, R. 1966. *Anal. Chem.* **38**, 1549–1553.
Sweeney, D. R., Leckman, J. F., Maas, J. W., Hattox, S., and Heninger, G. R. 1980. *Arch. Gen. Psychiatry* **37**, 1100–1103.
Takahashi, S., Godse, D. D., Warsh, J. J., and Stancer, H. C. 1977. *Clin. Chim. Acta* **81**, 183–192.
Tang, S. W., Stencer, H. C., Takahashi, S., Shephard, R. J., and Warsh, J. J. 1981. *Psychiatry Res.* **4**, 13–20.
Taylor, J. T., Freeman, S., and Brewer, P. 1981. *Clin. Chem.* **27**, 173–175.
Wilk, S., Gitlow, S. E., Clarke, D. D., and Paley, D. H. 1967. *Clin. Chim. Acta* **16**, 403–408.
Wilk, S., Davis, K. L., and Thacker, S. B. 1971a. *Anal. Biochem.* **39**, 498–501.
Wilk, S., and Mones, R. 1971b. *J. Neurochem.* **18**, 1771–1773.
Wolf, R. L., Mendlowitz, M., Roboz, J., and Gitlow, S. E. 1964. *J. Am. Med. Assoc.* **188**, 859–861.
Yeh, E. -L., Landis, D. H., and Maas, J. W. 1975. *Biochem. Med.* **14**, 411–416.
Zawad, J. S., and Brown, F. C. 1976. *Clin. Chim. Acta* **73**, 187–189.

6

Preliminary Characterization of Plasma MHPG in Man*

JAMES F. LECKMAN

JAMES W. MAAS†

Yale University School of Medicine, New Haven

I. Introduction

Catecholaminergic systems in the CNS and in the periphery are of critical importance in modulating a variety of basic survival-related behaviors, including eating, reproduction, and aggression (Antelman and

*This work was supported in part by NIMH grant nos. MH24393, MH30929, MH25642, the William T. Grant Foundation, and Mr. Leonard Berger.

†Present address: The University of Texas Health Science Center at San Antonio, San Antonio, Texas.

Caggiula, 1977). They have also been implicated in the pathogenesis of a number of neuropsychiatric disorders, including major affective disorders (Schildkraut, 1965; Bunney and Davis, 1965), schizophrenia (Lake *et al.*, 1980; Snyder *et al.*, 1973), Gilles de la Tourette syndrome (Cohen *et al.*, 1979; Shapiro *et al.*, 1973), Parkinson's disease (Hornykiewicz, 1973), and Huntington's chorea (Klawans, 1973). Catecholamines have also been implicated in the development of some forms of arterial hypertension (Bolme *et al.*, 1972; Elliott, 1979) and in abstinence syndromes (Gold *et al.*, 1978; Hoder *et al.*, 1981).

Strategies used to study the functioning of catecholamine systems in man have included postmortem studies of the relevant enzymes, receptors, neurotransmitters, and their metabolites; cerebrospinal fluid (CSF) studies of central catecholamines and their metabolites, as well as studies of urine and plasma. *In vivo* studies of urine and plasma offer many logistic advantages over the postmortem and CSF studies, but they suffer from being more indirect. Critical issues involve the degree to which the metabolites and the characteristics of enzymes and receptors found in periphery reflect or match the corresponding central moieties.

The purpose of this chapter is to offer a preliminary account of plasma measures of a major metabolite of norepinephrine (NE), 3-methoxy-4-hydroxyphenethyleneglycol (MHPG), in man. In the sections that follow, we shall briefly review the evidence that bears on the potential usefulness of plasma measures of MHPG levels in studying the activity of brain noradrenergic systems before examining the relevant human studies in patient and nonpatient populations.

II. Brain MHPG versus Other Metabolites as an Index of Brain NE Activity

The catabolism of NE to MHPG involves three widely distributed and largely nonspecific enzymes: monoamine oxidase (MAO), catechol-*O*-methyltransferase (COMT), and aldehyde reductase (AR), as reviewed in Chapter 1 of this volume (Tabakoff and DeLeon-Jones).

Although the formation of vanillylmandelic acid (VMA) can compete with MHPG production (Fig. 1), VMA does not appear to be a major metabolite of NE in brain (Ader *et al.*, 1978; Karoum *et al.*, 1976; Sjöquist, 1975). VMA exists in lower concentrations, and its distribution in various brain regions is substantially different from the pattern of distribution for NE and MHPG. The highest levels of VMA are found in the striatum as compared with NE and MHPG, where the highest levels

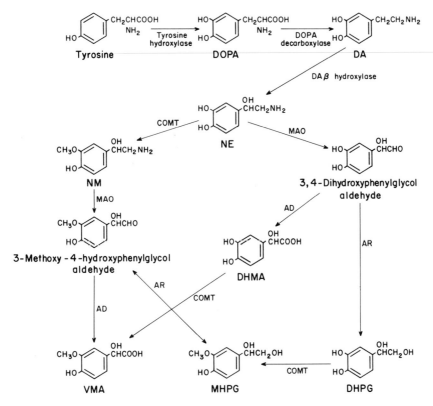

Fig. 1. Metabolic pathways involved in the synthesis and catabolism of norepinephrine (NE). Abbreviations: 3,4-dihydroxyphenylalanine (DOPA); dopamine (DA); catechol O-methyltransferase (COMT); monoamine oxidase (MAO); normetanephrine (NM); aldehyde dihydrogenase (AD); aldehyde reductase (AR); 3,4-dihydroxymandelic acid (DHMA); 3-methoxy-4-hydroxymandelic acid (VMA); 3-methoxy-4-hydroxyphenethyleneglycol (MHPG); and 3,4-dihydroxyphenethyleneglycol (DHPG).

are found in the hypothalamus (Duncan *et al.*, 1974; Karoum *et al.*, 1976; Tabakoff, 1977).

The most compelling evidence for brain MHPG being a better index of brain NE metabolism than VMA comes from experiments in which central NE systems were altered and changes in both metabolites monitored. Ader *et al.* (1978) found that electrical stimulation of noradrenergic locus coeruleus (LC) increased brain MHPG threefold, whereas no effect on VMA levels was found. Similarly, electrothermic destruction of the locus coeruleus produced a 50% decrease in brain MHPG levels compared with no change in VMA levels (Table I).

In contrast, dihydroxyphenethyleneglycol (DHPG), an immediate

TABLE I

Evidence for Alterations in Brain MHPG as an Index of NE activity

Change in brain concentration following:

Compound	LC[a] stimulation	LC[a] destruction	Stress[b]	6-OHDA[c]	Clonidine	Piperoxane
NE	Increased	Decreased	Increased	Decreased	Decreased	Increased
MHPG	Increased	Decreased	Increased	Decreased	Decreased	Increased
DHPG	NA[d]	NA	Increased	NA	Decreased	NA
VMA	No change	No change	NA	NA	NA	NA

[a] Noradrenergic locus coeruleus.
[b] Long periods of forced running, electrical foot shock, and cold stress.
[c] 6-Hydroxydopamine.
[d] NA = data not available.

precursor of MHPG (Fig. 1) is an important metabolite of NE in brain in its own right (Gale and Maas, 1977; Jimmerson *et al.*, 1979; Stone, 1973). Although less well studied, DHPG has a regional distribution similar to NE and MHPG in brain (Rutledge and Jonason, 1967). DHPG has also been shown in several animal species to be present in concentrations approaching those of MHPG in a variety of brain regions (Schanberg *et al.*, 1968).

As reviewed by DeMet and Halaris (1979) and Roth (Chapter 2, this volume), there is substantial evidence that *brain* levels of MHPG are a reliable index of central NE release and metabolism. These include studies of brain MHPG following (1) lesion or stimulation of the noradrenergic locus coeruleus, (2) experimentally induced stress, and (3) pharmacological agents known to affect central NE activity (Table I).

Electrothermic lesions of the LC have consistently resulted in decreased levels of MHPG in brain (Ader *et al.*, 1978; Arbuthnott *et al.*, 1973; Korf *et al.*, 1973a; Kostowski *et al.*, 1974). Conversely, electrical stimulation of the LC produces a consistent increase in levels of MHPG found in rat brain and spinal cord (Ader *et al.*, 1978; Bareggi *et al.*, 1978; Crawley *et al.*, 1979; Korf *et al.*, 1973a).

Experimentally induced stress (long periods of forced running, electrical foot shocks, and cold stress) have also been shown to increase brain levels of MHPG and DHPG in animals (Caesar *et al.*, 1974; Cassens *et al.*, 1980; Korf *et al.*, 1973b; Meek and Neff, 1973; Stone, 1973, 1975). Korf and co-workers (1973c) reported that stress did not increase levels of brain MHPG in LC-lesioned animals but did in sham-operated controls.

6-Hydroxydopamine (6-OHDA), an agent that destroys central catecholaminergic nerve terminals when administered ic, greatly reduces brain NE levels (Breese and Traylor, 1970). Similar decrements in brain MHPG levels have also been reported following 6-OHDA administration (Bareggi *et al.*, 1974; Helmeste *et al.*, 1979; Howlett *et al.*, 1975; Maas *et al.*, 1973).

Clonidine, an α_2-noradrenergic receptor agonist, has been shown to reduce NE turnover (Anden *et al.*, 1970) and to inhibit the spontaneous firing of the noradrenergic locus coeruleus (Cedarbaum and Aghajanian, 1976, 1977; Svensson *et al.*, 1975). Several investigators (Braestrup and Nielsen, 1976; Stone, 1976) reported that the acute administration of clonidine significantly reduced both MHPG and DHPG in rat brain, whereas the administration of phenoxybenzamine and aceperone, α-noradrenergic receptor blocking agents, significantly increased rat MHPG levels.

Maas and co-workers (1977), using an *in vivo* arteriovenous difference technique, reported that clonidine produced a significant drop in brain

MHPG production, whereas piperoxane, an α-noradrenergic antagonist, markedly increased brain MHPG production.

Having established that brain MHPG levels, in some species, reflect central NE release and metabolism, we need to consider the intervening factors that may affect plasma levels of MHPG.

III. Factors That Influence Plasma MHPG Levels

In addition to the activity of brain NE systems, there are a variety of factors, both central and peripheral, that can affect plasma levels of MHPG (Table II).

A. Central Factors

The factors that determine the amount of NE released into the synapse following depolarization are partially understood. α_2-Adrenergic presynaptic receptors regulate, via a calcium-dependent process, the amount of NE released following depolarization (Langer, 1974, 1977; Starke, 1977). These inhibitory receptors appear to be part of a negative feedback mechanism mediated by the neuron's own transmitter. Although most MHPG is formed extraneuronally following the release of

TABLE II
Factors that Influence Plasma MHPG Levels

Central factors
Activity of brain NE systems (release, associated with or independent of synaptic transmission, and metabolism of NE in brain)
Transport kinetics into cerebral circulation or CSF
Cerebral blood flow
Factors with both central and peripheral components
Activity of SNS (regulated centrally but determines the amount of NE released in periphery)
Rates of conjugation sulfate versus glucuronide (primarily peripheral)
Peripheral factors
Competing metabolic pathways for NE released from sympathetic nerve endings
Transport kinetics into peripheral circulation
Conversion to VMA
Factors influencing urinary excretion

NE from the nerve terminal, not all MHPG in brain is derived from NE release associated with synaptic transmission, as NE also appears to "leak" from nerve terminals. Similarly, the site of MHPG formation in brain is not solely extraneuronal (Nielsen and Braestrup, 1977). Intra-neuronal formation is the result of the rapid uptake of nor-metanephrine by the presynaptic terminal, which, in turn, is metabo-lized by intracellular MAO and AR (Fig. 1) (Hendley et al., 1970).

In contrast to NE, free MHPG is able to diffuse freely from brain sites and from the vicinity of peripheral sympathetic nerve endings across cell membranes (Kessler et al., 1976) to enter the CSF and plasma.

The kinetics and time course of these events in the brain have not been studied extensively. Karoum and co-workers (1976) reported that the half-life of MHPG in rat brain was 1.8 h. Species-specific differences would be expected given physical differences in the size and proximity of NE-rich areas to the ventricular system. Species differences in the degree of sulfate conjugation in brain would also affect the kinetics as MHPG-SO$_4$ is actively transported whereas free MHPG is not (Meek and Neff, 1973).

Evidence suggests that, although the site of sulfate conjugation is ex-traneuronal (Eccleston and Ritchie, 1973), conjugation probably occurs in the vicinity of the noradrenergic neurons, because in most animal species studied the regional distribution of the sulfate conjugates closely parallels the levels of MHPG and DHPG (Meek and Foldes, 1973; Meek and Neff, 1972). In man, brain MHPG exists predominantly in the free form with the concentration of conjugated MHPG being much lower (Bertilsson, 1973; Karoum et al., 1977a; Maas et al., 1976; Hattox, Chap-ter 5, this volume).

Less is known about the central formation of the MHPG glucuronide conjugate. Although this moiety is absent in rat brain, its presence in low concentrations in human brain has been reported (Karoum et al., 1977a).

B. Peripheral Factors

In brain, the reduction of the aldehydes formed by the action of MAO on NE and normetanephrine (NM) predominates over their oxidation, so that MHPG and, to a lesser extent, DHPG are the major metabolites of NE formed centrally. In the periphery, VMA is the major metabolite of NE (Goodall and Rosen, 1963). For a detailed discussion regarding the enzymology of the reductive versus oxidative pathways in brain and the periphery, see Chapter 1 of this volume. A portion of the MHPG found in urine and plasma derives from peripheral sites, particularly the sympathetic nervous system (SNS).

Free MHPG exists in low concentration (nanogram range) in plasma. Only a small fraction of MHPG is excreted in the urine unchanged. In plasma, the metabolic fate of free MHPG proceeds to conjugation with either sulfate or glucuronide moieties.

Once conjugated, MHPG is efficiently excreted in the urine. Shimizu and LaBrosse (1969) reported that, on the average, the amount of MHPG excreted as the sulfate conjugate was equal to the amount excreted as the glucuronide conjugate. The individual variation in this regard, however, was high. The amount excreted as free MHPG was uniformly low, accounting for only 8% of the total.

Another factor that may operate to limit the correspondence of central and peripheral MHPG levels in man is the conversion of MHPG to VMA in the peripheral circulation. Evidence has been presented that indicates that 40–50% of free MHPG injected intravenously is found in the urine as VMA (Blombery et al., 1980; Mårdh et al., 1980). The use of pharmacologic doses of MHPG employed in these studies, approximately three orders of magnitude greater than those produced by brain normally, leaves open to the question of the degree to which this conversion occurs under physiological conditions. This skepticism is supported by comparable studies in subhuman primates in which tracer amounts of labeled MHPG were administered and where it was found that only about 4% of MHPG was converted to VMA (Maas et al., unpublished observations). The kinetics and time course of the conversion of free MHPG to VMA have not been studied in plasma, per se, nor have the sites of the conjugation of free MHPG been determined. That this process may be more complex than it would intuitively seem to be is indicated by the finding of a lack of a significant correlation between plasma-free MHPG and plasma-conjugated MHPG (Sweeney et al., 1980).

IV. The Role of the SNS: Interaction of Central and Peripheral NE Systems

The amount of MHPG in plasma and urine that derives directly from brain has been an area of active investigation, with estimates ranging from 10 to 60% (for a review of this area see Chapter 3, this volume). These discrepancies may reflect species differences and other major methodologic differences, i.e., the use of radio tracer studies versus 6-

OHDA studies versus arteriovenous difference studies. However, recent work on the regulation of NE release, MHPG formation, and its subsequent metabolism in the periphery calls into question the value of trying to determine the precise proportion of plasma and/or urinary MHPG that is of central origin because there is increasing evidence that a functional interaction exists between central and peripheral NE systems. To the extent that central and peripheral NE systems form a single functional unit, defining precisely the amount of MHPG in plasma or urine that derives from central versus peripheral sites loses some of its importance. These issues of central–peripheral adrenergic interactions and the fractional contribution of brain MHPG to peripheral pools were reviewed in detail in Chapter 3.

V.   Correspondence of MHPG Levels in Brain, CSF, and Plasma

Consistent with the evidence of a functional interaction between central and peripheral NE systems and despite the effects of other potentially confounding factors, studies in primates have shown a direct correspondence among MHPG levels in brain, CSF, and plasma (Elsworth et al., 1980; Redmond et al., 1979). In one study of vervet monkeys in which various brain regions were studied, plasma-free MHPG was highly correlated with MHPG concentrations in most regions studied, including amygdala, hippocampus, hypothalamus, and occipital cortex (Elsworth et al., 1981). In addition, both NE and MHPG levels in CSF and plasma have been shown to be correlated in man (Jimerson et al., 1981; Lake et al., 1981). Clonidine, an α_2-noradrenergic receptor agonist, which reduces brain NE turnover and inhibits the firing of the LC (Anden et al., 1970; Starke et al., 1973; Svensson et al., 1975), also reduces the venous–arterial difference of MHPG in primates (Cedarbaum and Aghajanian, 1976, 1977; Maas et al., 1976) and reduces plasma MHPG levels in man (Leckman et al., 1980, 1981).

Crawley and co-workers (1978) reported that plasma levels of MHPG in the rat increased following electrical stimulation of the LC. Jimerson and co-workers (1979) found that immobilization stress and direct stimulation of the sympathetic outflow of pithed rats increased plasma levels of both MHPG and DHPG. In contrast, other investigators using comparable methods to assay plasma MHPG levels (Helmeste et al., 1979) were unable to observe differences in plasma MHPG concentrations following ic injection of 6-OHDA. This same group did report a clear fall (~36%) in plasma MHPG following ip injection of clonidine but concluded that this was not a central effect because there was no additional decrement in plasma MHPG when clonidine treatment was combined with debrisoquine, a peripheral MAO inhibitors. Evidence in monkeys, however, indicates that, although debrisoquine does *not* enter brain, it does reduce brain levels of MHPG by an obscure mechanism probably involving sympathetic afferents (Maas et al., 1979). Although this effect may account for Helmeste and co-workers' failure to observe a further decrement in plasma MHPG with the combined treatment of debrisoquine and clonidine, it does not explain the normal levels of brain MHPG following debrisoquine treatment.

In the aggregate, the available data do suggest that there are significant relationships between CNS noradrenergic function and plasma MHPG. The mechanisms by which such relationships might occur are reviewed by Maas and Leckman (Chapter 3, this volume).

VI. Plasma MHPG in Man: Emerging Clinical Applications

A. Plasma MHPG in Normal Control Subjects

1. Plasma-Free MHPG. A number of studies on plasma levels of free MHPG have recently been conducted (for a comprehensive review, see Hattox, Chapter 5, this volume). Gas chromatography–mass spectroscopy (GC–MS) measurement of MHPG in human plasma has revealed mean values of approximately 4.0 ng/ml with the range extending from 2.0 to 12.0 ng/ml. (Jimerson et al., 1981; Karoum et al., 1977b; Leckman et al., 1981; Maas et al., 1979; Swann et al., 1980; Takahashi et al., 1977; Young et al., Chapter 10, this volume).

Although there is less variance within than across subjects with regard to plasma levels of free MHPG under baseline conditions it appears that MHPG levels may be quite labile among some normal subjects. In a recent study of the effects of clonidine on plasma-free MHPG levels and blood pressure, we found a ±12% fluctuation in these MHPG levels over a 1-h period (8:00 to 9:00 A.M.) with a maximum fluctuation of ±43% in some patients (Leckman et al., 1980, 1981).

Diurnal variation of plasma-free MHPG levels may also occur in some subjects with clear increases in levels of plasma MHPG from 8:00 A.M. to 12:00 noon, with levels reaching a plateau in the afternoon (Leckman *et al.*, 1981; Sternberg *et al.*, 1981; Swann *et al.*, 1980) (Table IV). It was also found that increases may be accentuated by fasting (Swann *et al.*, 1980). The increase in levels of plasma-free MHPG is consistent with findings that urinary MHPG excretion in normal subjects increases during daytime hours, peaking in the afternoon and evening hours (Cymerman and Francesconi, 1975; Davis *et al.*, 1967; Hollister *et al.*, 1978; Potter *et al.*, Chapter 8, this volume; Wehr *et al.*, 1980).

No sex differences in plasma levels of free MHPG have been reported (Jimerson *et al.*, 1981). Other investigators have discussed increases in plasma-free MHPG levels as a result of increasing noradrenergic function with age (Young *et al.*, Chapter 10, this volume).

The effects of various drugs on plasma-free MHPG levels have also been investigated. In a study of nine normal male subjects, clonidine was administered in various doses (0, 1, and 5 µg/kg po). The 5 µg/kg doses produced a significant decrease from baseline and placebo levels of free MHPG in plasma, reaching a nadir between 3 and 4 h after dosage (Fig. 2). Substantial individual variation, however, was observed within and across subjects (Fig. 3). These studies did not address the question of the origin of the MHPG fall, brain effect versus decreased SNS activity versus peripheral effect versus some combination of these, but did suggest, because of the clonidine dosage, that the change in plasma levels may roughly reflect changes in central NE neuronal activity. In these

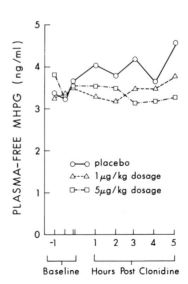

Fig. 2. Mean plasma-free MHPG (ng/ml) for nine normal male subjects following oral clonidine (1 and 5 µ/kg) and placebo.

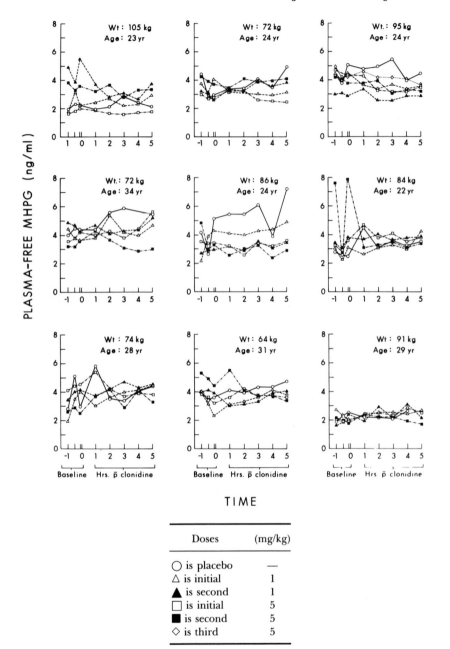

Fig. 3. Individual plasma-free MHPG (ng/ml) response in nine normal male subjects receiving oral clonidine (1 and 5 μg/kg) and placebo.

same studies, an unexpectedly close relationship between sitting and standing diastolic blood pressure and plasma-free MHPG was found (Leckman *et al.*, 1981).

The effects of debrisoquin on plasma MHPG have also been examined. Debrisoquin is a peripheral monoamine oxidase inhibitor (Medina *et al.*, 1969), which has been shown to reduce brain MHPG but not homovanillic acid (HVA) in animal populations (Maas *et al.*, 1979). In a study of six normal subjects, debrisoquin was found to reduce plasma levels of free MHPG (Swann *et al.*, 1980). In contrast to the clonidine studies, a correlation was found between standing systolic blood pressure and levels of free MHPG in plasma.

Correlations between plasma-free MHPG and urinary excretion of total MHPG have not been reported in normal adult control subjects. However, a significant correlation between plasma-free MHPG and CSF total MHPG has been reported (Jimerson *et al.*, 1981).

2. Plasma-Conjugated MHPG. Levels of conjugated MHPG in plasma of normal subjects show considerable variation in the three studies that have been performed (Karoum *et al.*, 1977b; Takahashi *et al.*, 1977; Jimerson *et al.*, 1981). Mean values range from 10 to 20 ng/ml. However, other studies have found plasma levels of combined MHPG conjugates to be as low as 11.9 and even 7.0 ng/ml (Jimerson *et al.*, 1981; Takahashi *et al.*, 1977). The issue of stability and possible diurnal variations in these measures has not been addressed in normal subjects. One study found that plasma-conjugated MHPG levels increase with age and are higher in male subjects than in female subjects (Jimerson *et al.*, 1981). The differential contribution of the sulfate and glucuronide conjugates to these findings awaits further study. No pharmacological trials involving plasma-conjugated MHPG in man have thus far been reported.

Surprisingly, plasma-conjugated and plasma-free MHPG appear to be unrelated (Jimerson *et al.*, 1981; Sweeney *et al.*, 1980). However, plasma-conjugated MHPG levels have also been reported to be correlated with CSF MHPG levels (Jimerson *et al.*, 1981).

The delineation of the relationship between plasma-conjugated MHPG and urinary MHPG excretion in normal subjects awaits additional data.

Unlike plasma-free MHPG, levels of plasma MHPG conjugates show an increase with age in adult subjects (Jimerson *et al.*, 1981). These investigators also found that men tend to have higher concentrations of conjugated MHPG in plasma than do women (Jimerson *et al.*, 1981).

3. Plasma-Total MHPG. In addition to studies that have investigated plasma-free and -conjugated MHPG levels separately, other studies of plasma-total MHPG have been reported in normal subjects (Dekirmen-jian and Maas, 1974; Halaris et al., 1977; Markianos and Beckmann, 1976). These studies have reported a broad range of baseline levels, varying from 10.9 ± 3.4 to 22.0 ± 0.6 ng/ml (Jimerson et al., 1981; Karoum et al., 1977b; Markianos and Beckmann, 1976; Takahashi et al., 1977). The stability of these measures has not been reported. However, one of these studies indicated that a diurnal increase in plasma-total MHPG levels similar to that seen in plasma-free MHPG levels may occur in some normal subjects (Markianos and Beckmann, 1976).

In another study, plasma-total MHPG was found to be related to a number of other biogenic amines; plasma-total MHPG correlated with CSF total MHPG and CSF norepinephrine levels (Jimerson et al., 1981). Pharmacological trials involving plasma-total MHPG have not been reported in normal control subjects.

B. Patients with Major Affective Disorders

1. Plasma-free MHPG. Plasma levels of free MHPG have been investigated in at least three studies under baseline conditions (Sweeney et al., 1980; Siever et al., 1981; Charney et al., 1981). Mean A.M. levels appear to be comparable to those reported in normal subjects under similar conditions. In 1 study of 10 endogenously depressed patients, baseline plasma-free MHPG levels were quite stable, and there was much less variance within individual patients than across patients (Table III) (Charney et al., 1981). This finding of little fluctuation of free MHPG levels is comparable to the results of Sweeney and co-workers (1980) in a heterogenous group of neuropsychiatric patients. Studies of depressed patients have not reported any diurnal variation in plasma-free MHPG levels (Charney et al., 1981; Sweeney et al., 1980) (Table IV) nor have sex or age effects been reported in this patient population.

There have been two reports on the effect of clonidine on plasma-free MHPG levels in depressed patients (Charney et al., 1981; Siever et al., 1981). Significant reductions were observed following either oral (Charney et al., 1981) or intravenous (Siever et al., 1981) administration. The magnitude of the fall in plasma concentration was comparable to that observed in normal control subjects and correlated with a drop in systolic blood pressure. No consistent acute behavior effects have been reported other than sedation.

In the study of Charney and co-workers (1981), an oral clonidine challenge was performed before and following 3 weeks of treatment with desmethylimipramine (DMI).

TABLE III

Variation within Subjects versus across Subjects for 8 to 9 A.M. Baseline Values of Plasma-Free MHPG

Diagnostic group	Source of variance	Sum of squares	df	Mean square	F ratio	Level of significance	N	Mean ± S.E.M.
Normal controls (Beckman et al., 1981)	Within subjects	3,839.8	8	480.0	3.85	$p < .0004$	9	3.3 ± 1.0
	Across subjects	15,701.1	126	124.6				
	Total	19,540.9	134					
Depressed (Charney et al., 1981)	Within subjects	40,458.7	9	4495.4	166.71	$p < .0001$	10	4.2 ± 1.8
	Across subjects	2,076.4	77	27.0				
	Total	42,535.1	86					
Schizophrenic (Sternberg et al., 1981)	Within subjects	13,414.3	9	1490.5	37.19	$p < .0001$	10	3.7 ± 1.5
	Across subjects	2,725.6	68	40.1				
	Total	16,139.9	77					

TABLE IV
Diurnal Change in Plasma-Free MHPG

Population	Investigators	N	Plasma-free MHPG (ng/ml)		
			A.M. Mean	P.M. Mean	p
Normal controls	Leckman et al., 1981[a]	9	3.3	4.5	.01
	Swann et al., 1981[b]	6	3.4	3.9	.05
	Sternberg et al., 1982[c]	11	3.8	4.5	.01
Depressed	Charney et al., 1981[a]	15	4.4	4.3	NS[e]
	Sweeney et al., 1980[d]	7	3.6	3.1	NS
Schizophrenic	Sternberg et al., 1982[c]	11	4.0	4.2	NS

[a] Measures at 8 A.M. versus 2 P.M.
[b] Measures at 8 A.M. versus 12 P.M.
[c] Measures at 8 A.M. versus mean 11:30 A.M., 12 P.M., and 1 P.M.
[d] Measures at 8 A.M. versus 4 P.M.
[e] NS = not significant.

DMI, alone, also produced a significant decrease in plasma levels of free MHPG in these depressed patients. Following 3 weeks of treatment with DMI, the effects of clonidine on both plasma-free MHPG and blood pressure were markedly attenuated. Although these findings are suggestive of the development of subsensitivity of α_2-adrenergic receptors during DMI treatment, as would be predicted from animal studies (Crews and Smith, 1978, 1980; Tang et al., 1978; McMillen et al., 1980; Sugrue, 1980; Sypraki and Fibjger, 1980), they do not clearly support the hypothesis that depression is associated with a hypersensitivity of α_2-adrenergic receptors (Leckman et al., 1980), because no significant differences in response to clonidine were observed between treatment responders and nonresponders either before or during treatment with DMI (Charney et al., 1981).

In an earlier study, we found that dextroamphetamine produced a modest fall in mean plasma-free MHPG concentrations in depressed patients (Sweeney et al., 1981).

2. Plasma-conjugated MHPG. No correlation between plasma-free and -conjugated MHPG was observed in a preliminary study of 5 depressed patients (Sweeney et al., 1980). Similarly, no significant correlation between plasma-free MHPG and urinary total MHPG was observed in a larger group of 10 patients, although this may have occurred because of 1 deviant value. Baseline levels of conjugated MHPG were comparable to those reported for normal subjects and were relatively stable over a several-day period (Sweeney et al., 1980). The same study failed to reveal any diurnal variation in conjugated MHPG levels (Sweeney et al., 1980).

3. Plasma-total MHPG. Total MHPG levels have been measured in plasma in a large number of affectively ill patients (Halaris, 1978; Halaris and DeMet, 1978, 1979, 1980). Although studies on the stability, diurnal variation, and sexual difference in plasma-total MHPG levels have not been described, a number of striking clinical and pharmacologic results ave been reported. Briefly, this body of data indicates that patients with a bipolar major affective disorder in the manic phase have high levels of plasma-total MHPG in contrast to normal subjects or depressed patient groups (Halaris, 1978; Halaris and DeMet, 1978, 1979). Other findings include transient increases in plasma-total MHPG following administration of imipramine and AHR-1118 in depressed patients (Halaris and DeMet, 1979, 1980). Decreases in plasma-total MHPG levels have also been reported in manic patients following lithium treatment (Halaris, 1978; Halaris and DeMet, 1978). Although these studies are promising, they need to be replicated, ideally using the more rigorous GC–MS methodology. The methodological difficulties involved in using gas GC alone are substantial (Halaris *et al.*, 1977). This method may underestimate the total amount of MHPG present. The mean value for total MHPG in the normal controls in the preceding studies was 7.9 ng/ml (Halaris *et al.*, 1977), whereas estimates of total MHPG based on GC–MS studies, in which free and conjugated MHPG were determined separately, yield considerably higher estimates of total MHPG in normal subjects of between 16.5 and 22.4 ng/ml (Jimerson *et al.*, 1981; Karoum *et al.*, 1977b; Takahashi *et al.*, 1977).

C. Schizophrenic Patients

Plasma-free MHPG. Two studies have presented data on plasma-free MHPG in schizophrenic patients (Sweeney *et al.*, 1980; Sternberg *et al.*, 1981). Schizophrenic patients were found to have morning baseline MHPG values within the same range as a group of normal controls and to have less variance in their baseline levels within individual patients than across patients. No diurnal increase in levels was observed (Sternberg *et al.*, 1981) (Table IV). Age and sex effects have not been studied.

The effects of clonidine (1 and 5 μg/kg) were also studied in this patient group. Interestingly, among schizophrenic patients, no effect on MHPG levels was observed after oral clonidine administration, although they did show a reduction in both systolic and diastolic blood pressure, which matched that of control subjects. This may indicate that schizophrenic individuals have a decreased number or functioning of the α_2-adrenergic receptors responsible for MHPG production and that there may be an uncoupling of the effects of clonidine on the LC versus the regions of the medulla oblongata responsible for the hypotensive effect of clonidine.

D. Patients with Other Neuropsychiatric Disorders

Plasma levels of MHPG have also been reported in at least two other neuropsychiatric disorders: Tourette's syndrome and infantile autism. These reports are discussed in Chapter 10, this volume by Young *et al.*

VII. Summary

Plasma measures of MHPG have been available for less than a decade. The measurement of the nanogram quantities of MHPG found in plasma using GC–MS is technically demanding and expensive. However, these debits are offset by the relative ease of plasma collection and the potential for obtaining serial specimens over relatively short intervals of time.

In the aggregate the available, emerging data indicate that there are significant relationships between CNS noradrenergic function and plasma MHPG levels.

The range of potential clinical applications of measures of plasma MHPG levels is broad and includes studies of syndromes in which adrenergic overactivity or underactivity has been implicated. This list includes essential hypertension, orthostatic hypotension, abstinence syndromes (opiate, alcohol), major affective disorders, schizophrenia, anxiety and phobic disorders, and the syndrome of Gilles de la Tourette. Study designs would be expected to vary from simply monitoring the natural course of disease states (abstinence syndromes, labile hypertension, bipolar illness) to performing provocative testing using specific physiological or pharmacological challenges under a variety of conditions. In addition, plasma MHPG measures may also allow more sophisticated studies of alterations in receptor sensitivities to emerge. It should not be forgotten, however, that practical questions concerning the lability of plasma-free and -conjugated MHPG, diurnal fluctuations, and relationships with age and sex and other state and trait variables remain to be answered.

Acknowledgments

The authors wish to thank Margrethe Cone for providing expert secretarial skills and Keith Caruso for his help in data analysis.

References

Ader, J. P., Muskiet, F. A. J., Jeuring, H. J., and Korf, J. 1978. *J. Neurochem.* **30**, 1213–1216.

Anden, M. E., Corridi, K., Fuxe, B., Hökfelt, T., Hökfelt, C., and Svensson, T. 1970. *Life Sci.* **9**, 513–523.

Antelman, S. M., and Caggiula, A. R. 1977. *Science* **195**, 646–653.

Arbuthnott, G. W., Christie, J. E., Crow, T. J., Eccleston, D., and Walter, D. S. 1973. *Exp. Neurol.* **41**, 411–417.

Bareggi, S. R., Marc, V., and Morsell, P. L. 1974. *Brain Res.* **75**, 177–180.

Bareggi, S. R., Markey, K., and Genovese, E. 1978. *Eur. J. Pharmacol.* **50**, 301–306.

Bertilsson, L. 1973. *J. Chromatogr.* **87**, 147–153.

Blombery, P., Kopin, I. J., Gordon, E. K., Markey, S. P., and Ebert, M. 1980. *Arch. Gen. Psychiatry* **37**, 1095–1098.

Bolme, P., Fuxe, K., and Lidbrink, P. 1972. *Res. Comm. Chem. Pathol. Pharmacol.* **4**, 657–697.

Braestrup, C., and Nielsen, M. 1976. *J. Pharmacol. Exp. Ther.* **198**, 596–608.

Breese, G. R., and Traylor, T. D. 1970. *J. Pharmacol. Exp. Ther.* **174**, 413–420.

Bunney, W. E., Jr., and Davis, J. M. 1965. *Arch. Gen. Psychiatry* **13**, 483–494.

Caesar, P. M., Hagne, P., Sharman, D. F., and Werdinius, B. 1974. *Br. J. Pharmacol.* **51**, 187–195.

Cassens, G., Roffman, M., Kuruk, A., Orsulak, P. J., and Schildkraut, J. J. 1980. *Science* **209**, 1138–1139.

Cedarbaum, J. M., and Aghajanian, G. K. 1976. *Brain Res.* **112**, 413–419.

Cedarbaum, J. M., and Aghajanian, G. K. 1977. *Eur. J. Pharmacol.* **44**, 375–385.

Charney, D. S., Heninger, G. R., Sternberg, D. E., Redmond, D. E., Leckman, J. F., Maas, J. W., and Roth, R. H. 1981. *Arch. Gen. Psychiatry* **38**, 1334–1340.

Cohen, D. J., Young, J. G., Nathanson, J. A., and Shaywitz, B. A. 1979. *Lancet* **2**, 551–553.

Crawley, J. N., Hattox, S. E., Maas, J. W., and Roth, R. H. 1978. *Brain Res.* **141**, 380–384.

Crawley, J. N., Roth, R. H., and Maas, J. W. 1979. *Brain Res.* **166**, 180–184.

Crawley, J. N., Maas, J. W., and Roth, R. H. 1980. *Brain Res.* **183**, 301–311.

Crews, T. F., and Smith, C. B. 1978. *Science* **202**, 322–324.

Crews, T. F., and Smith, C. B. 1980. *J. Pharmacol. Exp. Ther.* **215**, 143–149.

Cymerman, A., and Francesconi, R. F. 1975. *Life Sci.* **16**, 225–236.

Davis, V. E., Cashaw, J. L., Huff, J. A., Brown, H., and Nicholas, N. 1967. *Proc. Soc. Exp. Biol. Med.* **125**, 1140–1143.

Dekirmenjian, H., and Maas, J. W. 1974. *Clin. Chim. Acta* **52**, 203–210.

DeMet, E. M., and Halaris, A. E. 1979. *Biochem. Pharmacol.* **23**, 3043–3050.

Duncan, R. J. S., and Sourkes, T. L. 1974. *Biochem. Pharmacol.* **23**, 663–669.

Ebert, M. H., and Kopin, I. J. 1975. *Trans. Assoc. Am. Physicians* **28**, 256–264.

Eccleston, D., and Ritchie, I. M. 1973. *J. Neurochem.* **21,** 635–646.
Elliott, J. M. 1979. *Clin. Exp. Pharmacol. Physiol.* **6,** 569.
Elsworth, J. D., Roth, R. H., Stogin, J. M., Leahy, D. J., Moore, M. R., and Redmond, D. E., Jr. 1980. *Neurosci. Abstr.* **6,** 140.
Elsworth, J. D., Redmond, D. E., and Roth, R. H. 1982. *Brain Res.* **235,** 115–124.
Gale, S., and Maas, J. W. 1977. *J. Neural Transm.* **41,** 59–72.
Gold, M. S., Redmond, D. E., and Kleber, H. D. 1978. *Lancet i,* 599–602.
Goodall, McC., and Rosen, L. 1963. *J. Clin. Invest.* **42,** 1578–1588.
Halaris, A. E., DeMet, E. M., and Halaris, M. E. 1977. *Clin. Chim. Acta* **78,** 285–294.
Halaris, A. E. 1978. *Am. J. Psychiatry* **135,** 493–494.
Halaris, A. E., and DeMet, E. M. 1978. *Lancet i,* 670.
Halaris, A. E., and DeMet, E. M. 1979. *Catecholamines: Basic and Clinical Frontiers* (E. Usdin, I. J. Kopin, and J. Barchas, eds.), pp. 1866–1868. Pergamon Press, New York.
Halaris, A. E., and DeMet, E. M. 1980. *Prog. Neuropsychopharmacol.* **4,** 43–49.
Helmeste, D. M., Stancer, H. G., Coscina, D. V., Takahashi, S., and Warsh, J. J. 1979. *Life Sci.* **25,** 601–606.
Hendley, E. D., Taylor, K. M., and Snyder, S. H. 1970. *Eur. J. Pharmacol.* **12,** 167–179.
Hoder, E. L., Leckman, J. F., Ehrenkranz, R. A., Kleber, H., Cohen, D. J., and Poulsen, J. A. 1981. *N. Eng. J. Med.* **305,** 1284.
Hollister, L. E., Davis, K. L., Overall, J. E., and Anderson, T. 1978. *Arch. Gen. Psychiatry* **35,** 1410–1415.
Hornykiewicz, O. 1973. *Fed. Proc. Amer. Soc. Exp. Biol.* **32,** 183.
Howlett, D. R., Jenner, F. A., and Nahorski, S. R. 1975. *J. Pharm. Pharmacol.* **27,** 447–449.
Jimerson, D. C., Sun, C. L., Yamaguchi, I., and Kopin, I. J. 1979. *Catecholamines: Basic and Clinical Frontiers* (E. Usdin, I. J. Kopin, and J. Barchas, eds.), pp. 927–929. Pergamon Press, New York.
Jimerson, D. C., Ballenger, J. C., Lake, C. R., Post, R. M., Goodwin, F. K., and Kopin, I. J. 1981. *Psychopharmacol. Bull.* **17,** 86–87.
Karoum, F., Neff, N. H., and Wyatt, R. J. 1976. *J. Neurochem.* **27,** 33–35.
Karoum, F., Moyer-Schwing, J., Potkin, S. G., and Wyatt, R. J. 1977a. *Comm. Psychopharmacol.* **1,** 343–352.
Karoum, F., Moyer-Schwing, J., Potkin, S. G., and Wyatt, R. J. 1977b. *Brain Res.* **125,** 333–339.
Kessler, J. A., Fenstermacher, J. D., and Patlak, C. S. 1976. *Brain Res.* **102,** 131–141.
Kitchin, A. H., and Turner, R. W. D. 1966. *Br. Med. J.* **2,** 728–731.
Klawans, H. L. 1973. *The Pharmacology of Extrapyramidal Movement Disorders.* Karger, Basel.
Korf, J., Aghajanian, G. K., and Roth, R. H. 1973a. *Eur. J. Pharmacol.* **21,** 305–310.
Korf, J., Aghajanian, G. K., and Roth, R. H. 1973b. *Neuropharmacol.* **12,** 933–938.
Korf, J., Roth, R. H., and Aghajanian, G. K. 1973c. *Eur. J. Pharmacol.* **23,** 276–282.
Kostowski, W., Samanin, R., Bareggi, S. R., Marc, V., Garattini, S., and Valzelli, L. 1974. *Brain Res.* **82,** 178–182.
Lake, C. R., Sternberg, D. E., van Kammen, D. P., Ballenger, J. C., Ziegler, M. G., Post, R. M., Kopin, I. J., and Bunney, W. E. 1980. *Science* **207,** 331–333.
Lake, C. R., Gullner, H. G., Polinsky, R. J., Ebert, M. H., Zieger, M. G., and Bartler, F. C. 1981. *Science* **211,** 955–957.
Langer, S. Z. 1974. *Biochem. Pharmacol.* **23,** 1793–1800.
Langer, S. Z. 1977. *Br. J. Pharmacol.* **60,** 481–497.
Leckman, J. F., Maas, J. W., Redmond, D. E., Jr., and Heninger, G. 1980. *Life Sci.* **26,** 252–262.
Leckman, J. F., Maas, J. W., and Heninger, G. R. 1981. *Eur. J. Pharmacol.* **70,** 111–120.

Luria, M. H., and Freis, E. D. 1965. *Curr. Ther. Res.* **7,** 289–296.

Maas, J. W., and Landis, D. H. 1971. *J. Pharmacol. Exp. Ther.* **177,** 600–612.

Maas, J. W., Dekirmenjian, H., Garver, D., Redmond, D. E., and Landis, D. H. 1973. *Eur. J. Pharmacol.* **23,** 121–130.

Maas, J. W., Hattox, S. E., Landis, D. H., and Roth, R. H. 1976. *Brain Res.* **118,** 167–173.

Maas, J. W., Hattox, S. E., Landis, D. H., and Roth, R. H. 1977. *Eur. J. Pharmacol.* **46,** 221–228.

Maas, J. W., Hattox, S. E., Greene, N. M., and Landis, D. H. 1979. *Science* **205,** 1025–1027.

Maas, J. W., Martin, D. M., and Landis, D. H. 1982. Submitted for publication.

Mårdh, G., Sjöquist, B., and 'A'nggard, E. 1980. Presented at 54th Biennial International Symposium on Alcoholism, June.

Markianos, E., and Beckmann, H. 1976. *J. Neural Trans.* **39,** 79–93.

McMillen, B. A., Warmack, W., German, D. C., and Shore, P. A. 1980. *Eur. J. Pharmacol.* **61,** 239–246.

Medina, M. A., Giachetti, A., and Shore, P. A. 1969. *Biochem. Pharmacol.* **18,** 891–901.

Meek, J. L., and Neff, N. H. 1972. *Br. J. Pharmacol.* **45,** 435–441.

Meek, J. L., and Neff, N. H. 1973. *J. Pharmacol. Exp. Ther.* **184,** 570–575.

Meek, J. L., and Foldes, A. 1973. *Frontiers in Catecholamine Research* (E. Usdin and S. H. Snyder, eds.), p. 167. Pergamon Press, New York.

Nielsen, M., and Braestrup, C. 1977. *Naunyn-Schmiedeberg's Arch. Pharmacol.* **300,** 93–99.

Redmond, D. E., Jr., Roth, R. H., Hattox, S. E., Stogin, J. M., and Baulu, J. 1979. *Neurosci. Abstr.* **5,** 348.

Riederer, P., Birkmayer, W., Seemann, D., and Wuketich, S. 1977. *J. Neural Trans.* **41,** 241–251.

Rutledge, C. O., and Jonason, J. 1967. *J. Pharmacol. Exp. Ther.* **157,** 493–502.

Schanberg, S. M., Schildkraut, J. J., Breese, G. R., and Kopin, I. J. 1968. *Biochem. Pharmacol.* **17,** 247–254.

Schildkraut, J. J. 1965. *Am. J. Phsychiatry* **122,** 509–522.

Shapiro, A. K., Shapiro, E., and Wayne, H. 1973. *Arch. Gen. Psychiatry* **28,** 92–97.

Shimizu, H., and LaBrosse, E. H. 1969. *Biochem. Pharmacol.* **18,** 1643–1654.

Siever, L., Insel, T., and Unde, T. 1981. *J. Clin. Psychopharmacol.* **1,** 193–206.

Sjöquist, B. 1975. *J. Neurochem.* **24,** 199–201.

Snyder, S. H. 1973. *Am. J. Psychiatry* **130,** 61–67.

Solomon, H. M., Ashley, C., Spirt, N., and Abrams, W. B. 1969. *Clin. Pharmacol. Ther.* **10,** 229–238.

Starke, K., Endo, I., and Laube, H. D. 1973. *Naunyn–Schmiedeberg's Arch. Pharmacol.* **291,** 55–70.

Starke, K. 1977. *Rev. Physiol. Biochem. Pharmacol.* **77,** 1–124.

Sternberg, D. E., Charney, D. S., Heninger, G., Leckman, J. F., Landis, D. H., and Hafstad, K. M. 1982. *Arch. Gen. Psychiatry,* in press.

Stone, E. A. 1973. *J. Neurochem.* **21,** 589–601.

Stone, E. A. 1975. *Life Sci.* **16,** 1725–1730.

Stone, E. A. 1976. *Life Sci.* **19,** 1491–1498.

Sugrue, M. F. 1980. *Life Sci.* **28,** 377–384.

Svensson, T. H., Bunney, B. S., and Aghajanian, G. K. 1975. *Brain Res.* **92,** 291–306.

Swann, A., Maas, J. W., Hattox, S. E., and Landis, D. H. 1980. *Life Sci.* **27,** 1857–1862.

Sweeney, D. R., Leckman, J. F., Maas, J. W., Hattox, S., and Heninger, G. R. 1980. *Arch. Gen. Psychiatry* **37,** 110–113.

Sweeney, D. R., Leckman, J. F., Hattox, S. E., Heninger, G. R., and Maas, J. W. 1981. Unpublished data.

Sypraki, C., and Fibiger, H. C. 1980. *Life Sci.* **27,** 1863–1867.

Tabakoff, B. 1977. *Structure and Function of Monoamine Enzymes* (E. Usdin, N. Weiner, and M. B. H. Youdim, eds.), pp. 629–649. Marcel Dekker, New York.

Takahashi, S., Godse, D. D., Warsh, J. J., and Stancer, H. C. 1977. *Clin. Chim. Acta* **81,** 183–192.

Tang, S. W., Helmeste, D. M., and Stancer, H. C. 1978. *Naunyn–Schmiedeberg's Arch. Pharmacol.* **305,** 207–211.

Warsh, J. J., Godse, D. D., Cheung, S. W., and Li, P. P. 1981. *J. Neurochem.* **36,** 893–901.

Wehr, T. A., Muscettola, G., and Godwin, F. K. 1980. *Arch. Gen. Psychiatry* **37,** 257–263.

7

Relationship between Psychiatric Diagnostic Groups of Depressive Disorders and MHPG*

JOSEPH J. SCHILDKRAUT
Harvard Medical School, Boston

PAUL J. ORSULAK
Massachusetts Mental Health Center, Boston

ALAN F. SCHATZBERG
McLean Hospital, Belmont

ALAN H. ROSENBAUM
Henry Ford Hospital, Detroit

*This work was supported in part by Grant No. MH 15413 from the National Institute of Mental Health.

I. Introduction

The observation that certain pharmacological agents that produced alterations in mood and affective state in human subjects also produced significant effects on the disposition and metabolism of catecholamines in the brain served as the initial stimulus for research on the possible role of alterations in norepinephrine metabolism in the pathophysiology of the affective disorders (depressions and manias). Moreover, on the basis of these early observations, the possibility was suggested more than 15 years ago (Schildkraut, 1965) that different subgroups of patients with depressive disorders might be characterized by differences in the metabolism of norepinephrine and the physiology of noradrenergic neuronal systems. During the intervening years, many studies have provided data supporting this possibility. In this chapter we shall review selected aspects of the findings of these studies, focusing on those studies that have involved measurements of 3-methoxy-4-hydroxyphenethyleneglycol (MHPG).

It has often been strategic in this area of research for investigators to focus on only one or another of the neurotransmitters or neuromodulators thought to be involved in the pathophysiology of affective disorders. However, this strategic reductionism has not been based on the assumption that any single group of neurotransmitters or neuromodulators (e.g., catecholamines, indoleamines, acetylcholine, or endorphins), are of singular importance in the affective disorders or that all aspects of the pathophysiology of all types of affective disorders could be explained by alterations in any single neurochemical system. Indeed, the physiological and biochemical interactions of various neurotransmitter systems have been widely recognized for many years, and this concept is reinforced by findings documenting the very complex neuropharmacology of the drugs that produce alterations in human affective state, as well as by the biochemical, neurophysiological, and neuroanatomical complexities of the underlying neuronal systems within the brain. The situation is further complicated by the capacity of these neuronal systems for adaptive, homeostatic responses to pharmacological, physiological or environmentally induced perturbations.

Despite all of the inherent complexities of the central nervous system, and the evidence that many concomitant biochemical, physiological, environmental, and psychological factors may be involved in the pathogenesis of the affective disorders, the heuristic value of a "reductionistic" formulation, such as the catecholamine hypothesis of affective disorders (Schildkraut, 1965), has been demonstrated during the past 15 years by the expanding body of research on catecholamine metabolism in patients with affective disorders. This literature has been reviewed by many investigators during the intervening years (Baldessarini, 1975; Bunney, 1975; Bunney and Davis, 1965; Goodwin and Post, 1975; Goodwin and Sack, 1973; Maas, 1975, 1978, 1979; Mendels and Frazer, 1974; Prange et al., 1974; Schildkraut, 1965, 1970, 1973, 1974, 1977, 1978; Schildkraut et al. in press; Segal et al., 1974; Shopsin et al., 1974. Consequently, only selected aspects of the literature on the role of norepinephrine in depressive disorders will be summarized in this chapter.

II. Physiological Implications of Measurements of Urinary MHPG

During the 1960s findings from a number of studies suggested that MHPG or its sulfate conjugate was a major metabolite of norepinephrine in the human brain, as it was in the brains of a number of other species (Glowinski et al., 1965; Maas and Landis, 1968; Mannarino et al., 1963; Rutledge and Jonason, 1967; Schanberg et al., 1968a and 1968b). Moreover, it appeared that much of the norepinephrine originating in the brain was execreted in the urine as MHPG. In contrast, relatively little urinary norepinephrine, normetanephrine, epinephrine, metanephrine, or 3-methoxy-4-hydroxymandelic acid (VMA) appeared to derive from the central nervous system; and most appeared to originate in peripheral sources such as the sympathetic nervous system or the adrenal glands (Maas and Landis, 1971).

However, urinary MHPG may derive in part from the peripheral sympathetic nervous system as well as from the brain, and, as reviewed in other chapters in this volume, the exact fraction of urinary MHPG—which does in fact derive from norepinephrine originating in the brain—remains uncertain (see Schildkraut, 1978). For example, on the basis of a study in human subjects measuring venoarterial differences in the concentration of MHPG in plasma coming out of the brain (venous blood), as compared to plasma entering the brain (arterial blood), Maas et al. (1979) estimated that the average contribution by brain to the total body production of MHPG exceeded 60%. However, the findings of this study have been questioned by Blombery et al. (1980). These investigators reported that deuterium-labeled MHPG (when administered intravenously) is rapidly converted to VMA; on the basis of this finding they estimated that about half of urinary VMA is derived from MHPG and that only about 20% of urinary MHPG comes from norepinephrine originating in the brain. However, Blombery *et al.* (1980) did note that even if the majority of urinary MHPG was derived from peripheral sources (as suggested by their study) urinary MHPG could still be a biochemical measure of clinical value in subclassifying affective disorders or in predicting therapeutic response to specific forms of treatment.

Although one might intuitively expect levels of MHPG in the cerebrospinal fluid (CSF) to provide a better index of norepinephrine metabolism in the brain than does urinary MHPG, this does not appear to be the case. The confusing literature on studies of CSF MHPG in patients with affective disorders has been reviewed elsewhere (Schildkraut, 1978) and will not be considered in this chapter.

III. Longitudinal Studies of Urinary MHPG Levels in Patients with Bipolar Manic-Depressive Disorders

In a series of longitudinal studies of individual patients with naturally occurring or amphetamine-induced bipolar manic-depressive episodes, Schildkraut and his associates (Greenspan *et al.*, 1970; Schildkraut *et al.*, 1971, 1972; Watson *et al.*, 1972) found that levels of urinary MHPG were relatively lower during periods of depression and relatively higher during periods of mania or hypomania than during periods of remission. Similar findings have been observed by a number of other investigators (Bond *et al.*, 1972, 1975; DeLeon-Jones *et al.*, 1973; Post *et al.*, 1977), although all findings do not concur (Bunney *et al.*, 1972; Shopsin *et al.*, 1973). The changes in MHPG excretion appeared to precede the changes in clinical state in several of the studies demonstrating the relationship between MHPG excretion and affective state in patients with bipolar manic-depressive episodes (Bond *et al.*, 1972, 1975; DeLeon-Jones *et al.*, 1973), but this has not been observed in all studies (Post *et al.*, 1977).

All depressions, however, are not clinically or biologically homogeneous (Schildkraut, 1965) and all depressed patients do not excrete comparably low levels of MHPG (Maas *et al.*, 1968, 1972). Consequently, many investigators have gone on to explore the possibility that urinary excretion of MHPG, and possibly other catecholamine metabolites, might provide a biochemical basis for differentiating among the depressive disorders.

IV. Urinary MHPG Levels in Bipolar Manic-Depressive and Other Clinically Defined Subgroups of Depressive Disorders

Because MHPG excretion had been found to vary with clinical state in patients with bipolar manic-depressive disorders, it was of particular interest to compare urinary MHPG levels in bipolar manic-depressive depressions with MHPG levels in other clinically defined subtypes of depressive disorders that might represent biologically different entities. Because most bipolar manic-depressive depressions present clinically as endogenous depressive syndromes (Schildkraut and Klein, 1975), and because bipolar manic-depressive patients rarely show nonendogenous chronic characterological depressive syndromes (i.e., nonendogenous dysphoric depressive syndromes), unipolar nonendogenous chronic characterological depressions were initially used as a comparison group (Schildkraut et al., 1973a,b). This was done to minimize the likelihood of including in the comparison group patients with clinically latent bipolar manic-depressive disorders (i.e., bipolar patients who had not yet manifested their first hypomanic or manic episode). The findings of this initial study showed that urinary MHPG levels were significantly lower in patients with bipolar manic-depressive depressions than in patients with unipolar nonendogenous chronic characterological depressions (Schildkraut et al., 1973a,b).

This finding of reduced urinary MHPG levels in patients with bipolar manic-depressive depressions (when compared with MHPG levels in patients with unipolar depressions or in normal control subjects) has subsequently been confirmed in studies from a number of different laboratories (Beckmann and Goodwin, 1980; DeLeon-Jones et al., 1975; Edwards et al., 1980; Garfinkel et al., 1977; Goodwin and Post, 1975; Goodwin and Potter, 1979; Maas et al., 1973). Of particular interest is the study of Garfinkel et al. (1977), which showed that when the peripheral contribution of urinary MHPG was reduced with carbidopa (a decarboxylase inhibitor that does not cross the blood–brain barrier) the differences in urinary MHPG levels in bipolar manic-depressive depressions and control subjects became more pronounced and statistically significant.

Urinary MHPG levels have also been found to be reduced in patients with schizoaffective depressions—characterized by the occurrence of psychotic manifestations that are not solely affect consonant, in the absence of a history of chronic asocial, eccentric, or bizarre behavior (Schildkraut et al., 1978a); other investigators (Beckmann and Goodwin, 1980) have also reported a reduction of urinary MHPG levels in schizoaffective depressions. Further data on a larger series of patients matched for age and sex will be required before the findings on urinary MHPG levels in patients with schizoaffective depressions can be regarded as definitive. However, the comparable reduction in urinary MHPG levels in both bipolar manic-depressive depressions and schizoaffective depressions is consistent with the possibility that the schizoaffective disorders, when defined according to the criteria used in this research (Schildkraut *et al.*, 1978a), are clinically and biologically related to, or represent variants of, bipolar manic-depressive disorders. This relationship, which was proposed a number of years ago by Klein (1965), has also been suggested by the findings of other investigators (Taylor and Abrams, 1975; Procci, 1976).

In contrast to the reduction in urinary MHPG levels, observed in patients with bipolar manic-depressive and schizoaffective depressions when compared with values in patients with unipolar depressions, there were no differences in VMA excretion in these depressive subgroups (Schildkraut *et al.*, 1978a). This observation is of particular interest because, as previously indicated, it has been suggested that circulating MHPG may be converted to VMA, thus raising questions concerning the use of urinary MHPG as an index of norepinephrine metabolism in the brain (Blombery *et al.*, 1980). Although urinary norepinephrine levels tended to be lower in patients with bipolar manic-depressive and schizoaffective depressions when compared with values in patients with unipolar depressions, the differences were not statistically significant. Moreover, there were no differences in urinary levels of normetanephrine, epinephrine, or metanephrine, when values in patients with bipolar manic-depressive and schizoaffective depressions were compared with values in patients with unipolar depressions (Schildkraut *et al.*, 1978a).

V. Application of Multivariate Discriminant Function Analysis to Data on Urinary Catecholamines and Metabolites in Depressed Patients

Although MHPG was the only catecholamine metabolite that showed a pronounced difference when values in patients with bipolar manic-depressive depressions and unipolar nonendogenous chronic characterological depressions were compared, multivariate discriminant function analysis was used to explore the possibility that the other catecholamine metabolites might provide further information that would aid in differentiating among subtypes of depressions (Schildkraut *et al.*, 1978b). This analysis resulted in the development of a discrimination equation based on levels of urinary catecholamines and metabolites that provided an even more precise discrimination among subtypes of depressive disorders than did urinary MHPG levels alone.

This discrimination equation for the depression type (D-type) score was of the form

$$D\text{-type score} = C_1(MHPG) - C_2(VMA) + C_3(NE)$$
$$- C_4(NMN + MN)/(VMA) + C_0.$$

In this equation, low scores were related to bipolar manic-depressive depressions and high scores were related to unipolar nonendogenous depressions.

Preliminary validation of this discrimination equation was obtained in a further sample of depressed patients whose biochemical data had not been used to derive the equation. When individual values of the D-type scores and urinary MHPG levels in the patients with schizoaffective or bipolar manic-depressive depressions were compared to values in the patient with unipolar nonendogenous depressions, in this preliminary validation sample, there was no overlap and a wide separation of the D-type scores, whereas there was some overlap and less separation of the MHPG levels. Although this discrimination equation was generated mathematically to provide the best least-squares fit of the data, and although the terms were not selected by the investigators, it is tempting to speculate that the inclusion of VMA as well as other urinary catecholamines and metabolites (of peripheral origin) in this empirically derived equation may be correcting for that fraction of urinary MHPG that comes from peripheral sources rather than from the brain (Schildkraut *et al.*, 1978b).

VI. Identification of Possible Subtypes of Unipolar Depressive Disorders

In contrast to the relatively consistent findings showing that patients with bipolar manic-depressive depressions have low urinary MHPG levels, consistent findings have not been obtained in studies of urinary MHPG levels in patients with unipolar depressions. For example, Maas and his associates (DeLeon-Jones *et al.*, 1975; Maas, 1978; Taube *et al.*,

1978) have reported that patients with primary depressive disorders had reduced urinary MHPG levels, and Casper *et al.* (1977) have reported that patients with major depressive disorders had reduced MHPG levels. However, Goodwin and his associates (Beckmann and Goodwin, 1980; Goodwin and Post, 1975; Goodwin and Potter, 1979) have reported that urinary MHPG levels in patients with unipolar depressive disorders did not differ from values in control subjects, whereas Garfinkel *et al.* (1979) have reported that patients with unipolar depressive disorders excrete higher levels of MHPG than control subjects (both under drug-free conditions and while receiving carbidopa).

It is conceivable that diagnostic heterogeneity may account for these discrepancies because findings from our laboratory (Schildkraut *et al.*, 1978a) revealed a wide range of urinary MHPG levels in patients with unipolar depressive disorders, and because these findings have been confirmed and extended in subsequent studies (Schatzberg *et al.*, 1980a; Schildkraut *et al.*, 1981). Although the mean urinary MHPG level has been significantly lower in bipolar manic-depressive or schizoaffective depressions than in either unipolar depressions or age- and sex-matched controls in our studies, there were no significant differences from control values in the mean urinary MHPG levels in the total group of unipolar depressions or in various subgroups defined by the Research Diagnostic Criteria (RDC).

In a previously reported series of 16 patients with unipolar endogenous depressions, the mean value of urinary MHPG was 1950 μg/24 h (Schildkraut *et al.*, 1978a). In our enlarged sample, 26 of 50 patients with unipolar depressions had urinary MHPG levels >1950 μ/24 h whereas only 3 of 20 patients with bipolar manic-depressive or schizoaffective depressions had MHPG levels >1950 μg/24 h (χ^2 = 6.61; p <.025). Inspection of a scatter plot of the data on MHPG levels in this series of 70 depressed patients revealed what appeared to be a natural break in MHPG levels around 2500 μg/24 h, and suggested the possible existence of a subgroup of unipolar depressions with MHPG levels >2500 μg/24 h. For example, in this series 17 of 50 patients with unipolar depressions had urinary MHPG levels >2500 μg/24 h, whereas only 1 of 20 patients with bipolar manic-depressive or schizoaffective depressions had MHPG levels >2500 μg/24 h (χ^2 = 4.86; p <.05). Thus the data from this series of 50 patients with so-called unipolar depressive disorders further substantiates the biochemical heterogeneity of unipolar depressions, demonstrating that some patients have low MHPG levels (comparable to values seen in the bipolar manic-depressive or schizoaffective depressions) whereas others have high MHPG levels (sometimes higher than control values) and still others have MHPG levels in an intermediate range. Therefore, it is conceivable that differences in patient sampling may have accounted for the discrepancies (noted in the preceding paragraph) in the findings of the various studies that examined urinary MHPG levels in patients with unipolar depressive disorders.

The existence of a subgroup of unipolar depressions with elevated urinary MHPG levels is further suggested by the data from an independent series of patients with severe unipolar depressions studied by our collaborative research group (Rosenbaum et al., 1980a). Although the mean urinary free cortisol (UFC) level in the total sample of severely depressed patients was significantly higher than the control mean, these data revealed a subgroup of severely depressed patients with urinary MHPG levels >2500 μg/24 h who had the most markedly elevated UFC levels. As reported elsewhere (Rosenbaum et al., 1981), the relationship between UFC and urinary MHPG levels observed in this series of severely depressed patients did not appear to be secondary to anxiety. However, this relationship may, in part, have been due to the severity of the depressive disorders because preliminary data from a subsequent study has not revealed a similar correlation between UFC and urinary MHPG levels in patients with milder depressions.

One possibility that might explain our findings of a subgroup of severely depressed patients with high urinary MHPG levels and markedly elevated UFC levels is that in these patients high norepinephrine output may occur as a secondary response to an increase in cholinergic activity. This possibility is consistent with the hypothesis that central cholinergic factors may play a role in the etiology of depressive disorders (Janowsky et al., 1972) and is particularly intriguing in view of the findings of other investigators that (1) physostigmine (an anticholinesterase) and other pharmacological agents that increase brain cholinergic activity exacerbate depressive symptoms in depressed patients (Garver and Davis, 1979; Janowsky et al., 1972) and induce depressive symptoms in normal controls (Risch et al., 1980); (2) physostigmine produces an increase in plasma cortisol levels in normal controls (Risch et al., 1980); (3) physostigmine can overcome suppression of the hypothalamic pituitary-adrenal-cortical axis by dexamethasone in normal subjects, thereby mimicking the abnormal escape from dexamethasone suppression seen in some depressed patients who show cortisol hypersecretion (Carroll et al., 1980); and (4) physostigmine produces an increase in cerebrospinal fluid levels of MHPG in normal subjects (Davis et al., 1977).

Thus the markedly elevated UFC levels that we observed in some patients with severe unipolar depressive disorders could result from an increase in cholinergic activity, and the elevated urinary MHPG levels in these patients could represent a secondary noradrenergic response to such cholinergic hyperactivity. This formulation suggests the possibility that the anticholinergic effects of certain antidepressant drugs may contribute to their antidepressant effects in patients with this subtype of depressive disorder.

VII. Recent Studies of Pretreatment Urinary MHPG Levels as Predictors of Responses to Noradrenergically Active Antidepressant Drugs

Since the initial report of Maas *et al.* (1972), studies from a number of laboratories have indicated that pretreatment levels of urinary MHPG may aid in predicting responses to certain noradrenergically active tricyclic and tetracyclic antidepressant drugs that act, in part, by blocking the reuptake of norepinephrine. Specifically, depressed patients with "low" pretreatment urinary MHPG levels have been found to respond more favorably to treatment with imipramine (Beckmann and Goodwin, 1975; Cobbin *et al.*, 1979; Maas *et al.*, 1972, 1980; Rosenbaum *et al.*, 1980b; Schatzberg *et al.*, 1980–1981; Steinbook *et al.*, 1979), desipramine (Maas *et al.*, 1972), nortriptyline (Hollister *et al.*, 1980), or maprotiline (Rosenbaum *et al.*, 1980b; Schatzberg *et al.*, 1981) than do patients with "high" MHPG levels.

We have reported findings of a prospective study (Schatzberg *et al.*, 1980–1981) of urinary MHPG levels as a predictor of response to imipramine in 24 depressed patients who met RDC for major depressive disorders. In this series of patients with unipolar depressions, 13 had pretreatment urinary MHPG levels ≤ 1950 μg/24 h and 11 had MHPG levels >1950 μg/24 h. Patients were considered to have shown a favorable response to treatment with imipramine, in this study, if the Hamilton Depression Rating Scale score at 4 weeks was reduced by at least 60% from pretreatment baseline values. Using this criterion, favorable responses to imipramine at 4 weeks were observed in 9 of the 13 patients with pretreatment MHPG levels ≤ 1950 μg/24 h, but in only 3 of 11 patients with MHPG levels >1950 μg/24 h (Fisher Exact—$p = .05$).

In order to further explore the hypothesis that patients with low pretreatment levels of urinary MHPG will show a favorable response to antidepressant drugs acting preferentially on noradrenergic neuronal systems, in a prospective study, we have also examined pretreatment urinary MHPG levels as a possible predictor of antidepressant response to maprotiline, a noradrenergically active tetracyclic antidepressant drug (Schatzberg *et al.*, 1980b, 1981). This study included 28 depressed patients who met the RDC for major depressive disorders, 12 of whom had pretreatment MHPG levels ≤1950 μg/24 h whereas 16 had MHPG levels >1950 μg/24 h. In this study, as in the preceding one, a patient was considered to have shown a favorable response to treatment if the Hamilton Depression Rating Scale score at 4 weeks was reduced by at least 60% from the pretreatment baseline value. Using this criterion, 8 of the 12 patients with pretreatment MHPG levels ≤1950 μg/24 h showed a favorable response to maprotiline, whereas only 3 of 16 patients with MHPG levels >1950 μg/24 h showed a favorable response to treatment ($\chi^2 = 4.74$; $p < .05$). Moreover, in this study we also observed that the antidepressant responses to maprotiline occurred more rapidly and at lower doses in patients with pretreatment MHPG levels ≤1950 μg/24 h than in patients with MHPG levels >1950 μg/24 h. Although antidepressant responses were eventually observed in some patients with high pretreatment urinary MHPG levels, these responses tended to occur later in treatment and only after relatively higher doses of maprotiline (Schatzberg *et al.*, 1981).

As described in a preceding discussion, our findings have suggested that there may be at least three subtypes of unipolar depressive disorders that can be discriminated on the basis of differences in pretreatment urinary MHPG levels. In view of these findings, data from these two studies of pretreatment urinary MHPG levels as predictors of response to imipramine or maprotiline were combined in order to provide us with a large enough series of patients to compare treatment responses in these three groups. Although further studies in a larger series of patients will be required for confirmation, these findings suggest that depressed patients with elevated pretreatment MHPG levels (>2500 μg/24 h) may be more responsive to treatment with imipramine or maprotiline than are patients with intermediate pretreatment MHPG levels (1951–2500 μg/24 h) though neither group is as responsive to these drugs as are patients with low pretreatment urinary MHPG levels (≤1950 μg/24 h).

VIII.   Concluding Comments on Urinary MHPG Levels in Patients with Unipolar Major Depressive Disorders

In the light of the findings described in the preceding section, we have prepared a histogram showing the distribution of pretreatment urinary

MHPG levels in more than 100 patients with unipolar major depressive disorders on whom we had obtained data during the course of our various collaborative studies. This histogram revealed a clustering of patients with urinary MHPG levels above 2500 μg/24 h in addition to clusters occurring at lower MHPG levels (Schildkraut et al., 1982). Thus the natural distribution of urinary MHPG levels in this rather large series of patients with unipolar major depressive disorders provides further evidence suggesting the existence of a subgroup of patients with unipolar depressive disorders with urinary MHPG levels >2500 μg/24 h. When this series of patients with unipolar depressions was categorized following the RDC, there were no meaningful differences in urinary MHPG levels when values were compared in patients with major depressions, primary depressions, or endogenous depressions. Nor were there any differences between MHPG values in any of these subgroups of unipolar depressive disorders when compared with values in the matched control group. Thus it would appear that these clinical subtypes of major depressive disorders, distinguished by the RDC, do not represent subgroups that are homogenous with respect to urinary MHPG levels. In studies currently in progress, we are further attempting to identify clinical features that may characterize unipolar depressive disorders with low, intermediate, and high pretreatment urinary MHPG levels.

Thus the findings of our studies further substantiate the biochemical heterogeneity of the so-called unipolar depressive disorders. In these studies, we have found a wide range of urinary MHPG levels in patients with unipolar depressions, with some having low urinary MHPG levels comparable to values in the bipolar manic-depressive or schizoaffective group, others having high urinary MHPG levels (sometimes higher than control values), and still others having intermediate urinary MHPG levels. As noted in a preceding discussion, these findings may help to account for the fact that in various studies, patients with unipolar depressions have previously been reported to excrete reduced, elevated, or unchanged urinary MHPG levels when compared with normal controls.

Moreover, our findings suggest that there may be at least three biologically meaningful and therapeutically relevant subtypes of unipolar depressive disorders that can be discriminated on the basis of differences in urinary MHPG levels and that a number of different underlying pathophysiological mechanisms may be involved in these subtypes of unipolar depressions. Subtype I, with low pretreatment urinary MHPG levels, may have low norepinephrine output as a result of a decrease in norepinephrine synthesis or a decrease in its release from noradrenergic neurons. Subtype II, with intermediate urinary MHPG levels, may have normal norepinephrine metabolism but abnormalities in other neurochemical systems. Subtype III, with high pretreatment urinary MHPG levels, may have high norepinephrine output in response to subsensitive noradrenergic receptors (Schildkraut, 1973) and/or to an increase in cholinergic activity as described in Section VI.

A number of issues must be considered when interpreting such data on urinary MHPG levels in patients with affective disorders. For example, it is generally recognized that urinary MHPG levels in most depressed patients fall within the range of values observed in normal control subjects (Hollister et al., 1978). Thus although measurement of urinary MHPG levels may help to differentiate among subgroups of depressive disorders, urinary MHPG levels cannot be used to make a diagnosis of depression per se.

Moreover, as discussed elsewhere in this volume, urinary MHPG levels in depressed patients may vary in relation to many factors including phase of illness, anxiety, activity, blood pressure, diet, drug administration, and alcohol consumption (Beckmann et al., 1979; Goodwin et al., 1978; Howlett and Jenner, 1978; Muscettola et al., 1977; Sweeney et al., 1978; Wehr and Goodwin, 1977). In addition, some depressed patients may show alterations in timing of the circadian rhythm of MHPG excretion (Wehr et al., 1980). Elucidation of the physiological significance of these findings may be expected to contribute to our ultimate understanding of the role of norepinephrine metabolism in depressive disorders.

References

Baldessarini, R. J. 1975. Arch. Gen. Psychiatry 32, 1087–1093.
Beckmann, H., and Goodwin, F. K. 1975. Arch. Gen. Psychiatry 32, 17–21.
Beckmann, H., and Goodwin, F. K. 1980. Neuropsychobiol. 6, 91–100.
Beckmann, H., Ebert, M. H., Post, R., and Goodwin, F. K. 1979. Pharmakopsychiat. 12, 351–356.
Blombery, P. A., Kopin, I. J., Gordon, E. K., Markey, S. P., and Ebert, M. H. 1980. Arch. Gen. Psychiatry 37, 1095–1098.
Bond, P. A., Jenner, F. A., and Sampson, G. A. 1972. Psychol. Med. 2, 81–85.
Bond, P. A., Dimitrakoudi, M., Howlett, D. R., and Jenner, F. A. 1975. Psychol. Med. 5, 279–285.
Bunney, W. E., Jr. 1975. Psychopharmacol. Comm. 1, 599–609.
Bunney, W. E., Jr., and Davis, J. M. 1965. Arch. Gen. Psychiatry 13, 483–494.
Bunney, W. E., Jr., Goodwin, F. K., Murphy, D. L., House, K. M., and Gordon, E. K. 1972. Arch. Gen. Psychiatry 27, 304–309.

Carroll, B. J., Greden, J. F., Haskett, R., Feinberg, M., Albaby, A. A., Martin, F. I. R., Rubin, R. T., Heath, B., Sharp, P. T., McLeod, W. L., and McLeod, M. F. 1980. *Acta Psychiatrica Scand* **61**, (280), 183–199.

Casper, R. C., Davis, J. M., Pandey, G. N., Garver, D. L., and Dekirmenjian, H. 1977. *Psychoneuroendocrinol.* **2**, 105–113.

Cobbin, D. M., Requin-Blow, B., Williams, L. B., and Williams, W. O. 1979. *Arch. Gen. Psychiatry* **36**, 1111–1115.

Davis, K. L., Hollister, L. E., Goodwin, F. K., and Gordon, E. K. 1977. *Life Sci.* **21**, 933–936.

DeLeon-Jones, F. D., Maas, J. W., Dekirmenjian, H., and Fawcett, J. A. 1973. *Science* **179**, 300–302.

DeLeon-Jones, F., Maas, J. W., Dekirmenjian, H., and Sanchez, J. 1975. *Am. J. Psychiatry* **132**, 1141–1148.

Edwards, D. J., Spiker, D. G., Neil, J. F., Kupfer, D. J., and Rizk, M. 1980. *Psychiatry Res.* **2**, 295–305.

Garfinkel, P. E., Warsh, J. J., Stancer, H. C., Godse, D. D. 1977. *Arch. Gen. Psychiatry* **34**, 735–739.

Garfinkel, P. E., Warsh, J. J., and Stancer, H. C. 1979. *Am. J. Psychiatry* **136**, 535–539.

Garver, D. L., and Davis, J. M. 1979. *Life Sci.* **24**, 383–394.

Glowinski, J., Kopin, I. J., and Axelrod, J. 1965. *J. Neurochem.* **12**, 25–30.

Goodwin, F. K., and Post, R. M. 1975. *Biology of the Major Psychoses* (D. X. Freedman, ed.), pp. 299–332. Raven Press, New York.

Goodwin, F. K., and Potter, W. Z. 1979. *Catecholamines: Basic and Clinical Frontiers*, Vol. II (E. Usdin, and J. Barchas, eds.), pp. 1863–1865. Pergamon Press, New York.

Goodwin, F. K., and Sack, R. L. 1973. *Frontiers in Catecholamine Research* (E. Usdin, and S. A. Snyder, eds.), pp. 1157–1164. Pergamon Press, New York.

Goodwin, F. K., Cowdry, R. W., and Webster, M. H. 1978. *Psychopharmacology: A Generation of Progress* (M. Lipton, A. DiMascio and K. F. Killam, eds.), pp. 1277–1288. Raven Press, New York.

Greenspan, K., Schildkraut, J. J., Gordon, E. K., Baer, L., Aronoff, M. S., and Durell, J. 1970. *J. Psychiatr. Res.* **7**, 171–183.

Hollister, L. E., Davis, K. L., Overall, J. E., and Anderson, T. 1978. *Arch. Gen. Psychiatry* **35**, 1410–1415.

Hollister, L. E., Davis, K. L., and Berger, P. A. 1980. *Arch. Gen. Psychiatry* **37**, 1107–1110.

Howlett, D. R., and Jenner, F. A. 1978. *Br. J. Psychiat.* **132**, 49–54.

Janowsky, D. S., El-Yousef, M. K., Davis, J. M., and Sekerke, H. J. 1972. *Lancet* **2**, 632–635.

Klein, D. F. 1965. *Recent Advances in Biological Psychiatry*, Vol. 7 (J. Wortis, ed.), pp. 273–387, Plenum Press, New York.

Maas, J. W. 1975. *Arch. Gen. Psychiatry* **32**, 1357–1361.

Maas, J. W. 1978. *Ann. of Internal Med.* **88**, 556–563.

Maas, J. W. 1979. *Trends in Neurosci.* **2**, 306–310.

Maas, J. W., and Landis, D. H. 1968. *J. Pharmacol. Exp. Ther.* **163**, 147–162.

Maas, J. W., and Landis, D. H. 1971. *J. Pharmacol. Exp. Ther.* **177**, 600–612.

Maas, J. W., Fawcett, J. A., and Dekirmenjian, H. 1968. *Arch. Gen. Psychiatry* **19**, 129–134.

Maas, J. W., Fawcett, J. A., and Dekirmenjian, H. 1972. *Arch. Gen. Psychiatry* **26**, 252–262.

Maas, J. W., Dekirmenjian, H., and DeLeon-Jones, F. 1973. *Frontiers in Catecholamine Research* (E. Usdin, and S. Snyder, eds.), pp. 1091–1096. Pergamon Press, New York.

Maas, J. W., Hattox, S. E., Greene, N. M., and Landis, D. H. 1979. *Science* **205**, 1025–1027.

Maas, J. W., Bowden, C., Mendels, J., and Koscis, J. H. 1980. Presented at the 12th

Congress of the College Internationale Neuro-psychopharmacologicum, Goteborg, Sweden, June 22–26.

Mannarino, E., Kirshner, N., and Nashold, B. D., Jr. 1963. *J. Neurochem.* **10**, 373–379.

Mendels, J., and Frazer, A. 1974. *Arch. Gen. Psychiatry* **30**, 447–451.

Muscettola, G., Wehr, T., and Goodwin, F. K. 1977. *Am. J. Psychiatry* **134**, 914–916.

Post, R. M., Stoddard, F. J., Gillin, C., Buchsbaum, M. S., Runkle, D. C., Black, K. E., and Bunney, W. E., Jr. 1977. *Arch. Gen. Psychiatry* **34**, 470–477.

Prange, A. J., Jr., Wilson, I. C., Lynn, C. W., Alltop, L. B., and Stikleather, R. A. 1974. *Arch. Gen. Psychiatry* **30**, 56–62.

Procci, W. R. 1976. *Arch. Gen. Psychiatry* **33**, 1167–1178.

Risch, S. C., Cohen, R. M., Janowsky, D. S., Kalin, N. H., and Murphy, D. L. 1980. *Science* **209**, 1545–1546.

Rosenbaum, A. H., Maruta, T., Schatzberg, A. J., Orsulak, P. J., Jiang, N. S., and Schildkraut, J. J. 1980a. New Research Abstracts, American Psychiatric Association, Annual Meeting/May. NR13.

Rosenbaum, A. H., Schatzberg, A., Maruta, T., Orsulak, P. J., Cole, J. O., Grab, F. I., and Schildkraut, J. J. 1980b. *Am. J. Psychiatry* **137**, 1090–1092.

Rosenbaum, A. H., Maruta, T., Schatzberg, A. F., Orsulak, P. J., and Schildkraut, J. J. 1981. Presented at the 36th. Annual Meeting of the Society of Biological Psychiatry, Abstract 78.

Rutledge, C. O., and Jonason, J. 1967. *J. Pharmacol. Exp. Ther.* **157**, 493–502.

Schanberg, S. M., Schildkraut, J. J., Breese, G. R., and Kopin, I. J. 1968a. *Biochem. Pharmacol.* **17**, 247–254.

Schanberg, S. M., Breese, G. R., Schildkraut, J. J., Gordon, E. K., and Kopin, I. J. 1968b. *Biochem. Pharmacol.* **17**, 2006–2008.

Schatzberg, A. F., Orsulak, P. J., Rosenbaum, A. H., Gudeman, J., Kruger, E., Schildkraut, J. J., and Cole, J. O. 1980a. New Research Abstracts, American Psychiatric Association Annual Meeting/May. NR10.

Schatzberg, A. F., Rosenbaum, A. H., Orsulak, P. J., Cole, J. O., and Schildkraut, J. J. 1980b. Continuing Medical Education Syllabus and Scientific Proceedings in Summary Form, 133rd Annual Meeting of the American Psychiatric Association/May. p. 3.

Schatzberg, A. F., Orsulak, P. J., Rosenbaum, A. H., Maruta, T., Kruger, E. R., Cole, J. O., and Schildkraut, J. J. 1980–1981. *Comm. Psychopharmacol.* **4**, 441–445.

Schatzberg, A. F., Rosenbaum, A. H., Orsulak, P. J., Rohde, W. A., Maruta, T., Kruger, E. R., Cole, J. O., and Schildkraut, J. J. 1981. *Psychopharmacol.* **75**, 34–38.

Schildkraut, J. J. 1965. *Am. J. Psychiatry* **122**, 509–522.

Schildkraut, J. J. 1970. *Neuropsychopharmacology and the Affective Disorders.* Little, Brown and Company, Boston.

Schildkraut, J. J. 1973. *Ann. Rev. Pharmacol.* **13**, 427–454.

Schildkraut, J. J. 1974. *Ann. Rev. Med.* **25**, 333–348.

Schildkraut, J. J. 1977. *Depression: Clinical, Biological and Psychological Perspectives* (G. Usdin, ed.), pp. 166–197. Brunner Mazel, New York.

Schildkraut, J. J. 1978. *Psychopharmacology: A Generation of Progress* (M. Lipton, A. DiMascio, and K. F. Killam, eds.), pp. 1223–1234. Raven Press, New York.

Schildkraut, J. J., and Klein, D. F. 1975. *Manual of Psychiatric Therapeutics: Practical Psychopharmacology and Psychiatry* (R. I. Shader, ed.), pp. 39–61. Little, Brown and Company, Boston.

Schildkraut, J. J., Watson, R., Draskoczy, P. R., and Hartmann, E. 1971. *Lancet* **2**, 485–486.

Schildkraut, J. J., Keeler, B. A., Rogers, M. P., and Draskoczy, P. R. 1972. *Psychosomatic Med.* **34**, 470; plus erratum Psychosomatic Med. **35**, 274.

Schildkraut, J. J., Keeler, B. A., Grab, E. L., Kantrowich, J., and Hartmann, E. 1973a. *Lancet* 1, 1251–1252.

Schildkraut, J. J., Keeler, B. A., Papousek, M., and Hartmann, E. 1973b. *Science* 181, 762–764.

Schildkraut, J. J., Orsulak, P. J., Schatzberg, A. F., Gudeman, J. E., Cole, J. O., Rohde, W. A., and LaBrie, R. A. 1978a. *Arch. Gen. Psychiatry* 35, 1427–1433.

Schildkraut, J. J., Orsulak, P. J., LaBrie, R. A., Schatzberg, A. F., Gudeman, J. E., Cole, J. O., and Rohde, W. A. 1978b. *Arch. Gen. Psychiatry* 35, 1436–1439.

Schildkraut, J. J., Orsulak, P. J., Schatzberg, A. F., Cole, J. O., and Rosenbaum, A. H. 1981. *Psychopharmacol. Bull.* 17, 90–91.

Schildkraut, J. J., Orsulak, P. J., Schatzberg, A. F., and Rosenbaum, A. H. (in press). *Depression and Antidepressants* (E. Friedman, ed.), Raven Press, New York.

Schildkraut, J. J., Orsulak, P. J., Schatzberg, A. F., Cole, J. O., and Rosenbaum, A. H. 1982. *Biological Markers in Psychiatry and Neurology* (I. Hanin and E. Usdin, eds.), pp. 23–33. Pergamon Press, New York.

Segal, D. S., Kuczenski, R., and Mandell, A. J. 1974. *Biol. Psychiatry* 9, 147–159.

Shopsin, B., Wilk, S., Gershon, S., Roffman, M., and Goldstein, M. 1973. *Frontiers in Catecholamine Research* (E. Usdin and S. Snyder, eds.), pp. 173–180. Pergamon Press, New York.

Shopsin, B., Wilk, S., Sathananthan, G., Gershon, S., and Davis, K. 1974. *J. Nerv. Ment. Dis.* 158, 369–383.

Steinbook, R. M., Jacobson, A. F., Weiss, B. L., and Goldstein, B. J. 1979. *Curr. Ther. Res.* 26, 490–496.

Sweeney, D. R., Maas, J. W., and Heninger, G. R. 1978. *Arch. Gen. Psychiatry* 35, 1418–1423.

Taube, S. L., Kirstein, L. S., Sweeney, D. R. Heninger, G. R., and Maas, J. W. (1978). *Am. J. Psychiatry* 135, 78–82.

Taylor, M. A., and Abrams, R. 1975. *Am. J. Psychiatry* 132, 741–742.

Watson, R., Hartmann, E., and Schildkraut, J. J. 1972. *Am. J. Psychiatry* 129, 263–269.

Wehr, T. A., and Goodwin, F. K. 1977. *Handbook of Studies on Depression* (G. Burrows, ed.), pp. 283–301. Excerpta Medica, New York.

Wehr, T. A., Muscettola, G., and Goodwin, F. K. 1980. *Arch. Gen. Psychiatry* 37, 257–263.

8

Sources of Variance
in Clinical Studies of MHPG

WILLIAM Z. POTTER

National Institute of Mental Health, Bethesda, Maryland

GIOVANNI MUSCETTOLA

University of Naples, Italy

FREDERICK K. GOODWIN

National Institute of Mental Health, Bethesda, Maryland

I. Introduction

The use of 3-methoxy-4-hydroxyphenethyleneglycol (MHPG) determination as a tool in the diagnosis, treatment, and understanding of the etiology of primary affective illness requires a knowledge of the factors that influence concentrations of this norepinephrine (NE) metabolite in body tissues. Other chapters discuss variations in MHPG levels as a function of type of affective illness in adults or psychopathological states in children. In this chapter we shall discuss what are generally regarded as

MHPG: BASIC MECHANISMS
AND PSYCHOPATHOLOGY

"extraneous" sources of variance. Careful consideration of factors that can influence central and peripheral NE and/or MHPG concentration shows that extraneous sources of variance are not always separable from actual characteristics of the illness. For instance, changes in activity or anxiety may be associated with altered MHPG. Should this be considered as extraneous or as part of the illness? Should we consider altered MHPG levels to reflect a "state" or a "trait"? The "state versus trait" distinction depends on our level of understanding of the relationship between the pathophysiology of an illness and its symptoms. If we knew, for example, that alterations in urinary MHPG levels were an index of change in a central nervous system (CNS) function directly involved in the pathophysiology of depression, then a clearer interpretation of these changes would be possible.

Before examining these issues it will be useful to place the metabolic origins of urinary MHPG in perspective. The increasingly sophisticated efforts to identify the proportion of urinary MHPG that originates in the CNS are discussed in detail elsewhere (Chapter 3, in this volume). However, the interpretation of these studies is dependent on the assumption that MHPG is not converted to 3-methoxy-4-hydroxymandelic acid (VMA) in the periphery, an assumption that has been shown to be invalid in normal subjects (Blombery et al., 1980) as well as in a child with neuroblastoma (La Borosse, 1970)). Not only is MHPG extensively converted to VMA, but the extent of conversion is highly variable, probably even within the same individual (Blombery et al., 1980).

On the other hand, it is not self-evident that only MHPG formed in the CNS is relevant to studies in patients with affective illness (Goodwin and Potter, 1979). Certainly, "peripheral" changes of MHPG are prevalent in depression and mania and could be as important as its central formation. Furthermore, direct experimental evidence in animals indicates that central and peripheral noradrenergic systems may be interdependent (see Chapter 6, in this volume). Thus some structures involved in the central modulation of peripheral synaptic impulses are themselves catecholaminergic (Dahlstrom and Fuxe, 1965; Scriabine et al., 1976), whereas conversely, stimulation of peripheral nerves (saphenous, sural, or sciatic) in rat activates neurons of the locus coeruleus (Cedarbaum and Aghajanian, 1978). Direct stimulation of rat locus coeruleus produces a two- to threefold increase in plasma MHPG levels due in part, at least, to peripheral release of NE (Crawley et al., 1979). Subsequently, it was shown that this stimulation did not depend on intact coeruleus cells, thereby altering the interpretation of the connections responsible for the peripheral MHPG increase but not the fact of the increase itself (Crawley et al., 1980). In any event, increased levels of MHPG as an index of increased noradrenergic function can be a manifestation of events that originate centrally, peripherally, or both. Thus the question of the primary site(s) or process(es) that produce altered levels of MHPG is unanswerable with available methods.

However, in clinical studies we can ask questions that concern the extent to which altered MHPG concentration can be associated with specific aspects of affective illness. Methods used over the last decade permit us to study the sources of "normal" variance in urinary MHPG as well as variations that occur in illness.

Table I outlines the known potential sources of variance in urinary MHPG. The first group of variables consists of general population characteristics that seem to be related to neurotransmitters and their metabolites—age, sex, and body size. Activity, stress, illness, and drugs constitute another group of factors that may or may not be independent of the illness. Other groups include important temporal factors and personality variables. These too may or may not be independent of illness. The last group of variables are those that can be most clearly related to affective illness, although none have been shown to be completely illness-specific.

II. Interassay Variability

In order to assess the relative importance of the sources of variance identified in Table I, it is necessary to know the extent to which assays of MHPG are themselves sources of variance. Given the twofold range of reported values for the mean daily urinary excretion of MHPG in normals, there is *prima facie* evidence that assay variability may account for at

TABLE I
Sources of Variance in Clinical Studies of MHPG

Assay variability
Illness independent factors
  Age, Sex, and Body Size
Factors not necessarily independent of illness
  Diet, activity, stress, other illness and drugs
  Circadian and annual rhythms
  "Personality"
Illness dependent clinical state differences
  Activity, anxiety, psychosis, phase of illness

least some of the differences in "normative" data (for review see Goodwin and Potter, 1979). We have found that even within the same laboratory there is a 10–15% interassay coefficient of variation, and there is a systematic 20% overestimate of values obtained by gas chromatography with electron-capture detection as compared with values obtained using a mass spectrometric method as the reference standard (Muscettola *et al.*, 1981). Interpretation of any MHPG differences less than 20% must consider assay variability. Because it is impractical to make all comparisons dependent on values obtained within the same assay, one must be careful to distribute in a random fashion samples between all assays, so that urine from one specific group of subjects is not run in one batch whereas the comparison group is run in another. If this were done, for example, one might find a significant age difference in levels of urinary MHPG simply on the basis of assay variability. In the sources of variance studies we have surveyed, it is not always possible to know whether analyses were randomized. Some discrepancies between studies may, therefore, result from differences in laboratory methodology.

III. Age, Sex, and Body Size

Many significant differences in biochemical parameters in humans are associated with age. Cerebrospinal fluid (CSF) concentrations of the major metabolites of serotonin and dopamine increase markedly with age both in psychiatric patients and in controls; MHPG levels are less markedly increased in the 30–70-year age range (Asberg *et al.*, 1980). Because plasma NE concentrations are also known to increase with age (Lake *et al.*, 1977), one might expect parallel increases in levels of urinary MHPG if the relative contribution of the various sources of this metabolite remain the same. In a previous investigation, Shopsin *et al.* (1973) did not find a correlation between age and levels of urinary MHPG in patients and controls. Subsequently, however, the National Institute of Mental Health (NIMH) studies have shown a weak positive correlation in a group of depressed patients ($r = .3$, $n = 41$; Beckmann and Goodwin, 1980). A study comparing unmedicated chronic schizophrenics and controls found a significant ($p < .05$) positive correlation between age and MHPG-SO_4 excretion when both groups were considered together (Joseph *et al.*, 1976). Our most recent data based on a larger number of subjects ($n = 74$) reveal a significant but weak relationship between age and urinary MHPG in drug-free depressed patients

(Fig. 1). A similar but even stronger relationship ($r = .43$, $n = 88$, $p < .001$) was observed between age and levels of urinary MHPG for a combined group of depressed, manic, and normal subjects (Bowden *et al.*, 1981). Studies of normal volunteers show a similar relationship ($p < .07$); (Beckmann and Goodwin, 1980). The bulk of the evidence demonstrates that age should always be considered in analyses of group differences in urinary MHPG.

The contribution of sex to urinary MHPG is more clear-cut (Table II). Even though the absolute amounts reported many differ from study to study, within each study there is a consistent finding that control males excrete more MHPG than do females. In patient groups males also tend to excrete more although the difference is statistically significant in only one study (Maas *et al.*, 1973). These findings do not appear to be a function of body size and weight, although no study provides the necessary raw data to permit a pooled analysis. Moreover, the higher MHPG found in control males is consistent with the different sources of variance being important in controls and patients (see the following).

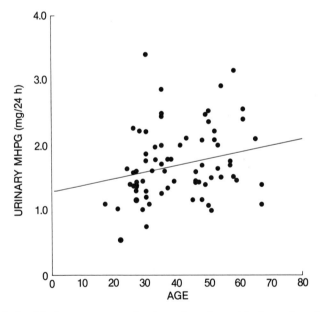

Fig. 1. Relationship between age and urinary 3-methoxy-4-hydroxyphenethyleneglycol (MHPG) in drug-free depressed unipolar and bipolar patients. MHPG values are means of an average of three 24 h periods for each patient. Subjects were inpatients restricted to a low monoamine diet (see Table III). Motor activity was not controlled. (Average urinary MHPG was $1.70 \pm .06$ mg/24 h, average age was 40.39 ± 1.46 years; where $r = .23$, $p < .05$, and $N = 74$.)

TABLE II
Sex Differences in Urinary MHPG

Study	Sex	N	Controls (mg/24 h)	N	Depressed patients (mg/24 h)
Fawcett et al., 1972	Male	—[a]	—	5	1.08 ± .16
	Female	—	—	6	0.93 ± .08
Maas et al., 1973	Male	19	1.67 ± .12	20	1.39 ± .09
	Female	21	1.35 ± .06	48	1.16 ± .06
Beckmann et al., 1979	Male	—	—	3	1.80 ± .62
	Female	—	—	9	1.63 ± .29
Sharpless, 1977	Male	—	—	10	2.02 ± .53
	Female	—	—	10	1.36 ± .47
	Male	6	2.11 ± .06	—	
	Female	5	1.62 ± .05	—	
Cobbin et al., 1979	Male	—	—	11	1.45 ± .26
	Female	—	—	24	1.28 ± .24
Coppen et al., 1979	Male	10	2.19 ± .23	10	1.73 ± .22
	Female	17	1.37 ± .08	13	1.48 ± .13
Beckmann and Goodwin, 1980	Male	7	1.44 ± .21	10	1.68 ± .20
	Female	8	1.23 ± .12	31	1.50 ± .10

[a] The dash indicates that data were not available.

Body height, known to contribute to variation of the serotonin metabolite 5-hydroxyindoleacetic acid in lumbar CSF, is not reported to influence CSF MHPG (Asberg et al., 1978; Goodwin et al., 1977; Wode-Helgodt and Sedvall, 1978).

IV. Environmental Factors

Such variables (diet, activity, stress, other illnesses, and drugs) may or may not be related to episodes of major affective illness and all have been reported to alter MHPG in patients and/or controls. Altered activity, in particular, may be viewed as a necessary component of certain depressions. Even if this is the case, activity and diet are variables, that at first glance, might be assumed to have a consistent relationship to levels of urinary MHPG across various populations. However, there are indications that MHPG response to dietary and activity changes may not be the same in depressed patients and in healthy controls. Therefore, studies that evaluate these relationships in controls cannot be extrapolated to depressed patients. Similarly, the marked sex differences in controls do not directly apply in patients as mentioned in the preceding section.

A. Diet

Although the amount of catecholamines ingested appears to have a negligible effect on the excretion of urinary catecholamines and their metabolites in normal volunteers (Cardon and Guggenheim, 1970; Rayfield *et al.*, 1972; Shaw and Trevarthen, 1958; Weetman *et al.*, 1976), there may be pronounced effects in patients (Muscettola *et al.*, 1977). The just-mentioned investigators used a paradigm in which hospitalized depressed patients and controls were switched from a "low monoamine diet" (Table III) to a dietary regimen in which they were encouraged to ingest the foods or beverages restricted in the low monoamine diet (except alcohol). Figure 2 illustrates the substantial increase in levels of urinary MHPG that was observed during the unrestricted diet condition in the patient group but not in the controls; subsequent study showed this effect to be independent of the sequence of dietary change. Preliminary follow-up data suggests that these effects may be state independent, for example, recovered depressed patients still showed significant increases in levels of urinary MHPG when changing from a restricted to an unrestricted diet.

Even before these studies, many investigators have chosen to control diet and have continued to do so (Maas *et al.*, 1973; Schildkraut *et al.*, 1978; Taube *et al.*, 1978), although others do not (Hollister *et al.*, 1978; Schildkraut *et al.*, 1973). One investigator (Sharpless, 1977) who placed volunteers and patients on a restricted catecholamine diet for 4 days found that levels of urinary MHPG decreased more in volunteers than in patients. This paradigm is obviously not identical to the one done by

TABLE III
NIMH Low Monoamine Diet

Excluded Beverages
  Chocolate, cocoa, wine, beer, alcohol, orange juice
Excluded Fruits and Nuts
  Banana, avocado, pineapple, plum, prune, orange, walnut, raisin, fig
Excluded Vegetables
  Tomato, broad bean, eggplant
Excluded meats, dairy products, and fish
  Chicken liver, herring, smoked fish, brain, aged cheese, sour cream

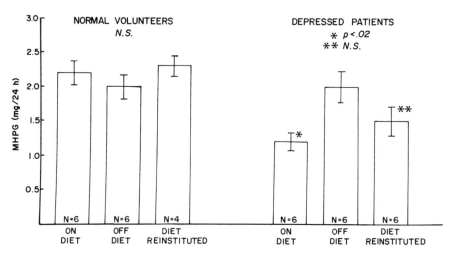

Fig. 2. Effect of discontinuing a low monoamine diet (Table III) in volunteers and depressed patients living on a research unit. Figure from Muscettola *et al.* (1977).

Muscettola *et al.* (1977) as already described. It has been suggested that diet control is not needed because no effect is noticeable using patient or volunteer *reports* of what they have eaten (Hollister *et al.*, 1978 and 1980a). Clearly, studies of actual diet and levels of urinary MHPG would be needed to support this impression. In light of the fact that subgroup differences have been identified in research centers where diet is controlled for the subgroup, it would appear prudent to continue this practice because diet clearly can contribute to variance of urinary MHPG in some circumstances.

B. Activity

As previously noted, altered activity can be viewed as a component of affective illness, especially bipolar, so that considering it as a source of variance may be relevant only in terms of forced activity change. Findings from several studies that have used different activity paradigms as well as different methods of quantitating activity are summarized in Table IV. Those studies that depend on retrospective comparisons of "agitation" or "retardation" in depressed subjects or self-reports in volunteers do not reveal an effect of activity on levels of urinary MHPG (DeLeon-Jones *et al.*, 1975; Hollister *et al.*, 1978; Taube *et al.*, 1978). NIMH studies (Beckmann *et al.*, 1979; Ebert *et al.*, 1972; Muscettola *et al.*, 1976) have consistently shown that experimentally induced increases in activity (telemetrically monitored) produce increased levels of urinary MHPG in patients but not in volunteers. Three of the four studies of volunteers show no increase in MHPG levels after "vigorous" exercise (see Table IV). The exception is a study using monitored ergometric exercise (cycling in place for 50 min at a rate sufficient to "go" 15 km carrying a light load), which did produce a definite increase in most but not all volunteers (Howlett and Jenner, 1978). Such a sustained effort is known to produce a marked increase in levels of peripheral NE; this may be large enough to produce increased levels of urinary MHPG, as well as other NE metabolites.

The NIMH studies (Table IV), which demonstrated that activity increased levels of urinary MHPG in patients but not in volunteers, are unique in that *all* subjects were living on the same research units and were on a controlled low monoamine diet (see the previous discussion and Table III). Twelve-hour urine samples were obtained, and the increase in levels of urinary MHPG was seen in the 7:00 A.M. to 7:00 P.M. collection that covered the period of increased activity (Beckmann *et al.*, 1979). The relationships between activity or levels of MHPG and levels of urinary NE or epinephrine (EPI) were also investigated in a subset of subjects. In the six patients who had the most marked increases of urinary MHPG levels during the activity period, a relationship to NE or EPI

TABLE IV
Studies on the Relationship Between Physical Activity and Urinary MHPG

Subjects	Experimental design	Urinary MHPG	Study
Depressed patients	Doubling of exercise telemetrically verified	Increase	Ebert *et al.*, 1972
Volunteers	2 h of "rigorous exercise"	No change	Goode *et al.*, 1973
Depressed patients	Comparison of agitated vs retarded diagnostic subgroups	No difference	DeLeon-Jones *et al.*, 1975
Depressed patients	Comparison of agitated vs retarded diagnostic subgroups	No difference	Taube *et al.*, 1978
Volunteers	Telemetered increase of activity	No change	Muscettola *et al.*, 1976
Depressed patients		Increase	Beckmann *et al.*, 1979
Volunteers	Self reports of being "active" or "sedentary"	No difference	Hollister *et al.*, 1978
Volunteers (teenage)	Monitored ergometric exercise	Increase (variable)	Howlett and Jenner, 1978
Depressed patients	Telemetered "restricted" vs "enhanced" activity with anxiety measurements	No change and no difference	Sweeney *et al.*, 1978

could not be shown, although average amounts excreted of both did increase nonsignificantly (Beckmann *et al.*, 1979). These findings on NE and EPI levels are consistent with those of Sweeney *et al.* (1978). In another subset of four patients, CSF and urine were obtained as a baseline and again following activity. As originally shown (Post *et al.*, 1973) activity did increase MHPG levels in the CSF, but in this small group only a nonsignificant increase in urinary MHPG levels was found (Beckmann *et al.*, 1979).

Naturalistic investigation of the relationship between activity and urinary MHPG levels both within and between subjects were made possible by the development of an activity monitor. Activity of inpatients at the NIMH is monitored by a nontelemetric device worn on the nondominant wrist. Preliminary results indicate that there is no overall correlation between activity and levels of urinary MHPG (F. K. Goodwin and T. A. Wehr, unpublished data). Within an individual patient, however, both circadian and longitudinal patterns of MHPG levels (24 h MHPG totals for weeks to months) are associated with patterns of activity, although a precise relationship has not been defined (see the following discussion of "clinical state differences").

An important study has shown that the level of anxiety during procedures designed to explore the relationship between activity and MHPG levels may be the most relevant variable (Sweeney *et al.*, 1978). In this study one group of patients rode an exercycle during some part of an "enhanced activity" period. Another group was placed on "restricted activity" that involved bed rest except for micturition or defecation. Movement was monitored telemetrically and anxiety was recorded on the Spielberger state anxiety scale, a self-rating instrument. According to these ratings some individuals in both the patient and the control groups experienced either increased or decreased levels of anxiety during enhanced activity, others during restricted activity. The data suggested that increases and decreases in urinary MHPG levels could be best accounted for by increased or decreased levels of anxiety, respectively, in both groups of subjects (see the following discussion). These data were based on 8-h urine samples. Interestingly, in their 24-h samples from the *postexperimental* periods (Table II in Sweeney *et al.*, 1978), there is a tendency for levels of urinary MHPG to increase in the enhanced activity group [1059 ± 98 (SEM) versus 926 ± 73 (SEM)]. Another notable feature of this study is the relatively low mean 24-h urinary MHPG level (.88–.93 mg/day) as compared with those reported by other investigators for groups of depressed patients (e.g., 1.36–1.93 mg/day—Goodwin and Potter, 1979; 1.21–1.95 mg/day—Schildkraut *et al.*, 1978). These differences, of course, may simply reflect assay variability across research laboratories (Muscettola *et al.*, 1981) or differences in patient population. Finally, the positive relationship between changes in state anxiety and MHPG levels appears to be primarily accounted for by *decreases* in both parameters during either restricted or enhanced activity (see Fig. 1 in Sweeney *et al.*, 1978). Only one of the few individuals who showed an *increase* in levels of urinary MHPG showed a change in anxiety. Interestingly, in the NIMH studies decreases of urinary MHPG levels during activity periods were not observed.

In light of both the differing results and differing experimental approaches it is not appropriate to draw a general conclusion concerning the relationship of activity to levels of urinary MHPG. It may well be that interactions between experimentally increased activity and the extent of concomitant anxiety and stress (see Section IV.C) are the overall determinants of whether or not the level of urinary MHPG changes. The negative relationship between levels of MHPG and activity in naturalistic studies is consistent with an interpretation that there is at most a modest effect of activity per se. On the other hand, activity is a parameter that *can* contribute to variations in urinary MHPG levels, although the appropriate "control" for this phenomenon is not readily apparent. Again, it should be remembered that the level of activity may be an inherent part of affective illness in which case there can be no independent "control."

C. Stress

Two studies are usually cited as proof that stress has a possible effect on urinary MHPG excretion; the first, in patients, shows increases during a 24-h intravenous procedure (Maas *et al.*, 1971); the second, in pilots ("normals"), shows increases during landing on aircraft carriers (Rubin *et al.*, 1970). To our knowledge these particular studies have not been replicated. A differential MHPG level response to stress as measured by average evoked potentials following visual and painful electrical stimuli was found between volunteers and patients (Buchsbaum *et al.*, 1981). Male normal volunteers alone showed a clear increase in levels of urinary MHPG whereas depressed patients did not. The most severely depressed patients showed no evidence of increased MHPG levels in response to the experimentally induced "stress." An unanswered question is the extent to which such non-illness-dependent stresses contribute to variations in levels of urinary MHPG. Obviously, collections following a period of unquestionable physical (e.g., pain) or mental (e.g., performing on an examination) stress are not appropriate for the generation of normative data and need to be further studied in their own right.

D. Illness and Drugs

It is predictable that medical illnesses that involve production of NE (e.g., Shagass' Syndrome) would influence levels of urinary MHPG. Other conditions such as alcohol withdrawal (a hyperadrenergic state) can also alter (increase) urinary MHPG levels (Hollister *et al.*, 1980b). Levels of urinary MHPG seem to be increased in asthmatics too, although this may be a function of their medication (Hollister *et al.*, 1980b). Drugs used in the treatment of psychiatric illness, hypertension, and bronchospasm are in general likely to alter catecholamines in many tissues, as well as the concentration of MHPG in urine (for review see Javaid, Chapter 4, in this volume). Subjects on medication or subjects with multiple illnesses (e.g., depression plus hypertension) *must be excluded* in compiling normative data. We find, for instance, a highly significant positive correlation between systolic blood pressure and urinary MHPG levels (Fig. 3), a relationship that is also found in hypertensive patients who do not have a diagnosis of psychiatric or other illness (Keiser, H., personal communication). A similar positive relationship ($r = .43-.46$) has been reported between sitting and standing diastolic blood pressure and plasma MHPG levels (Leckman *et al.*, 1981).

E. Summary

Thus urinary MHPG level findings in controls and patients with major affective disorders are influenced by a number of factors, which make variable and differential contributions. These factors must be considered in the interpretation of data, particularly in light of reports that urinary MHPG values in patients almost all fall within the normal range (Hollister *et al.*, 1978). Hence, investigators frequently compare subgroups who fall within the high or low normal range (see Chapters 7 and 9, by Schildkraut and van Kammen, respectively). It is essential to be aware of the factors that we have discussed that may "push" patients into either a high or low urinary MHPG range.

The most striking result that emerges from a consideration of the factors that influence urinary MHPG levels is that it may be impossible to provide true "control" groups. At least in terms of diet and activity, normals appear to show a different response than do depressed patients. Thus it is not sufficient that patients and volunteers being compared in a study simply be on the same diet and on the same activity paradigm. It is necessary to show within the patient or volunteer group that the diet or activity is not having significant effects on urinary MHPG levels. If, for instance, diet were not controlled (on the basis of experience in volun-

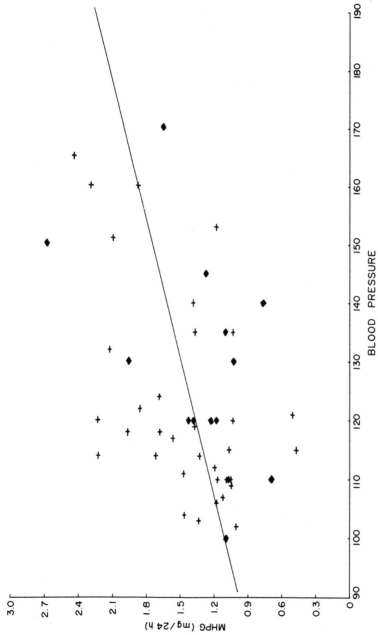

Fig. 3. Relationship ($p < .01$) between blood pressure and 24 h urinary MHPG excretion in depressed patients and normal controls. Subjects were on a low monoamine diet. Depressed patients are represented by a + and normal controls by a ◆, where $N = 48$ and $r = .46$. (Lewy and Goodwin, unpublished data).

teers), then differences in levels of urinary MHPG between a control and patient group would very likely be obscured.

V.   Circadian and Annual Rhythms

Most biochemical functions in humans and animals show daily variation and follow highly organized patterns that conform to 24-h periods. These patterns are not passive responses to the environment but seem to be driven by a pacemaker in the CNS (Moore, 1978). Circadian rhythms for establishing levels of norepinephrine and its metabolites have been identified in humans as well as in several animal species (for review see Table I in Wehr *et al.*, 1980). In a study of MHPG in normal subjects, a significant diurnal variation was noted that could be analyzed as a circadian pattern with a peak around 6 P.M. (Hollister *et al.*, 1978). This same peak time ("acrophase") was also identified in volunteers as part of a more extensive study of the circadian rhythm of MHPG levels (Wehr *et al.*, 1980). In this latter study the circadian MHPG pattern was compared with that of bipolar depressed patients living on the same unit as the volunteers (Fig. 4). The following two findings are apparent: both the amount and the pattern of urinary MHPG excretion were different in depressed patients. Although MHPG values were lower at all but one time, the pattern of the circadian rhythm in the patients showed an earlier peak (phase advance), which tended to reduce group differences during the day and exaggerate group differences at night (Wehr *et al.*, 1980). This finding of an earlier peak proves to be independent of the age difference between patients and volunteers. In addition to its theoretical implication (Wehr *et al.*, 1980) this finding may have important practical implications. Fixed time of day or 24-h integrative sampling procedures may either obscure or exaggerate differences between patient groups and controls. It may be possible to "exploit" this finding by comparing overnight urine levels in patient groups with those in controls, thereby greatly simplifying the procedures involved in doing urinary studies of MHPG levels. On the other hand, from a theoretical point of view, the shift in circadian pattern (phase shift) may itself prove to be an important phenomenon to study. This would necessitate around-the-clock sampling, an obviously complicating factor.

A high probability exists that an annual rhythm of levels of urinary MHPG will also be found. Preliminary studies of plasma norepinephrine levels (Lake and Wirz-Justice, unpublished data), CSF norepinephrine, and MHPG (Wirz-Justice, Wehr and Goodwin *et al.*, unpublished obser-

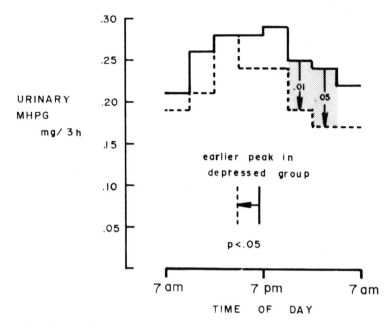

Fig. 4. Circadian rhythm of urinary MHPG in depressed bipolar patients and normal volunteers living on the same research unit. Figure from Wehr *et al.* (1980).

vations) measured at different times of the year (but at the same time of day) in various populations reveal significant annual fluctuations. Such annual fluctuations could account for the lack of stability of MHPG levels with respect to time observed in the group of normal volunteers (Hollister *et al.*, 1978). There is also the possibility that annual rhythms may not only be sources of variance but may be of special interest in terms of patients, e.g., differential suicide rates at different times of year.

In the interpretation of circadian and annual rhythms of urinary MHPG levels, it is not clear that one should "control" or "factor out" this variable; rather, investigators need to be aware of these factors, provide data that will permit better definition of patterns, and recognize that these sources of variance are important areas of study.

VI. Personality

Psychophysiological studies of anxiety in particular have revealed that altered noradrenergic function is associated with certain personality types (for review see Lader, 1980). Certain personality characteristics such as impulsivity have been highly correlated with the ratio of levels of urinary NE to epinephrine (for review see Hinton, 1980). Subjects in these studies were not, however, evaluated for possible changes in levels of urinary MHPG excretion.

Findings of a positive association between levels of MHPG in the CSF and "aggression" provide direct evidence of a relationship between levels of this NE metabolite and an aspect of personality (Brown et al., 1979). In this latter study there was an even more marked negative correlation of aggression with levels of the serotonin metabolite, 5HIAA, in the CSF (Brown et al., 1979). Studies in Scandinavia also show lower levels of 5HIAA in the CSF in patients who have higher Rorschach-based aggression scores (Asberg, 1980). Because low levels of 5HIAA are also associated with suicidal behavior (Asberg et al., 1976; Brown et al., 1979) this CSF amine metabolite may have important clinical implications.

Although the relationship between personality and/or behavioral profiles and levels of urinary MHPG has not been established, it should be kept in mind that this may prove to be important. The point made with other sources of variance can be repeated—not only may personality influence levels of urinary MHPG, but also whatever relationship that is found may contribute to our understanding of the pathophysiology of some types of depression.

VII. Clinical State Differences

The relationship between clinical state and levels of MHPG has been questioned since the outset of studies in affective illness. This relationship is most clearly demonstrable in comparisons of mania and depression in bipolar patients (see Chapter 7, in this volume). There is a general consensus that for each individual the mean levels of urinary MHPG or MHPG-SO$_4$ excretion during mania is greater than during depression. This fact stimulated numerous attempts to understand the extent to which the difference in activity level during mania and depression accounts for the differences in urinary MHPG levels. In one carefully studied manic-depressive patient, an increased, level of MHPG preceded the mania by as much as four days; the investigators concluded that activity or arousal alone could not explain the increased level of urinary MHPG (DeLeon-Jones et al., 1973).

The NIMH longitudinal studies of the "switch process" present a less clear picture. In a patient in whom behavior and daily urinary MHPG level was measured for 352 days, a variable relationship between mood and urinary MHPG level was found (Fig. 5). Even though the mood cycle and the MHPG cycle have identical *average* period lengths (as calculated by power spectral analysis), in some instances the increase in the level of MHPG precedes the mood change, in other instances it follows it. In the same patient it was possible to monitor mood, motor activity, and level of urinary MHPG through four cycles. From these data an "average cycle" profile was constructed (Fig. 6) (Wehr, 1977). As can be readily seen the timing of, for instance, maximal increase in activity does not parallel the maximum increase of the level of urinary MHPG. On the other hand, in the individual patient, average motor activity and the level of MHPG are elevated during all manic periods as compared with depressed periods (Fig. 6). Yet, as noted in a preceding section, there is no overall relationship between activity and MHPG levels across patients.

Thus we are faced with an association between activity and urinary MHPG levels that is highly variable and difficult to interpret. Moreover, the association between the timing of the association between level of urinary MHPG and mood within the same patient is also variable. These findings suggest that a few determinations of the level of MHPG are unlikely to provide much information concerning either the mood state or level of activity of an individual.

The longitudinal study just described (Figs. 5 and 6) also demonstrates that the phase of illness itself may have a variable relationship to urinary

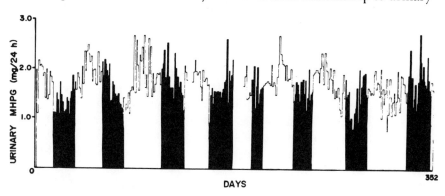

Fig. 5. Daily urinary MHPG in a single bipolar depressed patient for 352 days. Periods of depression in black with mean urinary MHPG being 1.62 ± .03 (159), of mania in white with mean urinary MHPG being 1.81 ± .02 (193) and p <.001. Severity of state not indicated (Muscettola, Wehr and Goodwin, unpublished data).

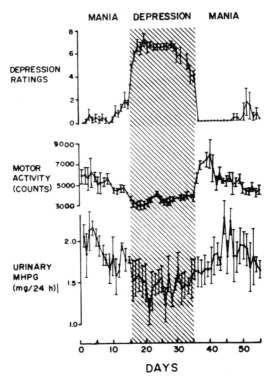

Fig. 6. An "average" mood cycle showing mean ± SEM of depression ratings, motor activity and urinary MHPG from four cycles of the same patient as in Fig. 5. For a more detailed description see Wehr (1977).

MHPG levels. At some points in depression levels of urinary MHPG may actually be higher than at some points in mania despite the *average* differences noted in a preceding discussion (see Fig. 5). And as a corollary, the average cycle profile reveals differences of levels of urinary MHPG within a particular phase. For instance, levels of MHPG are lower in early and late mania than in midmania (Fig. 6). Again, these findings indicate that caution is needed in the interpretation of small numbers of determinations of MHPG levels in an individual.

Anxiety considered as a symptom of depression may also influence urinary MHPG levels. In a small group of depressed males ($n = 10$) global anxiety ratings were fairly highly correlated ($r = .73$, $p < .05$) with levels of urinary MHPG although the same relationship was not seen in females (Beckmann and Goodwin, 1980). In this same study, global depression also correlated with levels of MHPG in males but not females. It was not possible to demonstrate that anxiety and depression were independent variables in this study. Using a different tool (the Spielberger State Anxiety Inventory) Sweeney *et al.* (1978) were also unable to show a relationship between baseline anxiety and urinary MHPG levels in a group of depressed female patients although induced *changes* in anxiety and MHPG levels did correlate (see the preceding discussions). In normal male volunteers Hollister *et al.* (1978) found no relationship between levels of MHPG and levels of anxiety. Whether or not the degree of anxiety in depressed male patients regularly influences levels of urinary MHPG needs further study.

Psychosis, obviously illness dependent, may also be positively related to levels of urinary MHPG (Beckmann and Goodwin, 1980). This relationship, however, has only been described in males and is not marked (r = .35). Psychosis has not been identified as a significantly contributing variable in other studies although the extent to which it has been considered is not clear.

VIII. Summary

In clinical investigations multiple sources of variance can influence urinary MHPG concentrations. Some such as age and sex have a constant effect whereas others such as diet and activity change levels of urinary MHPG only under certain experimental conditions or in certain populations. Thus "controlling" for a source of variance is not always appropriate or possible. It is therefore difficult to establish that alterations in urinary MHPG concentrations are specific to pathology. Moreover, even though the ultimate importance of MHPG studies to our understanding of the pathophysiology of psychiatric illness remains unclear, the methodological and conceptual issues reviewed here transcend the importance of this single metabolite. The issue of specificity is central to the interpretation of any clinical data whether they be in the sphere of biology or clinical phenomenology.

References

Asberg, M., Traskman, L., and Thoren, P. 1976. *Arch. Gen. Psychiatry* **33,** 1193–1197.
Asberg, M., Bertilsson, L., Rydin, E., Shalling, D., Thorén, P., and Traskman-Bendz, L. 1981. *Recent Advances in Neuropsychopharmacology* (B. Angrist, G. D. Burrows, M. Lader,

O. Liugjaerde, G. Sedvall, and D. Wheatley, eds.), pp. 257–271. Pergamon Press, New York.

Asberg, M., Bertilsson, L., Thoren, P., and Traskman, L. 1978. *Depressive Disorders* (S. Garattini, ed.), pp. 293–305. Verlag Stuttgart.

Beckmann, H., Ebert, M. H., Post, R., and Goodwin, F. K. 1979. *Pharmakopsychiat.* **12**, 351–356.

Beckmann, H., and Goodwin, F. K. 1980. *Neuropsychobiol.* **6**, 91–100.

Blombery, P. A., Kopin, I. J., Gordon, E. K., Markey, S. P., and Ebert, M. H. 1980. *Arch. Gen. Psychiatry* **37**, 1095–1098.

Bowden, C. L., Redmond, D. E., Swann, A., and Maas, J. D. 1981. *Psychopharmacol. Bull.* **17**, 70–72.

Brown, G. L., Goodwin, F. K., Ballenger, J. C., Goyer, P. F., and Major, L. F. 1979. *Psychiatry Res.* **1**, 131–139.

Buchsbaum, M. S., Muscettola, G., and Goodwin, F. K. 1981. *Neuropsychobiol.* **7**, 212–224.

Cardon, P. V., and Guggenheim, F. H. 1970. *J. Psychiatr. Res.* **7**, 263–273.

Cedarbaum, J. M., and Aghajanian, G. K. 1978. *Life Sci.* **23**, 1383–1392.

Cobbin, D. M., Requin-Blow, B., Williams, L. R., and Williams, W. O. 1979. *Arch. Gen. Psychiatry* **36**, 1111–1115.

Coppen, A., Rama, Rao, V. A., Ruthven, C. R. J., Goodwin, B. L., and Sandler, M. 1979. *Psychopharmacol.* **64**, 95–97.

Crawley, J. N., Roth, R. H., and Maas, J. W. 1979. *Brain Res.* **166**, 180–184.

Crawley, J. N., Maas, J. W., and Roth, R. H. 1980. *Brain Res.* **183**, 301–311.

Dahlstrom, A., and Fuxe, K. 1965. *Acta Physiol. Scand.* **64**, 1–36.

DeLeon-Jones, F., Maas, J. W., Dekirmenjian, H., and Fawcett, J. A. 1973. *Science* **170**, 300–302.

DeLeon-Jones, F. D., Maas, J. W., Dekirmenjian, H., and Sanchez, J. 1975. *Am. J. Psychiatry* **132**, 1141–1148.

Ebert, M. H., Post, R. M., and Goodwin, F. K. 1972. *Lancet* **11**, 766.

Fawcett, J., Maas, J. W., and Dekirmenjian, H. 1972. *Arch. Gen. Psychiatry* **26**, 246–251.

Goode, D. J., Dekirmenjian, H., Meltzer, H. Y., and Maas, J. W. 1973. *Arch. Gen. Psychiatry* **29**, 391–396.

Goodwin, F. K., Cowdry, R. W., and Webster, M. H. 1977. *Psychopharmacology—A Generation of Progress* (Lipton, M. DiMascio, and K. Killiam, eds.), pp. 1277–1288. Raven Press, New York.

Goodwin, F. K., and Potter, W. Z. 1979. *Neuropharmacology* (B. Saletu, ed.), pp. 127–137. Proceedings of the 11th CINP Congress. Pergamon Press, New York.

Hinton, J. W. 1980. *Handbook of Biological Psychiatry Part II Brain Mechanisms and Abnormal Behavior—Psychophysiology* (H. M. van Praag, M. H. Loder, O. J. Rafaelsen, and E. J. Sachar, eds.), pp. 285–314. Marcel Dekker, New York.

Hollister, L. E., Davis, K. L., Overall, J. E., and Anderson, T. 1978. *Arch. Gen. Psychiatry* **35**, 1410–1415.

Hollister, L. E., Davis, K. L., and Berger, P. 1980a. *Arch. Gen. Psychiatry* **37**, 1107–1110.

Hollister, L. E., Prusmack, J. J., Knopes, K., and Kanaske, K. 1980b. *Psychopharmacol.* **4**, 135–140.

Howlett, D. R., and Jenner, F. A. 1978. *Br. J. Psychiatry* **132**, 49–54.

Joseph, M. H., Baker, H. F., Johnstone, E. C., and Crow, T. J. 1976. *Psychopharmacol.* **51**, 47–51.

La Brosse, E. H. 1970. *J. Clin. Endocrinol.* **30**, 580–589.

Lader, M. H. 1980. *Handbook of Biological Psychiatry, Part II, Brain Mechanisms and Abnormal Behavior—Psychophysiology* (H. M. van Praag, M. H. Lader, O. J. Rafaelsen, and E. J. Sachar, eds.), pp. 225–248. Marcel Dekker, New York.

Lake, C. R., Ziegler, M. G., Coleman, M. D., and Kopin, I. J. 1977. *N. Eng. J. Med.* **296,** 208–209.

Leckman, J. F., and Heninger, G. R. 1981. *Eur. J. Pharmacol.* **70,** 111–120.

Maas, J. W., Dekirmenjian, H., and Fawcett, J. 1971. *Nature* **230,** 330–331.

Maas, J. W., Dekirmenjian, H., and Jones, F. 1973. *Frontiers in Catecholamine Research* (E. Usdin, and S. Snyder, eds.), pp. 1091–1096. Pergamon Press, New York.

Moore, R. Y. 1978. *Frontiers in Neuroendocrinology* (W. F. Ganong, and L. Martini, eds.), pp. 185–206. Raven Press, New York.

Muscettola, G., Wehr, T., and Goodwin, F. K. 1976. Central norepinephrine responses in depression versus normals. Presented at the Annual Meeting, American Psychiatric Association, New Research Abstracts, p. 8, Miami, Florida.

Muscettola, G., Wehr, T., and Goodwin, F. K. 1977. *Am. J. Psychiatry* **134,** 914–916.

Muscettola, G., Potter, W. Z., Gordon, E. K., and Goodwin, F. K. 1981. *Psychiatry Res.* **4,** 267–276.

Post, R. M., Kotin, J., Goodwin, F. K., and Gordon, E. K. 1973. *Am. J. Psychiatry* **130,** 67–72.

Rayfield, E. J., Cain, J. P., Casey, M. P., Williams, G. H., and Sullivan, J. M. 1972. *JAMA* **221,** 704–705.

Rubin, R. T., Miller, R. G., Clark, B. R., Plaud, R. E., and Arthur, R. J. 1970. *Psychosom. Med.* **32,** 589–597.

Schildkraut, J. J., Keeler, B. A., Papousek, M., and Hartmann, E. 1973. *Science* **181,** 762–764.

Schildkraut, J. J., Orsulak, P. J., Schatzberg, A. F., Gudeman, J. E., Cole, J. O., Rohde, W. A., and LaBrie, R. A. 1978. *Arch. Gen. Psychiatry* **35,** 1427–1433.

Scriabine, A., Clineschmidt, B. V., and Sweet, C. S. 1976. *Ann. Rev. Pharmacol. and Toxicol.* **16,** 113–123.

Sharpless, N. S. 1977. *Res. Comm. Chem. Pathol. Pharmacol.* **18,** 257–273.

Shaw, K. N. F., and Trevarthen, J. 1958. *Nature* **182,** 797–798.

Shopsin, B., Wilk, S., Gershon, S., Davis, K., and Suhl, M. 1973. *Arch. Gen. Psychiatry* **28,** 230–233.

Sweeney, D. R., Maas, J. W., and Heninger, G. R. 1978. *Arch. Gen. Psychiatry* **35,** 1418–1423.

Taube, S. L., Kirstein, L. S., Sweeney, D. R., Heninger, G. R., and Maas, J. W. 1978. *Am. J. Psychiatry* **135,** 78–82.

Weetman, R. M., Rider, P. S., Oei, T. D., Hempel, J. S., and Baehner, R. L. 1976. *J. Ped.* **88,** 46–50.

Wehr, T. A. 1977. *Ann. Intern. Med.* **87,** 319–335.

Wehr, T. A., Muscettola, G., and Goodwin, F. K. 1980. *Arch. Gen. Psychiatry* **37,** 257–263.

Wode-Helgodt, B., and Sedvall, G. 1978. *Comm. Psychopharmacol.* **2,** 177–183.

9

Urinary MHPG and Treatment Response: A Review

DANIËL P. VAN KAMMEN

National Institute of Mental Health, Bethesda, Maryland

I. Introduction

The clinical efficacy of tricyclic antidepressants such as imipramine, desimipramine (DMI), and amitriptyline is well established (Kessler *et al.*, 1978; Klerman, 1972; Morris and Beck, 1974). Other drugs such as lithium carbonate (Mendels *et al.*, 1979) and monoamine oxidase (MAO) inhibitors (Quitkin *et al.*, 1979) are effective in some depressed patients. Each of these drugs appears to be effective to a different degree with certain depressed patients. Statistical evidence of therapeutic efficacy does not provide the clinician with enough information for prescribing

MHPG: BASIC MECHANISMS
AND PSYCHOPATHOLOGY

ISBN 0-12-462920-2

the right drug for the right patient. Some patients may respond better to one type of antidepressant than to another, whereas others may fail to respond to any of the available antidepressant drugs. It usually takes several weeks before an adequate evaluation of the clinical response to tricyclic antidepressant treatment can be made. Clearly, an accurate prediction early in the illness concerning a patient's response to a certain antidepressant would be of great clinical importance. The medical tradition of response–prediction by careful diagnosis, using both clinical and biological means, has not reached the necessary sensitivity and specificity for treatment of depressive disorders. Traditional subclassifications, such as endogenous versus reactive, agitated versus retarded, hypersomniac versus hyposomniac, and endogenous versus anxious-neurotic depression, provide little help in choosing the right medication (Bielski and Friedel, 1976). Thus it seems timely to review those reports that have attempted to delineate groups of responding and nonresponding patients in order to provide the clinician with clear indications for prescribing the best antidepressant.

Attempts have been made to understand the etiology of depression by studying the biochemical effects of various compounds on certain biochemical systems in animals. Such attempts have led, for instance, to the formulation of the norepinephrine (NE) hypothesis of depression (Bunney and Davis, 1965; Schildkraut, 1965)—drugs that decrease NE activity could induce depression whereas drugs that increase NE activity would relieve depression—to the serotonin (5HT) hypothesis (Murphy et al., 1979; van Praag, 1980), as well as to attempts to predict antidepressant drug response (Bielski and Friedel, 1976; Goodwin et al., 1979). Because 3-methoxy-4-hydroxyphenethyleneglycol (MHPG) may reflect metabolism of NE by brain (see Chapter 3), it was hypothesized that studies of MHPG excretion levels would lead to the confirmation or rejection of this NE hypothesis. If low levels of MHPG excretion reflect an intrinsic NE deficit, such as that hypothesized to be present in depression, then drugs that allegedly raise NE activity should be effective (Fawcett and Siomopoulos, 1971; Goodwin et al., 1979).

This hypothesis is attractive in its simplicity. However, MHPG excretion does not relate to depression ratings (Beckmann and Goodwin, 1975, 1980; Beckmann and Murphy, 1977; Fawcett and Siomopoulos, 1971; Fawcett et al., 1972; Maas et al., 1972). Methodological problems have surfaced that question the early formulations of this hypothesis as well as the interpretability of MHPG excretion data (Goodwin and Potter, 1979). It is conceivable that depression is not mainly a disorder of the central nervous system (CNS) but may be systemic in nature. How specific the drug-free levels of urinary MHPG excretion data are for the understanding of the etiology of depression is discussed elsewhere in this volume. The focus here is on the potential use of MHPG excretion levels as a treatment-response predictor and on the relationship of antidepressant treatment effects on levels of MHPG excretion. This chapter reviews urinary MHPG antidepressant treatment-prediction studies from 1971 until 1981 that include only a few replication attempts such as for imipramine and amitriptyline response. Urine collection methodology, fluctuations of day-to-day levels, and the diagnostic implications of urinary MHPG levels will not be covered here.

Other potential predictors of antidepressant drug response, such as the D-type score (Schildkraut, 1978a,b), spinal fluid serotonin metabolite levels (Murphy et al., 1979; van Praag, 1980), dexamethasone suppression test, cortisol function and average-evoked response (AER) (Nurnberger et al., 1979) and REM latency are outside the scope of this review because they have not been evaluated yet vis-à-vis urinary MHPG excretion level and treatment response together except in one study (Maas et al., 1982). d-Amphetamine studies are also discussed, together with MHPG excretion level studies, because pretreatment urinary MHPG excretion level seems to relate to the acute behavioral response to d-amphetamine (Fawcett et al., 1971, 1972; Maas et al., 1972) and because this amphetamine effect may have predictive value for antidepressant drug response (Fawcett and Siomopoulos, 1971; Maas et al., 1972; van Kammen and Murphy, 1978, 1979). These attempts need to be replicated by other groups before this becomes clinically useful. In addition, the effects of drug treatment on MHPG excretion levels are presented.

II. Pretreatment MHPG and Drug–Response Prediction

A. d-Amphetamine Response

Beckmann et al. (1976), Fawcett et al. (1972), and Maas et al. (1972) observed that patients with low urinary MHPG excretion levels responded positively to d-amphetamine. We reported that pretreatment CSF MHPG in drug-free schizophrenic patients correlated significantly with the change in psychosis following iv d-amphetamine administration

($r = .58$, $p < .002$), suggesting that MHPG findings may not be of value for a drug response in affective disorder patients specifically but may be of value for drug response generally (van Kammen and Bunney, 1979).

B.   Tricyclic Antidepressants

Depressed patients who have responded to imipramine, de-simipramine, or nortriptyline treatment have been found to have lower pretreatment levels of urinary MHPG excretion than those who have not responded (Beckmann and Goodwin, 1975; Cobbin *et al.*, 1979; Fawcett *et al.*, 1972; Hollister *et al.*, 1980; Maas *et al.*, 1972, 1980; Rosenbaum, *et al.*, 1980; Schatzberg *et al.*, 1981). This predictive relationship has been reported for *d*-amphetamine responders as (Beckmann *et al.*, 1976; Fawcett *et al.*, 1972). Conversely, some researchers have found that amitriptyline responders tend to have "normal" or "high" urinary MHPG excretion levels compared with amitriptyline nonresponders (Beckmann and Goodwin, 1975; Cobbin *et al.*, 1979; Schildkraut, 1973), whereas other investigators were unable to observe such a relationship (Coppen *et al.*, 1979; Maas *et al.*, 1982; Sacchetti *et al.*, 1976; Spiker *et al.*, 1980). Imipramine and amitriptyline are used as prototype drugs for either NE or serotonin (5HT) deficiency depressions, although this division may be too simplistic. Drugs like amitriptyline or clomipramine (van Scheyen and van Kammen, 1979) or other drugs that facilitate central 5HT transmission may be more effective for patients with low levels of CSF 5HIAA—irrespective of MHPG urinary or CSF excreation levels— than imipramine, nortriptyline, or desimipramine (DMI), which may be more effective for patients with low MHPG concentration values. However, Maas *et al.* (1982) found a significant positive relationship between CSF 5HIAA levels and low urinary MHPG levels which was associated with a therapeutic response to imipramine. Coppen *et al.* (1979) found only high or normal levels of MHPG excretion in their depressed patients. Their study did not compare pretreatment MHPG levels in responders and nonresponders. Instead, they correlated pretreatment MHPG excretion levels with the changes in depression following a standard daily dose of only 150 mg/day of amitriptyline. Similarly, Sacchetti *et al.* (1976) reported that amitriptyline response was independent of pretreatment urinary MHPG excretion levels but this evaluation of the drug lasted for only 2 weeks and the dose was only 1.5 mg/kg body wt. The 2 patients with high pretreatment values in their study responded within 10 days. No significant correlations were reported. Thus these last two studies may not have adequately tested the hypothesis by dose and duration of treatment. Modai *et al.* (1979) found significantly lower levels of MHPG in 5 unequivocal responders to 150 to 200 mg/day for 5 weeks ($N = 15$).

The data of Cobbin and associates (1979) supported results from research studies with small groups of patients. Cobbin's study compared treatment outcome of a control group who had been treated with antidepressants according to physician's choice with two other groups of depressed patients who were treated according to urinary MHPG levels: Group A patients were treated with imipramine, desipramine, or nortriptyline if they had low pretreatment MHPG excretion levels and Group B patients were treated with amitriptyline if they had high or normal pretreatment MHPG excretion levels (Table I). Tricyclic antidepressants were given in daily doses of 200–300 mg/day. This study was performed with single-day determinations and, presumably, without dietary control in a routine clinical setting. Treatment outcome was significantly better for Groups A and B than for patients treated with antidepressants who were chosen by their treating psychiatrists. Interestingly, there were more subjects with very low MHPG levels ($N = 26$) than with high or normal levels ($N = 9$) in this group (Cobbin et al., 1979). It is unclear whether they corrected for disparate sample size in their statistical analysis. It is also possible that their control group was treated differently psychologically, which could account for the difference in outcome.

Spiker *et al.* (1980) did not find a significant relationship between pretreatment MHPG levels and response to amitriptyline in doses up to 200 mg. However, no direct comparisons were made between levels of six responders and six nonresponders. Blood levels of amitriptyline and nortriptyline were provided, although pretreatment urinary MHPG levels, response, and the two blood levels were not separately compared.

Maas *et al.* (1982) reported on a multicenter study in which low urinary MHPG excretion levels predicted imipramine response. High or moderate values did not predict amitriptyline response. On the other hand, low CSF 5HIAA values (assumed to predict amitriptyline response) were observed in patients with low urinary MHPG values. This finding may well establish the clinical usefulness of urinary MHPG levels for imipramine but not for amitriptyline response.

Hollister *et al.* (1980) studied *nortriptyline,* a major metabolite of amitriptyline, which has a similar effect on the NE system as imipramine. They also noted in their careful study that low MHPG levels predicted an antidepressant response to this drug.

Mianserin is a new tricyclic antidepressant (Zis *et al.*, 1979b) and the only reported MHPG prediction study is by Perry *et al.* (1978). No rela-

TABLE I

Urinary MHPG and Drug Response Prediction[a]

Authors[b]	Diagnosis[b]	Sex	Total (N)	MHPG pretreatment (mg/24 h)	MHPG during treatment (mg/24 h)	Comments
A. Amphetamine						
1. Fawcett et al., 1972	(8) PD (3) MD DN(2)	M = 6 F = 7	13			12 out of 13 patients were from Fawcett et al. 1970 (see Table II). Pretreatment MHPG vs d-amphetamine response ($r = .78$, $p < .01$). For NR 5/6 increased MHPG levels and for R 5/6 decreased MHPG levels.
d-Amphetamine						
2. Beckmann et al., 1976	(1) BPI (2) BPII (5) UP	M = 2 F = 6		(6) R 0.777 ± .15 (6)NR 1.115 ± .24	0.942 ± .241 [±14.8%] 0.843 ± .311 [−26.7%]	
Drug-free			8			R had nonsignificantly lower pretreatment levels. d-Amphetamine decreased MHPG levels minimally for responders, but increased levels in patients most activated (hypomanic). Li had no effect on placebo MHPG levels but attenuated behavioral and MHPG effects of amphetamine.
placebo				1.47 ± .11	1.47 ± .11	
d-Amphetamine				1.47 ± .11	1.20 ± .11[c]	
1-Amphetamine				1.47 ± .11	1.46 ± .02[d]	
d- + 1-Amphetamine				1.47 ± .11	1.27 ± .10[c]	
Lithium			8			
Placebo				1.52 ± .06	1.52 ± .06	
d-Amphetamine				1.52 ± .06	1.35 ± .07[d]	
1-Amphetamine				1.52 ± .06	1.48 ± .13[d]	
d- + 1-Amphetamine				1.52 ± .06	1.38 ± .09[d]	
B. Imipramine, Desimipramine						
1. Fawcett et al., 1972 (IMI or DMI)	(7) PD (3) MD (2) DN	M = 5 F = 7	12	(See under A.1, MHPG levels not provided for individual subjects treated with IMI and/or DMI)		Levels were lower than means of normal men (1.660 ± .085) and women (1.397 ± .063). Pretreatment MHPG vs. IMI/DMI response (4th week; $r = .84$, $p < .01$).

2. Maas et al., 1972	(a) (4) PD (4) MD (3) DN (1) SAD	M = 5 F = 7	12			During the 4th week a treatment response was noted. For pretreatment MHPG R vs. NR, p < .005, and for pretreatment MHPG MR vs. NR, p < .05. Sex difference was resolved by correcting for creatinine excretions. Ratio of MHPG level pretreatment–treatment was significantly larger in responders vs. nonresponders (p < .05).
	(4) R (4)MR (4)NR			0.715 ± .390[c] 0.980 ± .172[c] 1.39 ± .24[c]	0.740 ± .082[c] 0.860 ± .263[c] 0.815 ± .190[c]	
	(b) (7) PD (2) MD (6) DN (1) ID	M = 5 F = 11	16	1.062 ± .094[c]	(IMI/DMI: 4th week) (13) 0.920 ± .070[d]	MHPG treatment levels increased in improvers. MHPG pretreatment was correlated with pretreatment minus treatment depression ratings (r = .54, p < .05). MHPG pretreatment vs. % depression, r = .55, p < .05, (treatment–pretreatment ratio). MHPG pretreatment had no correlation with depression scores. Compared with values of 5 normal women: 1.362 mg ± .085; no response in patients with levels greater than the normal mean. Depression ratings of 4th week treatment vs. pretreatment MHPG, r = .72, p < .001. MHPG pretreatment was correlated with pretreatment minus 4th week treatment depression ratings, r = .55, p < .05. MHPG pretreatment was correlated with % depression, r = –.63, p < .05.
	(a) + (b)	F = 18	18	Females treated with IMI		

Table I continues

173

Table I (*continued*)

Authors[a]	Diagnosis[b]	Sex	Total (N)	MHPG pretreatment (mg/24 h)	MHPG during treatment (mg/24 h)	Comments
3. Beckmann and Goodwin, 1975 (9) R (7) NR	UP	M = 5	16	1.10 ± .07 1.83 ± .13	(4) 1.01 ± .07 (3) 1.30 ± .25	Patients were selected for good response or lack of response to IMI. Pretreatment MHPG, R vs. NR, $p < .001$. IMI decreases MHPG levels, $p < .01$. Treatment MHPG levels, R < NR.
4. Perry *et al.* 1978		M = 14 F = 12		—	—	No relationship between treatment and response to IMI and MHPG. After 3-wk treatment, 10/12 improved. No difference in clinical response to placebo or mianserin (see D.1).
5. Cobbin *et al.*, 1979 Group A Control	(3) BP (23) UP	M = 8 F = 18 —	43	0.890^f	1.478	IMI, DMI, or nortriptyline in 200–350 mg/day at least for one-month duration. 15–18 increased MHPG levels at follow-up in Group A, which was unexpected. For comparison with high or normal pretreatment MHPG, see C.5.
6. Schatzberg *et al.*, 1980 (9)R, (4)NR (3)R, (8)NR	UP + BPII	M = 11 F = 12	24	≤1.950 >1.950	— —	Fisher's exact $p = .05$ (IMI response). Pretreatment values below 1.950 mg/24 h related to response at 2 wk with 150 mg/day raised to 300 mg by week 3 and 4 if not responding well.

Study	Type	Sex	N	MHPG	Treatment MHPG	Comments
7. Rosenbaum et al., 1980	UP	M = 8 F = 5	13	.1950	—	4-wk protocol completed by 8 parts. 5–6 with levels below .1950 mg/24 h responded and 6/7 with levels above .1950 mg/24 h also responded. Improvements were not significantly different in the two groups.
8. Maas et al., 1982	—	—	—	—	—	Multihospital study of IMI and AMI.
C. Amitriptyline						
1. Schildkraut et al., 1973 (3) R (3) NR	(4) BP (2) UP	M = 1 F = 5	6	$7.96 \pm .50g$ $3.66 \pm .20g$	—	One amitriptyline NR later responded to imipramine.
2. Beckmann and Goodwin, 1975 (4) R (4) NR	UP	M = 3 F = 5	8	$2.17 \pm .09$ $1.21 \pm .09$	$1.67 \pm .40$ $1.00 \pm .20$	A small group of patients was selected according to unequivocal response or lack of response to AMI. See Beckmann and Goodwin (B.3). Treatment MHPG levels decreased; $R > NR$, anxiety vs. MHPG: $r = .51$, $p < .01$ ($N = 41$). Pretreatment MHPG; $IMI < AMI$, $p < .05$.
3. Sacchetti et al., 1976	(11) UP	M = 5	5	(a) 1.420 1.003 (b) 0.565 0.615 0.620	—	Retarded depression was the primary affective disorder. Diet was controlled. 1.5 mg/kg ($\pm$ 105 mg/day) AMI qd for only 16 days. Antidepressant response in high MHPG patients by day 5 and 10; in Group B one patient had no response, in two patients after day 13; the strongest response was in Group A and sustained no relationship between MHPG changes and change in depression.

Table I continues

175

Table I (continued)

Authors[b]	Diagnosis[b]	Sex	Total (N)	MHPG pretreatment (mg/24 h)	MHPG during treatment (mg/24 h)	Comments
4. Coppen et al., 1979 (26)	UP	M = 3 F = 9	12	—	—	Dose was only 150 mg/day for 6 weeks. In 9 females MHPG levels correlated nonsignificantly with # depression score (Hamilton); $r = .22, p = $ NS.
5. Cobbin et al., 1979 Group B	(4) BP (5) UP	M = 3 F = 6	6	2.980	1.310	Group B; normal to high MHPG levels AMI treatment (200–500 mg/day). For Group A, see B.5. Controls: treated with IMI, AMI, DMI, NT, protriptyline, or doxepine as physician choice ($N = 43$). Duration of treatment (mean) 2.4 ± 1.4 months; Groups A and B were treated according to pretreatment MHPG levels; no control group was treated independently. Group B higher in guilt ($p < .001$); agitation ($p < .006$); diurnal variation ($p < .05$); females in paranoia ($p < .02$). 6/6 in Groups A and B; females more depressed ($p < .001$) and more suicides ($p < .05$); no difference between UP and BP in MHPG levels. For Group A see B.4. Groups A and B had significantly better treatment results than for
Control		M = 14 F = 28	43			

Study	Diagnosis	Sex	N			Notes
6. Modai et al., 1979 (5) R (10) NR	BP	—	15	1.79 1.11	1.95 1.77	control group expressed in Hamilton rating changes ($p <$ .05) or absolute treatment rating scores ($p <$ .05); it is unclear whether or not statistical analysis controlled for sample size differences. MHPG levels for R vs. NS, $p <$ .05. All patients improved. MHPG rose significantly ($p <$ .05) in all patients. Severity of depression did not correlate with pretreatment MHPG levels.
7. Spiker et al., 1980 (6) R (6) NR		M = 5 F = 13	18	2.148 ± .822	2.253 ± 1.065 2.460 ± .541	25 days of treatment, 14 days of 200 mg/24 h, 6 patients responded. No relationship between pretreatment values and response. AMI and nortriptyline blood levels were given, but no corrections were made for a therapeutic window. Pretreatment values for responders and nonresponders were not given, only a nonsignificant correlation with response.
8. Maas et al., 1982						See B.8
D. Nortriptyline Hollister et al. 1980 (9) low (8) high	UP (11) RP (6)	—	17	1.510 (0.869–1.751) 2.514 (2.047–3.097)	NP	Blood levels were 50–150 mg/ml. Lowest; 5/6 improved. Highest; 0/6 improved.
E. Mianserin Perry et al., 1978	(8) DN (8) PD	M = 2 F = 13	15	—	Increase	3rd week evaluation. No relationship between MHPG and treatment response and no difference in response with

Table I continues

177

Table I (*continued*)

Authors[a]	Diagnosis[b]	Sex	Total (N)	MHPG pretreatment (mg/24 h)	MHPG during treatment (mg/24 h)	Comments
						imipramine (see B.4) or placebo.
F. Maprotiline						
Schatzberg *et al.*, 1981 (9)R, (1)NR (3)R, (9)NR	UP (RDC)			≤1.950 >1.950	— —	Range was .797 to 3.417 mg/24 h. 150 mg (2 wk) up to 300 mg (4 wk). Patients with and without dropouts and inadequate dosage ($\chi^2 = 6.71$, $p < .01$). Low MHPG patients responded better at 2 wk; at 4 wk there was no significant difference. Significance between high and low MHPG: low at 4 wk; high MHPG levels for responders also; significant differences were lost when dropouts and patients with inadequate doses were excluded. Higher plasma levels needed in patients with higher pretreatment MHPG levels. Preliminary report in which imipramine or maprotiline responders had low values; see Rosenbaum *et al.*, 1980
G. Lithium						
Beckmann *et al.*, 1977	(5) BPI (3) BPII (2) UP	F = 10	10			Pretreatment MHPG levels did not separate R from NR. MHPG levels: BPI < UP ($p = .05$). Increased MHPG levels ($p < .01$) in responders on
(4) R (6) NR				0.87 ± .27 1.52 ± .35	1.12 ± .32 1.16 ± .25	

178

Drug / Study	Diagnosis	Sex	N			Comments
H. Phenelzine Beckmann and Murphy, 1977	UP (6) BPI (5) BPII (1)	M = 3 F = 9	12	1.67 ± .25	0.75 ± .12	Pretreatment depression ratings correlated with % MHPG change, $r = .71$, $p < .01$. Pretreatment MHPG did not separate R from NR, but pretreatment MHPG correlated with MAO, $r = .54$, $p < .05$ (unexpected). Patients with hypomanic or manic response showed decrease in MHPG levels. drug. Only female patients were used.
I. Flupenthixol Joseph et al., 1979	AS	M = 15 F = 12	27			Outcome measure: social function at 12 months postrial. MHPG levels declined in placebo responders. No decline in placebo nonresponders or in actively treated. Neuroleptic improvers exhibited a relative increase in MHPG levels.
(9) male good				1.47 ± .35		
(6) male poor				2.52 ± .77[h]		
(6) female good				2.00 ± .81		
(6) female poor				2.00 ± .68		

[a] The following abbreviations are used in the table: AS, acute schizophrenia; BP, bipolar; BPI, bipolar with mania; BPII, bipolar with hypomania; DN, depressive neurosis; ID, involutional depression; MD, manic–depressive; MR, moderate responders; NR, nonresponders; PD, psychotic depression; R, responders; SAD, schizo affected depression; UP, unipolar. The dash indicates that data were not provided.
[b] The parenthetical number indicates the number of patients.
[c] $p < .05$
[d] p not significant
[e] MHPG levels measured in mgMHPG/mg creatinine/24 h.
[f] Average for only 6 males and 12 females.
[g] MHPG levels measured in mgMHPG/gm creatinine/24 h.
[h] $p < .02$

179

tionship between pretreatment MHPG levels and clinical response was observed. Neurotic and psychotic depressed patients were studied for 21 days. No data were provided to evaluate this study. Patients responded in the same way to mianserin as to placebo and to imipramine treatment; in other words, the authors did not control for spontaneous remissions in their sample.

C. Maprotiline

Maprotiline is the only tetracyclic that has been studied. Schatzberg *et al.* (1981) observed that patients with pretreatment MHPG levels below the median of 1.950 mg/24 h tended to respond sooner (2 weeks) and with lower doses than patients with higher MHPG levels. At 4 weeks, with exclusion of dropouts and patients who did not receive high enough doses, no significant predicting effects of urinary MHPG excretion levels could be observed. It is possible that at higher doses other neuronal systems also are activated (e.g., serotonin). A preliminary version of this study was published by Rosenbaum *et al.* (1980). This is one of the few studies that included a consideration of blood levels.

D. Lithium

The antidepressant effects of lithium have been acknowledged and accepted (Mendels *et al.*, 1979; Schou, 1979), although the APA Task Force on Lithium had declined earlier to list depression as an indication for lithium treatment (Cohen *et al.*, 1975). Lithium has also prophylactic effects in patients with recurrent unipolar depressions (Shou, 1979) but these effects may last "only" up to 5 years (J. D. van Scheyen, personal communication, 1979). The antidepressant effects of lithium may take longer to develop than the antimanic effects, which may occur from 3 to 10 days after treatment is started, depending on how rapidly therapeutic steady-state blood levels are obtained. Beckmann *et al.* (1975) observed a nonsignificantly lower pretreatment urinary MHPG excretion level in depressed patients who had experienced an antidepressant response to lithium. van Kammen and Murphy (1979) observed a correlation between the third-week antidepressant response to lithium and an acute increase in activation euphoria with *d*-amphetamine administration in depressed inpatients, but only in unipolar and female patients. Whether gender is a more important variable than a unipolar or bipolar diagnosis to interpret *d*-amphetamine data for lithium response in this population is uncertain, inasmuch as the bipolar patient group in this study was comprised primarily of men and the unipolar group comprised mainly of women.

The patients in the study by Beckmann *et al.* (1975) were all female but included only two unipolar patients. Consistent with our observation (van Kammen and Murphy, 1979), other researchers have reported that gender may indeed be an influence on the antidepressant response to lithium (Donnelly *et al.*, 1978). These results need to be replicated before further conclusions can be drawn. Unipolar patients may respond to lithium as well as bipolar patients. Thus bivariate correlational evaluations are more likely to be informative in the unipolar group where there is, presumably, a wider range in levels of urinary MHPG excretion than in the bipolar patient group, which tends to have low MHPG levels anyway. In a more homogeneous group with lower MHPG levels, other variables that are relatively more specific to the antidepressant response may take precedence.

E. Phenelzine

The only group that evaluated the relationship between response to an MAO inhibitor, such as phenelzine, and urinary MHPG levels reported negative results in unipolar depressed patients (Beckmann and Murphy, 1977). These authors noted that platelet MAO levels in unipolar depressed patients correlated with MHPG levels ($r = .54$, $p < .05$). Belmaker *et al.* (1974) did not observe a significant correlation between MAO and MHPG in a group of normal subjects, but such a relationship may be present in a depressed population with, presumably, a dysregulated NE metabolism. Several reports have shown differences between depressed and normal subjects in urinary MHPG response to environmental stimuli such as diet (Muscettola *et al.*, 1977) and activity and anxiety (Beckmann and Goodwin, 1980; Hollister *et al.*, 1978; Sweeney *et al.*, 1978, 1979). Therefore, the significant MAO–MHPG correlation reported by Beckmann and Murphy (1977) requires replication in another depressed population. Edwards *et al.* (1979) studied MHPG excretion levels and platelet MAO levels in depressed and normal subjects but did not relate the two parameters to one another.

F. Drug-induced Mania

Zis *et al.* (1979a) studied the pretreatment MHPG levels of bipolar depressed patients who had switched into mania or hypomania on tricyclic antidepressants. They noted that the pretreatment levels correlated with the latency of onset of mania–hypomania (time on tricyclic antidepressant prior to occurrence of manic or hypomanic behavior; $r = .86$, $p < .001$); that is, patients with low MHPG levels tended to be more vulnerable to development of manic or hypomanic behavior. Beckman and Murphy (1977) noted that unipolar patients who became manic or hypomanic on phenelzine, an MAO inhibitor, had lower pretreatment MHPG excretion levels than patients who did not become manic, regardless of their antidepressant response to phenelzine. van Scheyen *et al.* (1979) reported 7 manic episodes in 50 previously diagnosed unipolar depressed patients (14%) who were treated with either amitriptyline or clomipramine and noted latency or mania in those patients who switched correlated with the age of onset of mania ($r = .92$, $p < .01$), as well as with duration of manic behavior ($r = .83$, $p < .02$). The latter two variables also correlated significantly with each other ($r = .82$, $p < .05$). Platelet MAO activity in five male patients correlated nonsignificantly with the latency of onset of mania ($r = .82$) (van Kammen *et al.*, 1980). Unfortunately, no pretreatment levels of urinary MHPG data were available (van Kammen *et al.*, 1980; van Scheyen and van Kammen, 1979). It is possible that this type of treatment response (i.e., induction of mania or hypomania) is more dependent on pretreatment levels of MHPG and NE than the therapeutic treatment response. The results of this section are summarized in Table II. The reader is cautioned and referred to Table I for further details. Only a few drugs have been studied adequately and with appropriate methodology.

TABLE II

Tentative Relationships between Antidepressant Drug Response and Pretreatment MHPG as Reported in the Literature Pretreatment Urinary MHPG Excretion

Drug	Low	Normal	High
d-Amphetamine	+[a]	±[b]	0
Imipramine	+	±	0
Desimipramine	(+)[c]	±	0
Nortriptyline	(+)	±	0
Amitriptyline		Probably no relationship	
Mianserin	?[d]		
Maprotiline	(+)	(+ In higher doses and later)	
Lithium		Possible relationship	
Phenelzine		No relationship	

[a] + indicates positive relationship with drug response.
[b] ± indicates uncertain relationship.
[c] (+) indicates possible prediction of drug response (similar to that of imipramine) but too few studies done to be conclusive.
[d] ? indicates that studies gathered inadequate information to draw conclusions.

III.   Drug Treatment Effects on MHPG Excretion

In evaluating these studies we assume that the changes in MHPG levels are expressions of the immediate drug effects on NE metabolism rather than on excretion by the kidney (see Table I).

A.   *d*-Amphetamine Effects

d-Amphetamine increases (Roffman *et al.*, 1977), decreases (Engberg and Svensson, 1979), or shows a varying effect (Calderini *et al.*, 1975) on MHPG levels in animals. In depressed patients Beckmann and associates (1976) noted that some patients with a strong response to *oral d*-amphetamine tended to show an increase in MHPG excretion levels whereas those who did not excreted a lower level of MHPG. Lithium pretreatment abolished a *d*-amphetamine-induced decrease in MHPG excretion levels (Beckmann *et al.*, 1976). This *d*-amphetamine-induced decrease is probably the primary drug effect, whereas the increase may represent a secondary response to activation of other biochemical systems or a rebound phenomenon. No information is available as to whether or not levels of urinary or CSF 5HIAA or homovanillic acid (HVA), the major dopmaine metabolite, would predict *d*-amphetamine response. In our drug-free schizophrenic patients levels of CSF MHPG but not of CSF HVA or 5HIAA predicted the change in psychosis following 20 mg dosage of *d*-amphetamine iv ($r = .58, p < .002$) (van Kammen *et al.*, 1982).

B.   Tricyclic Antidepressants

1. Imipramine Effects. Cobbin *et al.* (1979), Fawcett *et al.* (1972), and Maas *et al.* (1972) reported a decrease in urinary MHPG excretion in nonresponders to imipramine treatment and an increase or no change in responders. In contrast, Beckmann and Goodwin (1975) reported a decrease in all patients irrespective of response. The discrepancy among the groups may have been a result of low pretreatment values that normalized with improved behavior. Perry *et al.* (1978) studied 14 neurotic and psychotic depressed patients for 3 weeks and observed an increase. Their data are hard to interpret. They seemed to have used less than optimal doses, and no information was provided on the conditions under which the urine samples were collected (i.e., 1 or more days, which day of hospitalization, etc.).

2. Amitriptyline Effects. According to Beckmann *et al.* (1975) and to Schildkraut (1973, 1978a, 1978b), amitriptyline decreases MHPG excretion because all tricyclic antidepressants decrease deamination of NE in animal brain, presumably by blocking NE uptake. It is also conceivable that there is a decrease in NE synthesis and release. Apparently amitriptyline is more effective in 5HT deficiency depressions (i.e., low 5HIAA levels in urine or in CSF) (Goodwin *et al.*, 1979; Murphy *et al.*, 1979; van Praage, 1980). Coppen *et al.* (1979), Maas *et al.* (1982), Modai *et al.* (1979), and Spiker *et al.* (1980) reported that the change in MHPG and pretreatment MHPG levels did not predict amitriptyline response, thereby raising doubts about a role for NE in the amitriptyline response. Sacchetti *et al.* (1976) noted that MHPG level changes were unrelated to clinical response. The latter two studies may not have used sufficiently high daily doses (150 mg/day and 1.5 mg/kg, respectively). Furthermore, if the treatment evaluation takes place before 3 weeks (Perry *et al.*, 1978; Sacchetti *et al.*, 1976), such a study will not give interpretable data. Modai *et al.* (1979) found an increase in MHPG in 9 out of 15 bipolar depressed patients.

3. Mianserin Effects. Perry *et al.* (1979) reported an increase in levels of urinary MHPG during mianserin treatment but no individual or group data were given.

C. Lithium Effects

Beckmann *et al.* (1975) reported an increase in MHPG excretion in responders to lithium and a variable increase or decrease in the nonresponders.

D. Phenelzine Effects

Beckmann and Murphy (1977) noted that phenelzine decreased MHPG excretion levels regardless of response, although MHPG levels were not decreased very much. Phenelzine decreases the firing rate of the locus coeruleus and decreases MHPG production (Costa *et al.*, in press). Obviously, other MAO inhibitors such as deprenyl, which has amphetamine as a metabolite, or clorgyline need to be studied.

E. Summary

In summary, the results of the studies of drug effects on urinary MHPG excretion are confusing and hard to interpret. Improvement, drug effects, changes in activity, eating habits, sleep, etc. may have affected the urinary excretion data.

IV. Discussion

Low urinary MHPG excretion levels appear to predict a positive response to imipramine, desipramine, nortriptyline, and d-amphetamine and possibly to maprotiline (Rosenbaum, et al., 1980; Schatzberg et al., 1980, 1981). Beckmann and Goodwin (1975a) and Schildkraut (1973, 1978a) indicated a therapeutic response to amitriptyline in those depressed patients with high pretreatment levels of MHPG, but this could not be confirmed (Maas et al., 1982). Other negative prediction studies for amitriptyline frequently had design problems or failed to report enough data to be evaluated. Of the researched articles only the negative study by Coppen et al. (1979) and the multicenter study by Maas et al. (1980) evaluated MHPG and 5HIAA excretion (or CSF 5HIAA) for the same patient population. The studies show, however, that there is considerable overlap in MHPG levels between the two drug responder groups. Presumably, low MHPG excretion levels may predict amitriptyline response in those who metabolize amitriptyline mainly into nortriptyline. On the other hand, the concentration cut-off point for "low" MHPG levels of Schildkraut is above the mean of nonresponders by other investigators. A clinical reality remains that some patients will respond to each of the two drugs whereas others will respond to neither of them. Furthermore, there is just one single positive report about maprotiline response and a negative one for mianserin response, which suggests that clinical application is premature as a predictor for specific antidepressant drug response other than for drugs like imipramine (Maas et al., 1982).

Beckmann and Goodwin (1975), Maas et al. (1972), and Perry et al.

(1978) reported an increase with tricyclic antidepressants in responders, but Spiker *et al.* (1980) did not observe this. Pickar *et al.* (1978) noted an increase with change in clinical state. It is therefore necessary to control for spontaneous recovery, particularly in studies that evaluate patients immediately following admission (Perry *et al.*, 1978) and to ensure adequate treatment dose, i.e., blood levels.

Low urinary MHPG excretion levels seem to be as effective as a possible response predictor for *d*-amphetamine as they are for imipramine (Fawcett *et al.*, 1972; Goodwin *et al.*, 1979; Maas *et al.*, 1972; Maas *et al.*, 1982). That significant correlations between responses to acute oral *d*-amphetamine and to chronic treatment with tricyclic drugs were observed is intriguing (Table III). There is increasing evidence that plasma drug levels of tricyclic antidepressants (Kessler, 1978; Reisby *et al.*, 1977; Robinson *et al.*, 1979) and of *d*-amphetamine (Ebert *et al.*, 1976) relate to the respective behavioral responses. Either the two drugs use similar metabolism and absorption pathways or, as with lithium, certain minimal blood levels need to be obtained to observe clinical change. A question may be raised whether these results only indicate that the brain can or cannot respond with a change in behavior to pharmacological interventions. Such studies obviously need to be replicated. Although unipolar depressed patients are presumably more likely to respond to imipramine than to lithium, those patients with low urinary MHPG levels and a positive response to *d*-amphetamine should have some antidepressant response to lithium. This is an extrapolation that needs to be tested in the appropriate patient population with carefully designed methodology. On the other hand, van Kammen and Murphy (1978, 1979) did not find a significant correlation between platelet MAO activity and *d*-amphetamine or imipramine response in depressed patients, whereas lithium responders tended to have (nonsignificantly) higher platelet MAO activity than nonresponders (van Kammen and Murphy, 1979; Nurnberger *et al.*, 1979).

Differences in urinary MHPG excretion levels between males and females and between bipolar and unipolar patients have been reported. Generally, reports included more women than men (Beckmann *et al.*, 1975, 1977; Cobbin *et al.*, 1979; Coppen *et al.*, 1979; Fawcett and Siomopoulos, 1971; Fawcett *et al.*, 1972; Maas *et al.*, 1972; Schildkraut, 1973) and more unipolar (Beckmann *et al.*, 1977; Cobbin *et al.*, 1979; Coppen *et al.*, 1979; Sacchetti *et al.*, 1976; Schatzberg, in press) than bipolar patients. This limits the generalizability of the findings. Bipolar patients are frequently described as having lower MHPG levels than unipolar patients, but no difference in response to imipramine or amitriptyline has been reported in these two diagnostic categories separately. Beckmann and Goodwin (1980) observed that by correcting for systolic blood pressure, MHPG differences between these two diagnostic subgroups disappeared. Purportedly, amitriptyline affects 5HT systems more than it does NE systems, whereas this may be the opposite for imipramine (Goodwin *et al.*, 1979; Murphy *et al.*, 1979; van Praag, 1980). On the other hand, nortriptyline, which is a metabolite of amitriptyline, has effects similar to imipramine. One wonders whether retarded bipolar depressed patients would respond better to imipramine than to amitriptyline.

Several authors (Shaw *et al.*, 1973; Tang *et al.*, 1981) found that spinal fluid, plasma, and urinary excretion levels of MHPG did not change in similar directions with changes in clinical state or activity. This raises further questions about the interpretations of MHPG levels and drug response.

If MHPG excretion levels vary as much in schizophrenic patients (Taube *et al.*, 1978) as they do in depressed patients and normal controls, similar drug-prediction studies could be done for antipsychotic drug response in schizophrenia. To date, only one group has reported such a study looking for outcome at 12 months (Table I) (Joseph *et al.*, 1976). However, in our own experience adequate urinary collections are hard to obtain in psychotic patients and particularly in those who are ambivalent or negativistic (van Kammen *et al.*, unpublished observations). Hollister *et al.* (1978, 1980) expressed the same concerns for depressed patients. These difficulties might explain why most studies employ small numbers of subjects. If future studies establish *plasma* MHPG levels as a drug-response predictor, such technical problems will be solved (for a review of plasma MHPG see Leckman and Maas, Chapter 6, this volume).

A pattern is emerging for clinical applicability of urinary MHPG excretion levels as a moderate predictor of treatment response for some antidepressant drugs (i.e., imipramine, desimipramine, and nortriptyline) and drug induction of mania or hypomania (Beckmann and Murphy, 1977; Zis *et al.*, 1979a). Unfortunately, MHPG values appear discrepant across studies (see Table I), and treatment evaluations are frequently inadequate (e.g., too short, no drug levels available, no control for spontaneous recovery, etc.). Furthermore, studies of relationships between MHPG and the response to newer drugs, such as mianserin or maprotiline, are of a preliminary nature and no reports are available for zimelidine, iprindole, ludiomil, trazodone, nomifensine, fluoxetene, and others. It appears timely to do carefully controlled, well-designed prospective studies with large numbers of patients such as that reported by Maas *et al.* (1982). Tentatively, antidepressant drugs with a

TABLE III

Drug Response Prediction by d-Amphetamine[a]

Authors	Diagnosis[b]	N	d-Amphetamine response				Comments
			Δ Activation	Δ Euphoria	Δ Depression	Δ Thinking disturbance cluster	
A. Imipramine or Desimipramine							
1. Fawcett and Siomopoulos, 1971	(8) PD	13	—	—	—	—	2 × 15 mg d-amphetamine was administered po. Δ amphetamine vs. 3rd week depression Δ: $r = .66$, $p < .05$; Δ amphetamine vs. 4th week depression Δ: $r = .69$, $p < .05$. If suicide (not improved) and early discharge (is improved) included: $r = .76$ (3rd week) and $r = .89$ (4th week), $p < .01$. 12 of 13 patients included in Fawcett et al. (1972) study.
	(3) MD						
	(2) DN						
Amphetamine response	(7)R, (6)NR						
Imipramine response	(8)R, (5)NR						
2. van Kammen and Murphy, 1978	(9)UP	13	.61[c]	.61[c]	−.48[d]	—	The acute self-rated change following d-amphetamine and the 4th week treatment response to imipramine. 30 mg d-amphetamine was administered po in the A.M. d-Amphetamine response: no relationship with MAO. Self-ratings correlated significantly with observed ratings ($r = .49 − .85$, $p < .05 − .001$).
	(4)BP						
B. Lithium							
1. van Kammen and Murphy, 1979	(11) UP	18	.29	.28	−.30	—	30-mg d-amphetamine were administered in the A.M. Lithium response: no relationship with platelet MAO in men and women with either d-amphetamine or lithium response.
	(7) BP		.79[e]	.68[d]	−.56[f]	—	
	(10) Women		−.04	−.12	−.12	—	
	(8) Men		.49[f]	.49[f]	−.45[f]	—	
	(11) UP		−.06	−.17	−.17	—	
	(7) BP		.75[d]	.67[d]	−.45	—	
	(9) UP Women						
2. van Kammen et al., 1981	S	20	—	—	—	−.60	20-mg d-amphetamine were administered iv in the A.M. A 3rd week lithium response was noted. In drug free schizophrenic patients a stepwise multiple regression predicted the autopsychotic effect of lithium (for the total group $r^2 = .43$, $p = .003$; for the psychic group $r^2 = .54$, $p ≤ .02$; for the nonpsychotic depressed group $r^2 = .52$, $p = .03$).
	(10) P					−.60	
	(10) NPD					−.78	
	(11) Men					−.73	
	(9) Women					−.15	

[a] The following abbreviations are used in the table: BP, bipolar; DN, depressive neurosis; MD, manic-depressive; NPD, nonpsychotic depressive; NR, nonresponders; P, psychotic; PD, psychotic depression; R, responders; S, schizophrenic; UP, unipolar. The dash indicates that data were not provided.
[b] The parenthetical number indicates the number of patients.
[c] $p < .01$.
[d] $p < .05$ (2 tailed).
[e] $p < .001$ (2 tailed).
[f] $p < .05$ (1 tailed).

major effect on NE could be chosen for depressed patients with low MHPG excretion levels. The 5HIAA findings by Maas *et al.* (1982) and the reports by Schatzberg *et al.* (1980, 1981) support the notion that the concept of affective illness caused by or associated with abnormality in only one neurotransmittor system is somehow too simple. Evaluating less explored potential "markers" of response prediction with levels of urinary MHPG excretion for predicting subsequent clinical response might be one such research approach. At present, urinary MHPG level determination appears to have some limited value in the choice of some antidepressant medications, i.e., imipramine, desipramine, or nortriptyline response. The utility of pretreatment urinary MHPG levels in the choice of other antidepressants is either limited or needs to be determined by future research.

V. Summary

Depressed patients who respond to imipramine, desimipramine, and nortryptiline have lower pretreatment levels of 24-h urinary 3-methoxy-4-hydroxyphenethyleneglycol (MHPG) than either nonresponders or responders to amitriptyline. Overlap, however, occurs in urinary MHPG levels for subjects who respond subsequently to either drug. Only a few unreplicated studies with lithium, MAO inhibitors, and other tri-, tetra-, or bicyclic antidepressants have been published with mixed results. Low MHPG excretion levels may be a predictor of the latency time of onset of drug-induced mania as well. *d*-Amphetamine response may predict imipramine response also. In drug response prediction studies, adequate duration of treatment, dose, or drug level need to be assured and spontaneous recovery rate controlled in order to provide interpretable results. Preliminary studies with MHPG excretion levels and *d*-amphetamine suggest that those two could be used together as "predictors" for clinical response to imipramine treatment. Pretreatment urinary MHPG levels appear to have some limited clinical value as a single aid for choosing certain antidepressants.

Acknowledgment

The author gratefully acknowledges Dorothy Drake for typing assistance and William Z. Potter, M. D., Ph.D., and Giovanni Muscettola, Ph.D., for reading the manuscript.

References

Beckmann, H., and Goodwin, F. K. 1975. *Arch. Gen. Psychiatry* **32**, 17–21.

Beckmann, H., and Goodwin, F. K. 1980. *Neuropsychobiol.* **6**, 91–100.

Beckmann, H., and Murphy, D. L. 1977. *Neuropsychobiol.* **3**, 49–55.

Beckmann, H., St. Laurent, J., and Goodwin, F. K. 1975. *Psychopharmacologia* **42**, 277–282.

Beckmann, H., van Kammen, D. P., Goodwin, F. K., and Murphy, D. L. 1976. *Biol. Psychiatry* **11**, 377–387.

Belmaker, R., Beckmann, H., Goodwin, F. K., Murphy, D. L., Pollin, W., Buchsbaum, M., Wyatt, R., Ciaronella, P., and Lamprecht, F. 1974. *Life Sci.* **16**, 275–280.

Bielski, R. J., and Friedel, R. O. 1976. *Arch. Gen. Psychiatry* **33**, 1479–1489.

Bunney, W. E., Jr., and Davis, J. M. 1965. *Arch. Gen. Psychiatry* **13**, 483–494.

Calderini, G., Morselli, P. L., and Garattini, S. 1975. *Eur. J. Pharmacol.* **34**, 345–350.

Cobbin, D. M., Requin-Blow, B., Williams, L. R., and Williams, W. O. 1979. *Arch. Gen. Psychiatry* **36**, 1111–1115.

Cohen, I. M., Bunney, W. E., Jr., Cole, J. O., Fieve, R., Gershon, S., and Prien, R. F. 1975. *Am. J. Psychiatry* **132**, 997–1001.

Coppen, A., Rama Rao, V. A., Ruthven, C. R. J., Goodwin, B. L., and Sandler, M. 1979. *Psychopharmacol.* **64**, 95–97.

Crawley, J. N., Maas, J. W., Roth, R. M. 1979. *Psychopharmacol. Bull.* **15**(2), 27–29.

Donnelly, E. F., Goodwin, F. K., Waldman, I. N., Murphy, D. L. 1978. *Am. J. Psychiatry* **135**, 552–556.

Ebert, M. H., van Kammen, D. P., and Murphy, D. L. 1976. *Pharmacokinetics, Psychoactive Blood Levels and Clinical Response* (L. Gottschalk and S. Merlis, eds.), pp. 157–169. Spectrum Publications, New York.

Edwards, D. J., Spiker, D. G., Kuper, D. J., and Neil, J. F. 1979. *Catecholamines: Basic and Clinical Frontiers* (E. Usdin, I. Kopin, and J. Barchas, eds.), pp. 1869–1871. Pergamon Press, New York.

Engberg, G., and Svensson, T. N. 1979. *Life Sci.* **24**, 2245–2254.

Fawcett, J. A., and Siomopoulos, V. 1971. *Arch. Gen. Psychiatry* **25**, 247–255.

Fawcett, J. A., Maas, J. W., and Dekirmenjian, H. 1972. *Arch. Gen. Psychiatry* **26**, 246–251.

Goodwin, F. K., Cowdry, R. W., and Webster, M. N. 1979. *Psychopharmacology: A Generation of Progress* (M. A. Lipton, A. Dimascio, and K. F. Killam, eds.), pp. 1277–1288. Raven Press, New York.

Goodwin, F. K., and Potter, W. Z. 1979. *Catecholamines—Basic and Clinical Frontiers,* Vol. II (E. Usdin, I. Kopin, and J. Barchas, eds.), pp. 1863–1865. Pergamon Press, Oxford.

Hollister, L. E., Davis, K. L., Overall, J. E., and Anderson, T. 1978. *Arch. Gen. Psychiatry* **35**, 1410–1415.

Hollister, L. E., Davis, K. L., and Berger, P. A. 1980. *Arch. Gen. Psychiatry* **37**, 1107–1110.

Joseph, M. N., Baker, H. F., Johnstone, E. C., and Crow, T. J. 1976. *Psychopharmacol.* **51**, 47–51.

Kessler, K. A. 1978. *Psychopharmacology: A Generation of Progress* (M. A. Lipton, A. DiMascio, and K. F. Killam, eds.), pp. 1289–1302. Raven Press, New York.

Klerman, G. L. 1972. *J. Psychiatr. Res.* **9**, 253–270.

Maas, J. W., Fawcett, J. A., and Dekirmenjian, H. 1972. *Arch. Gen. Psychiatry* **26**, 252–267.

Maas, J. W., Kocsis, J. H., Bowden, C. L., Davis, J. M., Redmond, D. E., Hanin, I., Robbins, E., and Mendels, J. 1982. *Psychological Medicine,* in press.

Mendels, J., Ramsey, T. A., Dyson, W. L., and Frazier, A. 1979. *Lithium: Controversies and*

Unresolved Issues (T. B. Cooper, S. Gershon, N. S. Kline, and M. Schou, eds.), pp. 35–47. Excerpta Medica, New York.

Modai, I., Apten, A., Giolomb, M., and Wijsenbeek, M. 1979. *Neuropsychobiol.* **5,** 181–184.

Morris, J. B., and Beck, A. T. 1974. *Arch. Gen. Psychiatry* **30,** 667–674.

Murphy, D. L., Campbell, I., and Costa, J. L. 1979. *Psychopharmacology: A Generation of Progress* (M. A. Lipton, A. DiMascio, and K. F. Killam, eds.),

Muscettola, G., Wehr, T., and Goodwin, F. K. 1977. *Am. J. Psychiatry* **134,** 914–916.

Nurnberger, J. I. Jr., Gershon, E. S., Murphy, D. L., Buchsbaum, M. S., Goodwin, F. K., Post, R. M., Lake, C. R., Guroff, J. J., and McGinniss, M. H. 1979. *Lithium: Conflicts and Unresolved Issues* (T. B. Cooper, S. Gershon, N. S. Kline, and M. Schou, eds.), pp. 241–256. Excerpta Medica, New York.

Pickar, D., Sweeney, D. R., Maas, J. W., and Heninger, G. R. 1978. *Arch. Gen. Psychiatry* **35,** 1378–1383.

Perry, G. F., Fitzsimmons, B., Shapiro, and L. Irwin, P. 1978. *Br. J. Clin. Pharmacol.* **5,** 355–415.

Quitkin, F., Rifkin, A., and D. F. Klein 1979. *Arch. Gen. Psychiatry* **35,** 749–760.

Reisby, N., Gram, L. F., Bech, P., Nagy, A., Peterscn, G. O., Ortmann, J., Ibsen, I., Dencker, S. J., Jacobsen, O., Krautwald, O., Søndergaard, I., and Christiansen, J. 1977. *Psychopharmacol.* **54,** 263–272.

Robinson, D. S., Cooper, T. B., Ravaris, C. L., Ives, J. O., Nies, A., Bartlett, D., and Lamborn, K. R. 1979. *Psychopharmacol.* **63,** 223–231.

Roffman, M., Kling, M. A., Casses, G., Orsulak, P. J., Reigle, T. G., and Schildkraut, J. J. 1977. *Comm. Psychopharmacol.* **1,** 195–201.

Rosenbaum, A. H., Schatzberg, A. F., Maruta, T., Orsulak, P. J., Cole, J. O., Grab, E. L., and Schildkraut, I. J. 1980. *Am. J. Psychiatry* **137,** 1090–1092.

Sacchetti, E., Smeraldi, E., Cagnasso, M., Biondi, P. A., and Bellodi, L. 1976. *Int. J. Pharmacopsychiatry* **11,** 157–162.

Schatzberg, A. F., Rosenbaum, A. H., Orsulak, P. J., Rohde, W. A., Maruta, T., Kruger, E. R., Cole, J. O., and Schildkraut, J. J. 1981. *Psychopharmacol.* **73,** 34–38.

Schatzberg, A. F., Orsulak, P. J., Rosenbaum, A. H., Maruta, T., Kruger, E. R., Cole, J. O., and Schildkraut, J. J. 1980. *Comm. Psychopharmacol.* **4,** 441–445.

Schildkraut, J. J. 1965. *Am. J. Psychiatry* **122,** 509–522.

Schildkraut, J. J. 1973. *Am. J. Psychiatry* **130,** 695–699.

Schildkraut, J. J. 1978a. *Depression: Clinical, Biological and Psychological Perspectives* (E. Usdin, ed.), pp. 166–197. Brunner Mazel, New York.

Schildkraut, J. J. 1978b. *Psychopharmacology: A Generation of Progress* (M. A. Lipton, A. DiMascio, and K. J. Killam, eds.), pp. 1223–1234. Raven Press, New York.

Schou, M. 1979. *Arch. Gen. Psychiatry* **36,** 849–851.

Shaw, D. M., O'Keefe, R., MacSweeney, D. A., Brooksbank, B. W. L., Noguera, R., and Coppen, A. 1973. *Psycho. Med.* **3,** 333–336.

Spiker, D. G., Edwards, D., Hansen, J., Neil, J. F., and Kupfer, D. J. 1980. *Am. J. Psychiatry* **137,** 1183–1187.

Sweeney, D. R., Maas, J. W., Heninger, G. R. 1978. *Arch. Gen. Psychiatry* **35,** 1418–1423.

Sweeney, D. R., Maas, J. W., Pickar, D. 1979. *Catecholamines: Basic and Clinical Frontiers* (E. Usdin, I. J. Kopin, and J. Barchas, eds.), pp. 1917–1919. Pergamon Press, New York.

Tang, S. W., Stancer, M. C., Takahashi, S., Shephard, R. J., and Hank, J. J. 1981. *Psychiatry Res.* **4,** 13–20.

Taube, S. L., Kirstein, L. S., Sweeney, D. R., Heninger, G. R., Maas, J. W. 1976. *Am. J. Psychiatry* **135,** 78–82.

van Kammen, D. P., and Murphy, D. L. 1978. *Am. J. Psychiatry* **135,** 1179–1184.

van Kammen, D. P., and Murphy, D. L. 1979. *Neuropsychobiol.* **5,** 266–273.

van Kammen, D. P., and Bunney, W. E., Jr. 1979. *Catecholamines: Basic and Clinical Frontiers* (E. Usdin, I. J. Kopin, and J. Barchas, eds.), pp. 1896–1898. Pergamon Press, New York.

van Kammen, D. P., Bunney, W. E., Jr., Docherty, J. P., Marder, S. R., Ebert, M. H., Rosenblatt, J. E., and Rayner, J. N. 1982. *Am. J. Psychiatry* **139,** 991–997.

van Kammen, D. P., van Scheyen, J. D., and Murphy, D. L. 1980. *Biol. Psychiatry* **15,** 565–573.

van Praag, H. M. 1980. *Compr. Psychiatry* **21,** 30–43.

van Scheyen, J., and van Kammen, D. P. 1979. *Arch. Gen. Psychiatry* **36,** 560–565.

Zis, A. P., Cowdry, R. W., Wehr, T. A., Muscettola, G., and Goodwin, F. K. 1979a. *J. Psychiatr. Res.* **1,** 93–99.

Zis, A. P., and Goodwin, F. K. 1979b. *Arch. Gen. Psychiatry* **36,** 1097–1107.

10

Clinical Studies of MHPG in Childhood and Adolescence*

J. GERALD YOUNG
DONALD J. COHEN
BENNETT A. SHAYWITZ
GEORGE M. ANDERSON
JAMES W. MAAS†

Yale University School of Medicine, New Haven

*The research was supported in part by MHCRC grant MH30929, CCRC grant RR00125, NICHD grant HD-03008, the W. T. Grant Foundation, the MacArthur Foundation, Mr. Leonard Berger, and The Solomon R. & Rebecca D. Baker Foundation, Inc.

†Present address: The University of Texas Health Science Center at San Antonio, San Antonio, Texas.

MHPG: BASIC MECHANISMS
AND PSYCHOPATHOLOGY

I.   Introduction

Attention, arousal, anxiety, activity level, movement, affect, appetite, sleep, memory, and learning are dimensions of behavior affected by the neuropsychiatric disorders of childhood. Psychotic disorders afflict approximately 6 per 10,000 children (Fish and Rityo, 1979), mental retardation affects 1 to 3% of the population (Work, 1979), and a "moderate" disturbance, such as attention deficit disorder (ADD) and hyperactivity, has a prevalence of 4 to 10%, depending on the criteria used (Eisenberg, 1979; Silver, 1979). In order to understand the underlying biology of the disorders affecting so many children, clinical research has focused on neuronal systems that regulate these behaviors (Young and Cohen, 1979). Brain noradrenergic systems, for example, have been implicated in all these areas of function (Amaral and Sinnamon, 1977; Mason and Fibiger, 1979a,b; Redmond and Huang, 1979). Several research groups have studied brain norepinephrine (NE) metabolism in children by measurement of 3-methoxy-4-hydroxyphenethyleneglycol (MHPG), the major metabolite of NE in the brain (Maas and Landis, 1968; Schanberg *et al.*, 1968; Tabakoff and DeLeon-Jones, Chapter 1), based on the possibility that levels of MHPG in body fluids provide an index of noradrenergic activity (Crawley *et al.*, 1978, 1979, 1980, 1981; DeMet and Halaris, 1979; Hancock and Fougerousse, 1976; Korf *et al.*, 1973a; Maas *et al.*, 1976, 1977, 1979a; Nygren and Olson, 1977; and Roth, Chapter 2).

II.   MHPG in Body Fluids

Consideration regarding units of measurement, sources of variance, and optimal collection period for MHPG samples obtained from children are initially based on adult data. It is often assumed that the adult findings hold true for children and adolescents, but maturational effects alter metabolic processes, and a new look at each parameter in childhood is required. One of the first steps for any pediatric investigator is mapping the flow of developmental change.

A.   Units of Expression for MHPG in Body Fluids

MHPG levels in cerebrospinal fluid (CSF), plasma, and urine are expressed in concentration units (e.g., μg MHPG/ml urine), although the concentration unit for urinary MHPG is then converted to another form of expression in order to assess metabolite production over a longer time interval, or in relation to an index of body size and metabolic rate. Urinary MHPG concentration is most commonly expressed as μg/24 h, a reflection of total noradrenergic function over a full day, so that transient changes tend to be obliterated. A second method used to express urinary MHPG concentration takes advantage of the relatively stable production of creatinine from day to day in an individual (Greenblatt *et al.*, 1976); specification of the urinary creatinine is useful for demonstrating that the 24-h urine collection was complete (particularly important when collecting specimens from such difficult patient groups as autistic children). In addition, expression of the urinary MHPG level as μg MHPG/mg creatinine relates MHPG production to general body metabolism and minimizes the effects of minor loss of urine in 24-h collections. A third method corrects for the confounding effects of body size by expressing urinary MHPG levels as μg MHPG/24 h/m^2 of body surface area (Tietz, 1976). The results obtained by use of the three methods are highly correlated. Continued change in body size and metabolic function during childhood makes the use of units that take this into account particularly important. Expression of urinary MHPG levels according to mg creatinine or m^2 of body surface is the most direct method for children, although covarying for these effects during data analysis is an alternative approach. If one of these methods is not used, comparison of MHPG levels across individuals or groups can give specious results.

The alternative units for MHPG in body fluids reflect different clinical applications. Cerebrospinal fluid (CSF) MHPG may monitor brain noradrenergic activity most directly, serving as a critical reference for the physiological relevance of the other two measures. CSF MHPG reflects central noradrenergic activity over a relatively short time interval; the probenecid technique is not used to estimate turnover of the parent amine over a longer time interval because MHPG is not an acid metabolite whose egress is blocked by probenecid [as is homovanillic acid (HVA)] (Kessler *et al.*, 1976). Plasma MHPG levels are subject to short-term influences of both a physiological (diurnal variation, pulsatile secretion) (Leckman and Maas, 1981) and environmental (stress) nature (Cassens *et al.*, 1980; Korf *et al.*, 1973b). Clinical measurement of plasma MHPG levels requires stringent control over the circumstances in which it is obtained, and several sequential samples are necessary, particularly in children who may be confused and frightened by hospitalization.

Urinary MHPG levels are a less sensitive measure for short-term changes in noradrenergic function, but 24-h urine collections are optimal for assessing "baseline" noradrenergic function in situations in which it is judged likely to be profoundly altered (e.g., in disease states or after prolonged stress). In this case, its muted response to short-term change is an advantage. Most clinical studies of MHPG in childhood have utilized 24-h urine collections.

MHPG exists in free and conjugated (sulfate and glucuronide) forms in body fluids and is reported as free, conjugated, or total MHPG (the sum of the first two) (DeMet and Halaris, 1979). MHPG is largely in the free form in human brain, so that measurement of free MHPG is most useful for clinical studies using CSF and plasma samples (Leckman and Maas, Chapter 3 and Hattox, Chapter 5). Only a small proportion (8%) of urinary MHPG is in the free form, and total MHPG appears to be the most suitable measurement for urine samples (Hattox, Chapter 5). Maturational processes may alter the distribution of these forms of MHPG, and they need to be examined in childhood.

B. Sources of Variance in Clinical Studies of MHPG Levels

Studies of adults indicate that plasma-conjugated MHPG (Jimerson et al., 1981) and urinary total MHPG levels (Maas et al., 1973) are higher in men than women, but no sex-related difference in plasma-free MHPG levels has been shown. Studies of MHPG levels in children include few girls, so that sex-based differences cannot be evaluated.

The pulsatile release of MHPG into plasma is a source of considerable variance (Maas et al., 1980). An estimated mean hour-to-hour variation of $\pm 12\%$ in adults, with a maximum individual change of 43%, necessitates the use of sequential samples (Leckman and Maas, Chapter 6, this volume) in order to avoid errors when establishing baseline values and interpreting the response to challenge by stress or medication. The marked variance observed in adults will be assumed to characterize children until specific studies have been completed. Optimal assessment of the physiology of MHPG production and clearance in the plasma requires the determination of two or more levels at baseline conditions, followed by three or more determinations following an acute intervention.

A slight increase in MHPG excretion for normal adults occurs at 4:00 to 6:00 in the afternoon (Hollister et al., 1978; Wehr et al., 1980), whereas plasma MHPG levels appear to reach a peak at noon (Leckman et al., 1980; Swann et al., 1980; Sweeney et al., 1980). Comparison of 12-h samples in children did not show any differences between daytime and nighttime urinary MHPG levels (Brown et al., 1981). Clarification of diurnal changes requires thorough studies; in the interim, clinical studies should hold the time of sampling stable across individuals and studies.

The coefficient of variation for urinary 24-h MHPG levels in adults over a few days is 13%; when measured over a longer period (several weeks), the coefficient of variation increases to 25% (Hollister *et al.*, 1978). No comparable studies have been completed in children. Our preliminary investigation of urinary-free catecholamines has indicated a marked day-to-day variance, in which autistic children with low mean urinary-free catecholamine levels show high-normal levels on occasional days. Because there appeared to be a correspondance between urinary-free catecholamines and MHPG levels in pilot studies of autistic children (Young *et al.*, 1978, 1979), the urinary MHPG levels might be similarly subject to wide daily variation. One study of intrasubject variability of noradrenergic function in hyperactive children showed large mean coefficients of variation for supine plasma NE (20%) and DBH (27%) across days (Mikkelsen *et al.*, 1981). Until this source of variance is examined, studies utilizing single 24-h collections must be interpreted with caution.

C.   Collection Period for Urinary MHPG

The difficulty of obtaining 24-h urine samples makes the collection of urinary MHPG over shorter time periods very attractive, but the degree of correspondence among 24-h, 12-h, 6-h, and smaller samples is not yet known. (For an example of the potential information to be derived from successive short collection periods, see Potter *et al.*, Chapter 8, this volume, and Wehr *et al.*, 1980.) Presumably, a minimal time interval is reached at which the urinary MHPG levels begin to reflect transient influences on MHPG production in a way similar to plasma MHPG levels; the urinary measure then becomes useful in a new way, at the same time that it loses its capacity to reflect an integrated longer period of baseline noradrenergic function. Short collection periods ranging from one to a few hours have been used in studies of urinary catecholamines and are particularly practical for biological assessment of a child in his normal environment. Catecholamine levels are known to be very responsive, so that short collections might be more likely to reflect any environmental determinants under study. Similarly, because novelty influences catecholamine levels, it is advantageous for the collection to take place in the child's usual environment (Frankenhaeuser, 1975).

III.   24-Hour Urinary MHPG in Childhood

A.   Hyperactive Children

Hyperactive boys may have lower mean 24-h urinary MHPG levels than normal boys, but the distributions of the hyperactive and control groups overlap broadly (Shekim *et al.,* 1977; 1979a, 1979b), and there are dissenting studies (Khan and Dekirmenjian, 1981; Rapoport *et al.,* 1978; Wender *et al.,* 1971). A number of studies have attempted further discrimination of characteristics of the hyperactive boys in relation to MHPG excretion levels. These have included (1) investigation of the response to drugs acting on catecholamine neuronal systems (*d*-amphetamine, levodopa–carbidopa, and piribedil); (2) comparison of subgroups with normal to high pretreatment urinary MHPG levels to those with low MHPG levels, including their drug response and their association with clinical variables; (3) the relationship of drug response to the presence or absence of soft neurological signs; and (4) simultaneous measurement of levels of other urinary metabolites. MHPG excretion is also decreased in nonhyperactive, learning-disabled children when compared to controls (Shekim and Dekirmenjian, 1978). A reduction in 24-h urinary MHPG level in hyperactive or learning-disabled boys is not specific to these diagnostic groups, and its meaning requires further study (Table I).

When *d*-amphetamine is administered to hyperactive boys, MHPG excretion decreases (Brown *et al.,* 1981; Shekim *et al.,* 1977, 1979a, 1979b), an effect observed in some adult patient groups (Fawcett *et al.,* 1972). Other investigators describe a decrease that fails to reach statistical significance in normal and hyperactive subjects (Rapoport *et al.,* 1978; Wender *et al.,* 1971). The time at which the urinary MHPG levels response to amphetamine is measured may be a critical factor in that one study (Brown *et al.,* 1981) suggests that there may be a progressive decline in urinary MHPG levels for a week or more (Table II).

These findings mean that *d*-amphetamine simultaneously reduces symptoms, but aggravates the metabolic abnormality suggested to be a marker for the illness (low urinary MHPG level). There is no simple clinical–biological relationship to explain the possible reduction in urinary MHPG levels in hyperactive boys. Studies of the effects of carbidopa–levodopa and piribedil in hyperactive boys make this point again. According to the hypothesis that some children with hyperactivity might have a relative dopamine deficiency, L-dopa should be a beneficial medication. Although L-dopa does lead to a reduction in hyperactivity and some improvement in a vigilance measure, the overall effects are much less substantial than those achieved with d-amphetamine (Langer et al.,1981). The partial clinical improvement is accompanied by the expected increase in urinary MHPG levels (due to administration of large amounts of precursor, Table III), in contrast to the decrease observed with amphetamine-induced clinical improvement. Another attempt to bolster dopaminergic function in these children, by administering piribedil (a dopamine agonist), failed to elicit clinical improvement (Brown, 1979). Thus three drugs administered in order to achieve a similar effect on catecholamine systems led to a good clinical response, a partial clinical response, and a lack of response, along with inconsistent effects on urinary MHPG levels.

Division of hyperactive boys into those with normal to high MHPG excretion levels and those with low urinary MHPG levels does not lead to any association between high or low MHPG excretion levels and clinical variables. In fact, in both the normal-high and -low MHPG groups, the clinical responders to d-amphetamine show a reduction in MHPG excretion levels, whereas the nonresponders do not, regardless of their baseline MHPG level (Shekim et al., 1979b), consistent with another study in which clinical responders to d-amphetamine had a decrease in urinary MHPG levels whereas one nonresponder showed an increased MHPG excretion level (Brown et al., 1981). The responder group, which shows a decrease in urinary MHPG levels following d-amphetamine, also has more soft neurological signs (Shekim et al., 1979a); the presence of soft neurologic signs has previously been suggested as a predictor for favorable clinical response to stimulants (Satterfield et al., 1973).

Reduction in urinary MHPG during a single dose trial with d-amphetamine might serve as a metabolic marker for the subgroup of hyperactive children most likely to benefit; it also might begin to clarify the underlying molecular mechanism for symptom reduction. Among the 21 hyperactive boys studied before and after d-amphetamine treatment by Shekim and his colleagues, there were 15 responders and 6 nonresponders. The responders showed a reduction in urinary MHPG levels after stimulant treatment, whereas nonresponders did not (Shekim et al., 1979b). In addition, pretreatment urinary MHPG levels were higher in responders than in nonresponders. The percentage change in conduct problems and activity (measured by Factors I and IV on Conners Teacher Questionnaire) after treatment was correlated with the percentage change in urinary MHPG levels (Shekim et al., 1979b). Although further studies of noradrenergic metabolism in hyperactive

TABLE I

24-Hour Urinary MHPG Levels During Childhood

Subject group and investigators	N and Status		Urinary MHPG (mean ± SD)			Urinary creatinine	Urinary volume
			μg/24 h	μg/24 h/m²	μg/mg Creatinine		
Normal boys							
Khan and Dekirmenjian, 1981	10	opts[b]	648.9	384	.67	701.4	—[f]
McKnew and Cytryn, 1979	18	opts	—	1092 ± 109[a]	—	—	—
Rapoport et al., 1978	14	opts	960 ± 400	—	1.80 ± .73	587 ± 207	605 ± 459
Shekim et al., 1979b	13	opts	1042 ± 243	925 ± 161	1.66 ± .31	642 ± 173	—
[a]Wender et al., 1971	6	inpts[c]	—	—	1.62 ± .33	—	—
Young et al., 1979	9	inpts	766 ± 132	—	.92	837 ± 177	802 ± 197
Normal bedridden orthopedic patients							
McKnew and Cytryn, 1979	9	inpts	—	504 ± 32[a]	—	—	—

	N						
Chronically depressed children							
McKnew and Cytryn, 1979	9	inpts	—	753 ± 64[a]	—	—	—
Hyperactive boys							
Brown et al., 1981	8	inpts	—	—	1.74 ± .49	—	—
Khan and Dekirmenjian, 1981	10	opts	829.5	777	1.17	733	—
Langer et al., 1981	6	inpts	670 ± 310	—	1.73 ± .61	—	—
Rapoport et al., 1978	13	opts	1180 ± 470	—	1.69 ± .31	733 ± 367	625 ± 382
Shekim et al., 1979b	23	inpts	740 ± 306	687 ± 245	1.22 ± .47	640 ± 212	—
[d]Wender et al., 1971	9	inpts	—	—	1.43 ± .66	—	—
Infantile autism							
Young et al., 1979	5	inpts	538 ± 149	—	.81	622 ± 288	1210 ± 496
CSNA[e]							
Shekim et al., 1980	1	inpt	70 ± 23	90 ± 29	.22 ± .08	351 ± 131	514 ± 151

[a] SEM
[b] opts refers to outpatients
[c] inpts refers to inpatients
[d] includes one girl
[e] CSNA refers to Congenital Sensory Neuropathy with Anhydrosis
[f] The dash indicates that data were not available.

TABLE II
24-Hour Urinary MHPG Response to d-Amphetamine in Hyperactive Boys

Subject group and Investigators	N	Dose	Pretreatment	μg MHPG/mg creatinine (mean ± SD) Posttreatment			
				1 Day	3 Days	8 Days	14 Days
Normal subjects							
Rapoport et al., 1978	14	.5 mg/kg/day	1.80 ± .73	1.50 ± .47	—[d]	—	—
Hyperactive subjects							
Brown et al., 1981	8	.74 mg/kg/day	1.74 ± .49	—	1.42 ± .27	1.31 ± .22[a]	—
Rapoport et al., 1978	13	.5 mg/kg/day	1.69 ± .31	1.41 ± .48	—	—	—
Shekim et al., 1979b	21	.5 mg/kg/day	1.20 ± .47	—	—	—	.83 ± .29[b]
[c]Wender et al., 1971	9	10–20 mg/day	1.43 ± .66	—	—	—	1.30 ± .58

[a] $< .05$ (posttreatment vs. pretreatment levels)
[b] $p < .01$
[c] includes one girl
[d] The dash indicates that data were not available.

TABLE III
24-Hour Urinary MHPG Response to Carbidopa–Levodopa in Hyperactive Boys[a]

| | Baseline | 3 Weeks posttreatment | |
		Placebo	Carbidopa–Levodopa
N	6	6	6
Dosage	—[d]	—	60/600 mg/day
Urinary MHPG			
μg/24 h	670 ± 310	610 ± 310	1,030 ± 610[b]
(mean ± SD)			
μg/mg, creatinine	1.73 ± 0.61	1.75 ± 0.80	3.09 ± 1.28[c]
(mean ± SD)			

[a] From Langer et al. (1982).
[b] $p < .05$
[c] $p < .01$ ANOVA
[d] The dash indicates that no active medication was administered.

children could lead to discrimination of a subgroup amenable to treatment with stimulants, the molecular basis for differences in metabolic response in responder and nonresponder groups is a much more complicated problem. Also, because responders have higher urinary MHPG levels than nonresponders, the reduced mean urinary MHPG level for the entire hyperactive group might be due to the inclusion of the nonresponder group. Decreased urinary MHPG levels might be a nonspecific finding unrelated to this diagnostic group or indicative of a poor prognosis.

Another method for establishing the meaning of MHPG levels in childhood disorders is simultaneous measurement of levels of other urinary metabolites [e.g., urinary normetanephrine (NM), metanephrine (MN), and homovanillic acid (HVA)]. Homovanillic acid, the major metabolite of dopamine (DA), may be an index of concurrent central and peripheral dopaminergic effects of the stimulants; the methylated urinary catecholamine metabolites, NM and MN, derive predominantly from peripheral metabolic pools. Urinary HVA does not differentiate hyperactive and control groups or responders from nonresponders nor is it altered following d-amphetamine administration (Brown et al., 1981; Rapoport et al., 1978; Wender et al., 1971). Similarly, urinary MN levels are not a consistent discriminator of these clinical groups (Shekim et al., 1979b; Wender et al., 1971). On the other hand, urinary NM levels are increased in both hyperactive and learning-disabled boys as compared to normal controls (Shekim et al., 1979b; Shekim and Dekirmenjian, 1978; Wender et al., 1971). Urinary NM levels are not significantly altered by

d-amphetamine and are similar in responder and nonresponder groups. The MHPG : NM ratio, suggested to reflect central versus peripheral noradrenergic activity, is sharply reduced in hyperactive and learning-disabled groups, but is not altered by d-amphetamine (Shekim et al., 1979b).

Levels of vanillylmandelic acid (VMA), a product of peripheral NE metabolism, are increased by administration of carbidopa–levodopa to hyperactive boys, as are MHPG levels (Langer et al., 1981). This parallel change may reflect increased NE synthesis, both centrally and peripherally, subsequent to precursor administration. However, plasma NE levels do not increase, just as they show no increase after d-amphetamine administration in most studies (Langer et al., 1981, and personal communication concerning a more recent study; Mikkelsen et al., 1981; Rapoport et al., 1978; Wender et al., 1971).

An alternative strategy for distinguishing central and peripheral contributions to MHPG and HVA production is the use of debrisoquin sulfate, a monoamine oxidase inhibitor (Karoum et al., 1974; Medina et al., 1969). The peripheral output of HVA is diminished by debrisoquin without affecting central HVA production because debrisoquin does not cross the blood–brain barrier. However, in contrast to its lack of effect on CNS HVA production debrisoquin does decrease central MHPG production by an unknown mechanism, so that there is a significantly greater reduction of plasma MHPG levels than plasma HVA levels (Maas et al., 1979b). Low doses of debrisoquin produce a reduction reaching approximately 80% of human plasma HVA and MHPG produced peripherally, so that 75% of the plasma metabolites are derived from brain. During debrisoquin treatment, plasma MHPG and HVA levels are correlated (Swann et al., 1980). Our initial studies of debrisoquin as a treatment for the postulated noradrenergic excess in some Tourette's syndrome (TS) patients suggest its utility for dissecting noradrenergic and dopaminergic functions in this disorder; following a few days of debrisoquin treatment, a child's plasma HVA level was quite low, in agreement with the reduced DA turnover indicated by low CSF–HVA levels (Cohen et all, 1978).

B. Affective Disorders of Childhood

Children hospitalized with chronic depression have reduced urinary MHPG levels as compared to normal outpatient boys (Table I) (McKnew and Cytryn, 1979); the values are similar to the reduction in urinary

MHPG levels found in subgroups of adults with depression (Maas *et al.*, 1973). The broad range of values in the control group overlaps the range of MHPG levels among depressed patients and extends to much higher levels. A straightforward interpretation of these findings is discouraged by results obtained in a third group: hospitalized children who suffered a leg fracture 3 or more weeks prior to sample collection. They were carefully screened to exclude other physical or mental disorders. Their mean urinary MHPG excretion level was lower than either of the other two groups, and the range of values was very narrow among the eight patients (McKnew and Cytryn, 1979). Because their mean urinary MHPG level was significantly lower than that of the depressed children, the meaning of reduced MHPG levels in childhood depression is unclear. An initial explanation suggested that the relative urinary MHPG levels for the three groups reflect their activity levels; the bedridden fracture patients would be expected to have lower activity levels than depressed patients. However, some studies of adults have not demonstrated a relationship between activity levels and urinary MHPG excretion levels, whereas others have (Hollister *et al.*, 1978; Sweeney *et al.*, 1979). (Beckmann *et al.*, 1976; Ebert *et al.*, 1972; Post *et al.*, 1973; for a detailed discussion of this issue, see Potter *et al.*, Chapter 8, this volume.) Finally, simultaneous measurement of urinary NE and VMA levels in the three groups of children showed no differences across the groups for these compounds. Because urinary VMA and NE levels have also been suggested to reflect activity levels, some other explanation for the group differences in MHPG levels must also be considered. A tentative hypothesis of these investigators is that bedridden orthopedic patients experience a suppression of their "general arousal system" in response to their helplessness following an injury (McKnew and Cytryn, 1979).

An early study of affective disorders in children included one hypomanic child. Although his urinary NE and VMA levels were not markedly different than the mean for the control group, his urinary MHPG level was quite low (463 ± 49 $\mu g/m^2/24$ h) (Cytryn and McKnew, *et al.*, 1974).

C. Infantile Autism

Infantile autism is a more severe and pervasive disorder than hyperactivity or depression. Such children are characterized by impaired bonding and social relationships, language and cognitive deficits, speech abnormalities, involuntary sterotypic movements, and a desire to maintain a sameness in their surroundings. Most are very active and suffer from impaired regulation of arousal, attention, and anxiety (Fish and Ritvo, 1979). Autistic children have reduced 24-h urinary MHPG levels as compared to same-aged normal boys, both groups studied as inpatients (Young et al., 1979). Similar urinary volumes and creatinine excretion in the two groups indicate that the difficult urine collections from these children were complete. The reduction in MHPG excretion levels is not related to activity levels because most autistic patients are very active even while hospitalized.

Simultaneous measurement of free catecholamine excretion in these autistic children showed them also to be reduced in comparison to the control group (Young et al., 1978). The method for the determination of urinary-free catecholamines measures NE and epinephrine, but not dopamine. Free NE accounts for 80–90% of the free catecholamines measured (Crout, 1961). Although free catecholamines are predominantly derived from peripheral noradrenergic activity, two points suggest that this measure could be useful in studies of infantile autism. First, disturbances in attention and arousal can be monitored through cardiovascular indices of sympathetic function and might be correlated with peripheral fluid concentrations of NE, the sympathetic neurotransmitter. Cardiovascular correlates are altered in autism (Cohen and Johnson, 1977). Second, there is reason to expect a correspondance between urinary levels of free NE and MHPG because the locus coeruleus may exert a regulatory influence on peripheral sympathetic function through extensive pathways to the brainstem and spinal cord. In this sense, even peripherally derived MHPG is responsive to prevailing central noradrenergic activity (Crawley et al., 1978, 1979, 1980a,c; Hancock and Fougerousse, 1976; Nygren and Olson, 1977).

The disordered regulatory mechanisms in autism (including repetitive sterotypic movements, rushes of anxiety, impaired attention and arousal, and hyperactivity in many children) led to the anticipation of increased noradrenergic function in autism. The unexpected reduction might reflect a developmental vulnerability or a response to persistent stress and anxiety, but its actual origin, and whether it is primary or secondary, needs further study (Young et al., 1978).

Although 24-h urinary MHPG levels have not been measured in mentally retarded children, the levels in seven adults with Down syndrome were not different than controls; 24-h urinary HVA levels were significantly reduced in Down's syndrome patients (Mann et al., 1980). These results suggest that urinary MHPG levels are not simply reduced in all severe neuropsychiatric disorders of childhood but might be the basis for discrimination among some groups.

D. Congenital Sensory Neuropathy

Congenital sensory neuropathy with anhydrosis (CSNA) is a rare syndrome, thought to be inherited in an autosomal recessive pattern, whose symptoms reflect a disorder of the autonomic nervous system (ANS). It is characterized by an absence of deep and superficial pain sensitivity, disturbed thermoregulation, absence of sweating, vasomotor instability (erythematous blotching of skin), aplasia of dental enamel, mental retardation, self-mutilation, hypoglycemia, blond hair, blue or blue-green eyes, and fair complexion. These patients fail to produce a flare in response to intradermal histamine or to perspire in response to pilocarpine. Abnormalities on psychophysiological measures are also present; for example, serially presented auditory signals do not induce the usual phasic electrodermal activity (Daniel et al., 1980). Assessment of sympathetic nervous system (SNS) function of a child with CSNA, through measurement of levels of urinary metabolites, led to intriguing findings. The 24-h urinary levels of both MHPG and NM were markedly lower than those in an age-, weight-, and height-matched group of four boys, with the extreme reduction in levels reflecting both central and peripheral loss of noradrenergic function. Urinary VMA levels were also decreased as compared with those from seven hyperactive boys, as would be expected with SNS impairment. On the other hand, urinary metanephrine levels, representing principally the activity of the adrenal medulla, were not abnormal. Urinary HVA levels, reflecting dopaminergic function, were also not reduced when corrected by creatinine excretion (Shekim et al., 1980).

The pattern of the patient's metabolic excretion fits the profile predicted by the clinical symptoms of impaired SNS function: impaired central and peripheral noradrenergic dysfunction and intact dopaminergic and adrenal medullary (epinephrine) function.

E. Normal Boys

The levels of urinary MHPG established for normal boys in various studies are generally similar (Table I). It is important that the normal range be determined with accuracy because it overlaps the distributions of clinical groups with abnormal mean MHPG levels. At this point, disorders reported to include abnormal MHPG excretion levels are characterized by a mean decrease, with a mean increase in only one study (Khan and Dekermenjian, 1981). The mean MHPG excretion level for normal boys may eventually be lower than that indicated by the initial studies. The sources of variance described earlier need to be carefully delineated in future studies, particularly clarification of day-to-day changes and establishment of age-related norms.

IV. Cerebrospinal Fluid and Plasma MHPG in Childhood

Until recently, clinical investigators were unable to measure CSF and plasma MHPG levels, due to the very low concentrations (1–20 ng/ml) in these fluids. Measurement requires the use of gas chromatography–mass spectrometry (GC–MS) for accurate, reliable determinations in the lower concentration range (<10 ng/ml), especially when small variance is critical, rather than the more widely available gas chromatographic methods used for measurement of urinary MHPG levels (see Chapter 5, this volume). A new liquid chromatographic method for the determination of CSF MHPG levels is reliable, simple, and inexpensive (Anderson et al., 1981), so that determinations of CSF MHPG levels will now be more easily included in studies of noradrenergic metabolism.

Differences in the interpretation of urinary, plasma, and CSF MHPG levels, the sources of variance peculiar to each, and their potential applications were discussed in a preceding section. The choice of free, conjugated, or total MHPG levels in plasma or CSF was also described; free MHPG is the principal form produced by human brain metabolism, and studies in childhood have utilized this measure.

A. CSF-Free MHPG in Infantile Autism and Tourette's Syndrome

Because of ethical constraints on performing a lumbar puncture, CSF MHPG levels cannot be determined in normal children; but these levels might be measured in essentially normal contrast groups (children worked up for recurrent headaches, dizziness, etc., with no abnormal neurological or laboratory findings). Using CSF MHPG levels of adult neuropsychiatric patients for comparison, the CSF MHPG levels of six medication-free autistic boys were normal. CSF MHPG levels measured in six children with Tourette's syndrome (TS) of chronic multiple tics, each of whom either received probenecid loading or recently discontinued a medication, were distributed into two groups. Four patients were within the "normal" range, whereas two TS patients had increased

CSF MHPG levels (near 15 ng/ml) (Fig. 1). The two patients with increased CSF MHPG levels suggest a subgroup of Tourette's syndrome patients with increased noradrenergic activity, perhaps responsive to treatment with agents that reduce central noradrenergic activity, such as clonidine (Young *et al.*, 1981c).

B. Plasma-Free MHPG in Normal Boys, Infantile Autism, and Tourette's Syndrome

Plasma MHPG levels of normal boys were within the "normal" range for adults. Autistic and TS patients who had not received any medication for a month or longer also had plasma MHPG levels in this range (Fig. 2). However, among seven TS patients taking medication, two had increased plasma-free MHPG levels; each had discontinued a medication active at the dopamine receptor 3 weeks before venipuncture (pimozide and haloperidol) (Young *et al.*, 1981c). Elevated plasma-free MHPG levels in these children might indicate a subgroup of TS patients with impaired noradrenergic function or might be drug induced. Increased plasma-free MHPG levels in these patients could be related to an interac-

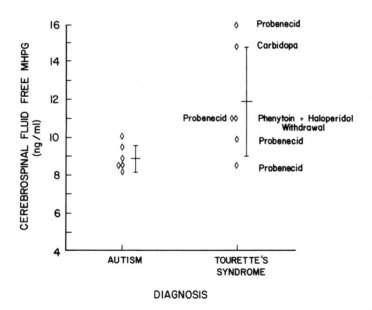

Fig. 1. Cerebrospinal fluid free MHPG levels in patients with Tourette's Syndrome (medicated) and infantile autism (not medicated).

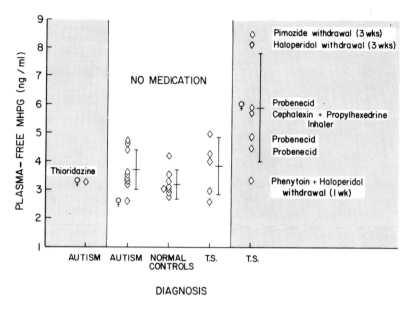

Fig. 2. Plasma-free MHPG levels in medicated and nonmedicated subjects: infantile autism, Tourette's Syndrome (TS), and normal controls. Three female patients are indicated; the remainder are males.

tion of the NE and DA neuronal systems, secondary to a supersensitive DA receptor following withdrawal of an agent active at the receptor.

C. Response of CSF and Plasma-Free MHPG to Clonidine

Clonidine is a partial noradrenergic agonist that, when administered in low doses, preferentially acts at the afferent input to the principal nucleus of noradrenergic cell bodies in the brain, the locus coeruleus. Low doses of clonidine reduce the firing rate of neurons in the locus coeruleus and the production of MHPG in brain by selective activation of presynaptic α_2-receptors (Anden *et al.*, 1970; Cedarbaum and Aghajanian, 1977; Svensson *et al.*, 1975). Elevated CSF-free MHPG in a TS patient suggested a subgroup of TS patients with increased noradrenergic activity that might be responsive to an agent that reduces brain noradrenergic activity (Cohen *et al.*, 1979a). An open trial of clonidine indicated that it achieves substantial symptom reduction in approximately 70% of TS patients (Cohen *et al.*, 1979b, 1980).

The level of CSF-free MHPG was measured in a single patient before and after a challenge dose of clonidine. His baseline level of 14.8 ng/ml was reduced to 10.4 ng/ml free MHPG after 1 month of clonidine treatment, accompanied by a good clinical response (Young *et al.*, 1981b).

Three TS patients, unmedicated for at least 1 month, were given challenge doses of medication, and plasma-free MHPG levels were obtained at baseline, 2, and 22 h following medication administration. A 25–40% reduction in plasma-free MHPG levels was observed following a challenge dose of clonidine (two severely disturbed patients) or haloperidol (a single patient with mild symptoms). All three patients had a good clinical response when treated with the challenge medication. Plasma-free MHPG levels have not yet been measured in a medication-free nonresponder (Young *et al.*, 1981b).

Challenge doses of clonidine given while a (responder) patient is on a maintenance dose indicate that a metabolic response can still be achieved. Plasma-free MHPG levels, which had been very high at baseline in one patient, were reduced in the two postclonidine samples. The other responder given a clonidine challenge dose (while on a maintenance dose) had a 40% increase in plasma-free MHPG level at the 2-h postclonidine point, before it was eventually reduced below baseline at 22 h. One patient, who did not have a good clinical response while on maintenance clonidine, also did not have a decrease in plasma-free MHPG level following clonidine challenge (Young *et al.*, 1981b). Further studies of clinical nonresponders will help clarify the relationship between plasma-free MHPG levels and clinical response to clonidine.

The use of other medications at the time of a clonidine trial tends to obscure changes in plasma-free MHPG levels. For example, while plasma MHPG levels might decrease during haloperidol treatment, it might increase during acute withdrawal from haloperidol.

A trial of clonidine was also attempted for two adolescent girls and one young adult man with infantile autism and led to a slight aggravation of their symptoms. Clonidine challenge produced a 40% increase in plasma-free MHPG level in the autistic girl in whom it was measured (Young *et al.*, 1981b).

V. Correspondence of MHPG Levels Measured Simultaneously in CSF, Plasma, and Urine

A strong correlation between plasma-free and urinary total MHPG levels in eight normal boys (Fig. 3) suggests that noradrenergic function

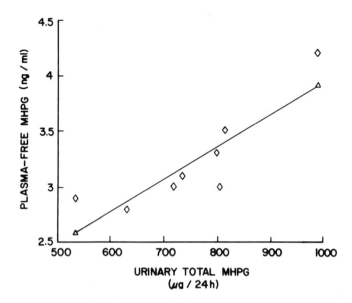

Fig. 3. Relationship between plasma-free MHPG and urinary total MHPG levels in normal boys. Mean age was 11.8 ± 1.6 years, mean plasma-free MHPG level was 3.2 ± .5 μg/24 h, and mean urinary total MHPG level was 753 ± 136 μg/24 h; where $r = .87, p = .005, N = 8$, and $y = 1.04 + .003x$.

may be sufficiently stable for it to be reflected in both plasma and urinary measures (Young *et al.*, 1981c). This is in contrast to the lack of correlation between plasma-free MHPG and urinary total MHPG levels observed in nine adult neuropsychiatric patients, although an outlier may have confounded this potential relationship (Sweeney *et al.*, 1980). In studies of normal adults, significant positive correlations between (1) plasma-free or -conjugated MHPG and CSF total MHPG levels (Jimerson *et al.*, 1981) and (2) urinary total MHPG and CSF-free MHPG levels (Maas *et al.*, 1982) indicate that there might be a correspondence among MHPG levels in the three body fluids. The small number of subjects in these studies, developmental changes in the pattern of NE secretion and metabolism, sampling inconsistency due to the secretion of free MHPG into the plasma in pulses (rather than continuously), the conversion of MHPG to VMA in the periphery (Blombery *et al.*, 1980), and the underlying disease in the patient group are among the factors that might contribute to discrepancies. The number of patients with simultaneous MHPG determinations in two or three body fluids must be increased and specific conditions affecting their relationships studied before the relationships among these measures can be established.

VI. Developmental Changes in MHPG Levels

Investigation of the relationship between age and MHPG level in human physiological fluids has generated mixed results, but the preponderance of evidence points to increasing noradrenergic function with age. An increase in urinary total MHPG, plasma-free MHPG, and plasma-conjugated MHPG levels appears to occur in normal subjects (Jimerson et al., 1981). Increasing CSF-free MHPG levels has been suggested in patients with infantile autism and Tourette's syndrome (a nonsignificant increase in small patient groups) (Young et al., 1981c), but CSF MHPG levels did not change with age in a large group of patients with a variety of neurological disorders (Seifert et al., 1979). Urinary total MHPG increases with age in autistic children (Young et al., 1979).

These inconsistencies in reported developmental effects on MHPG levels will be clarified (1) when they are established in normal subjects, without the confounding impact of disease; (2) when they are measured in large subject groups; and (3) when individuals are followed over long periods of time rather than relying on cross-sectional studies at a specific age. In addition, the direction of change with age depends on the specific period of life in which it is determined: childhood, adolescence, adulthood, or old age. Finally, a sense of developmental changes in function of a neuronal system can be assessed in humans only through indirect studies of multiple compounds related to the neurotransmitter for the neuronal system; this includes synthesizing and catabolic enzymes, precursors, metabolites, and the neurotransmitter and its receptor. Assessment of all these components of a neuronal system describes its developmental profile and how this profile is related to the development of other neuronal systems. This type of assessment of multiple studies suggests that the NE neuronal system shows increasing activity through childhood and adolescence, whereas the dopaminergic system shows decreasing activity (Young et al., 1981a). When developmental profiles are established in normal subjects, investigation of patient groups might indicate an alteration in the developmental pattern of a neuronal system for a specific patient group. For example, there are preliminary differences in the pattern of development of some compounds related to noradrenergic function in autistic children, which serve as a model for this type of investigation (Young *et al.*, 1981a).

VII.   Functional Significance of MHPG Levels

MHPG levels are assessed in relation to clinical indices, such as diagnostic groups and behavioral dimensions, or other neurochemical or neuroendocrine measures, in order to establish their functional significance. For example, changes in MHPG levels following clonidine are accompanied by effects on behavior, altered levels of other metabolites, and a selective neuroendocrine response; the various effects are not simultaneous and vary in magnitude. The marked increase of growth hormone (GH) following clonidine (Lal *et al.*, 1975; Gil-Ad *et al.*, 1979) is a more robust, acute response than the change in plasma MHPG levels (Leckman *et al.*, 1980, 1981; Young *et al.*, 1981b), suggesting that clonidine might have clinical application as a GH stimulation test and that GH response might be a sensitive test of brain function in some neuropsychiatric disorders. In a more basic way, the discrete effects of clonidine on specific clinical parameters (blood pressure, sedation, and motor regulation) reflect the distinct action of clonidine effects on specific noradrenergic neuronal subsystems (hypothalamic, brainstem, etc.) in relation to the more general noradrenergic effect presumably reflected in MHPG levels (Rudolph *et al.*, 1980). Because these effects are neither simultaneous nor of the same magnitude evaluation of other regulatory influences (such as dopaminergic or serotonergic effects) will help to dissect components of critical control mechanisms acting on individual parameters.

An example of the initial direction of such studies is a comparison of plasma MHPG and HVA levels before and after a 12-week trial of clonidine in 6 TS patients. There were significant increases after 12 weeks of clonidine in the baseline morning levels of both plasma MHPG (15% increase) and plasma HVA (77% increase) (Leckman *et al.*, 1982; Leckman and Maas, Chapter 6, this volume). Although the specific physiological mechanisms underlying these metabolic changes will require extensive investigation, the data suggest an interaction between the noradrenergic and dopaminergic systems in these patients. This interaction may mediate an increase in central DA turnover from the apparently low baseline turnover found in TS (Cohen *et al.*, 1978, 1979a, Leckman and Maas, Chapter 6, this volume).

VIII. Overview

Clinical studies of MHPG levels in childhood give encouraging evidence for the utility of MHPG levels as a clinical measure of noradrenergic function. MHPG levels may be useful in the discrimination of diagnostic groups or specific dimensions of behavior and for studying the maturation of the noradrenergic system. Because MHPG levels are altered by medications used in childhood disorders, MHPG has a potential use as a clinical marker guiding treatment choice. Initial work indicates a correspondence among MHPG levels in the three body fluids, suggesting the clinical relevance of plasma and urinary levels for estimating central noradrenergic activity. The broad range of behaviors and symptoms affected by noradrenergic function in children makes the prospect of monitoring the activity of this neuronal system a challenging impetus for further biological studies in childhood disorders.

Acknowledgments

We are grateful to Ms. M. E. Kavanagh, Ms. K. Burgess, Ms. J. Detlor, Ms. J. Holliday, Ms. D. Harcherik, Mr. H. Landis, Ms. E. Waldron, and Drs. B. Caparulo, G. Heninger, S. Hattox, and J. Leckman for their assistance in these studies; to M. Carey, R.N., M. Genel, M.D., and the staff of the Children's Clinical Research Center for patient care and research assistance; and to Ms. M. Cone for preparation of the manuscript.

References

Amaral, D. G., and Sinnamon, H. M. 1977. *Prog. Neurobiol.* **9,** 147–196.
Anden, M. E., Corrodi, H., Fuxe, K., Hökfelt, B., Hökfelt, T., Rydin, C., and Svensson, T. 1970. *Life Sci.* **9,** 513–523.
Anderson, G. M., Young, J. G., Cohen, D. J., Shaywitz, B. A., and Batter, D. K. 1981. *J. Chromatogr.* **222,** 112–115.

Beckmann, H., van Kammen, D. P., Goodwin, F. K., and Murphy, D. L. 1976. *Biol. Psychiatry* **11**, 377–387.

Blomberry, P. A., Kopin, I. J., Gordon, E. K., Markey, S. P., and Ebert, M. H. 1980. *Arch. Gen. Psychiatry* **37**, 1095–1098.

Brown, G. L., Ebert, M. H., Hunt, R. D., & Rapoport, J. L. 1981. *Biol. Psychiatry* **16**, 779–787.

Brown, G. L., Ebert, M. H., Mikkelsen, E. J., Buchsbaum, M., and Bunney, W. E., Jr. 1979. Dopamine agonist piribedil in hyperactive children, presented at annual meeting of American Psychiatric Association, Chicago, 1979. *Syllabus and Scientific Proceedings*, pp. 254–255.

Cassens, G., Roffman, M., Kuruc, A., Orsulak, P. J., and Schildkraut, J. J. 1980. *Science* **209**, 1138–1140.

Cedarbaum, J. M., and Aghajanian, G. K. 1977. *Eur. J. Pharmacol.* **44**, 375–385.

Cohen, D. J., and Johnson, W. T. 1977. *Arch. Gen. Psychiatry* **34**, 561–567.

Cohen, D. J., Shaywitz, B. A., Caparulo, B., Young, J. G., and Bowers, M. B., Jr. 1978. *Arch. Gen. Psychiatry* **35**, 245–250.

Cohen, D. J., Shaywitz, B. A., Young, J. G., Carbonari, C. M., Nathanson, J. A., Lieberman, D., and Bowers, M. B., Jr. 1979a. *J. Am. Acad. Child Psychiatry* **18**, 320–341.

Cohen, D. J., Young, J. G., Nathanson, J. A., and Shaywitz, B. A. 1979b. *Lancet*, Sept. 15, 551–553.

Cohen, D. J., Detlor, J., Young, J. G., and Shaywitz, B. A. 1980. *Arch. Gen. Psychiatry* **37**, 1350–1357.

Crawley, J. N., Hattox, S. E., Maas, J. W., and Roth, R. H. 1978. *Brain Res.* **141**, 380–384.

Crawley, J. N., Maas, J. W., and Roth, R. H. 1979. *Catecholamines: Basic and Clinical Frontiers* (E. Usdin, I. J. Kopin, and J. Barchas, eds.), pp. 678–680. Pergamon Press, New York.

Crawley, J. N., Maas, J. W., and Roth, R. H. 1980. *Brain Res.* **183**, 301–311.

Crawley, J. N., Roth, R. H., and Maas, J. W. 1981. *Brain Res.* in press.

Crout, J. R. 1961. *Standard Methods of Clinical Chemistry* (D. Seligson, ed.), pp. 62–80. Academic Press, New York.

Cytryn, L., McKnew, D. H., Jr., Logue, M., and Desai, R. B. 1974. *Arch. Gen. Psychiatry* **31**, 659–661.

Daniel, A., Shekim, W. O., Koresko, R. L., and Dekirmenjian, H. 1980. *Develpm. Behav. Ped.* **1**, 49–53.

DeMet, E. M., and Halaris, A. E. 1979. *Biochem. Pharmacol.* **28**, 3043–3050.

Ebert, M. H., Post, R. M., and Goodwin, F. K. 1972. *Lancet* **2**, 766.

Eisenberg, L. 1979. *Basic Handbook of Child Psychiatry* (J. D. Noshpitz, ed.), Vol. II, pp. 439–453. Basic Books, New York.

Fawcett, J., Maas, J. W., and Dekirmenjian, H. 1972. *Arch. Gen. Psychiatry* **26**, 246–251.

Fish, B., and Ritvo, E. R. 1979. *Basic Handbook of Child Psychiatry* (J. D. Noshpitz, ed.), Vol. II, pp. 249–304. Basic Books, New York.

Frankenhaeuser, M. 1975. *Emotions—Their Parameters and Measurement* (L. Levi, ed.), pp. 209–234. Raven Press, New York.

Gil-Ad, I., Topper, E., and Laron, Z. 1979. *Lancet* **2**, 278–280.

Gold, M. S., Donabedian, R. K., and Redmond, D. E., Jr. 1978. *Psychoneuroendocrinol.* **3**, 187–194.

Greenblatt, D. J., Ransil, B. J., Harmatz, J. S., Smith, T. W., Duhme, D. W., and Koch-Weser, J. 1976. *J. Clin. Pharmacol.* **16**, 321–328.

Hancock, M. B., and Fougerousse, C. L. 1976. *Brain Res. Bull.* **1**, 229–234.

Hollister, L. E., Davis, K. L., Overall, J. E., and Anderson, T. 1978. *Arch. Gen. Psychiatry* **35**, 1410–1415.

Jimerson, D. C., Ballenger, J. C., Lake, C. R., Post, R. M., Goodwin, F. K., and Kopin, I. J. 1981. *Psychopharmacol. Bull.* **17,** 86.

Karoum, F., Wyatt, R. J., and Costa, E. 1974. *Neuropharmacol.* **13,** 165–176.

Kessler, J. A., Gordon, E. K., Reid, J. L., and Kopin, I. J. 1976. *J. Neurochem.* **26,** 1057–1061.

Khan, A. U., and Dekirmenjian, H. 1981. *Am. J. Psychiatry* **138,** 108–110.

Korf, J., Aghajanian, G. K., and Roth, R. H. 1973a. *Eur. J. Pharmacol.* **21,** 305–310.

Korf, J., Aghajanian, G. K., and Roth, R. H. 1973b. *Neuropharmacol.* **12,** 933–938.

Lal, S., Tolis, G., Martin, J. B., Brown, G. M., and Guyda, H. 1975. *J. Clin. Endocrin. Metabol.* **41,** 827–832.

Langer, D. H., Rapoport, J. L., Brown, G. L., Ebert, M. H., and Bunney, W. E., Jr. 1982. *J. Am. Acad. Child Psychiatry* **21,** 10–18.

Leckman, J. F., Maas, J. W., Redmond, E., Jr., and Heninger, G. R. 1980. *Life Sci.* **26,** 2179–2185.

Leckman, J. F., Maas, J. W., and Heninger, G. R. 1981. *Eur. J. Pharmacol.* **70,** 111–120.

Leckman, J. F., Cohen, D. J., Young, J. G., Anderson, G. M., Detlor, J., Harcherik, D. F., Heninger, G. R., and Shaywitz, B. A. 1982. Effects of acute and chronic clonidine on plasma catecholamine metabolites in Tourette's syndrome. Submitted for publication.

McKnew, D. H., Jr., and Cytryn, L. 1979. *J. Amer. Acad. Child Psychiatry* **18,** 608–615.

Maas, J. W., and Landis, D. H. 1968. *J. Pharmacol. Exp. Ther.* **163,** 147–162.

Maas, J. W., Dekirmenjian, H., and Jones, F. 1973. *Frontiers in Catecholamine Research* (E. Usdin and S. H. Snyder, eds.), pp. 1091–1096. Pergamon Press, New York.

Maas, J. W., Hattox, S. E., Landis, D. H., and Roth, R. H. 1976. *Brain Res.* **118,** 167–173.

Maas, J. W., Hattox, S. E., Landis, D. H., and Roth, R. H. 1977. *Eur. J. Pharmacol.* **46,** 221–228.

Maas, J. W., Hattox, S. E., Greene, N. M., and Landis, D. H. 1979a. *Science* **205,** 1025–1027.

Maas, J. W., Hattox, S. E., and Landis, D. H. 1979b. *Biochem. Pharmacol.* **28,** 3153–3156.

Maas, J. W., Hattox, S. E., and Landis, D. H. 1980. *Life Sci.* **26,** 929–934.

Maas, J. W., Kocsis, J. H., Bowden, C. L., Davis, J. M., Redmond, D. E., Hunin, I., Robins, E., and Mendels, J. 1982. *Psycholog. Med.* in press.

Mann, D. M. A., Lincoln, J., Yates, P. O., and Brennan, C. M. 1980. *Lancet* **2,** 1366–1367. (Dec. 20, 27)

Mason, S. T., and Fibiger, H. C. 1979a. *Life Sci.* **25,** 1949–1956.

Mason, S. T., and Fibiger, H. C. 1979b. *Life Sci.* **25,** 2141–2147.

Medina, M. A., Giachetti, A., and Shore, P. A. 1969. *Biochem. Pharmacol.* **18,** 891–901.

Mikkelsen, E., Lake, C. R., Brown, G. L., Ziegler, M. G., and Ebert, M. H. 1981. *Psychiatry Res.* **4,** 157–169.

Nygren, L. G., and Olson, L. 1977. *Brain Res.* **132,** 85–93.

Post, R. M., Kopin, J., Goodwin, F. K., and Gordon, E. K. 1973. *Am. J. Psychiatry* **130,** 67.

Rapoport, J. L., Mikkelsen, E. J., Ebert, M. H., Brown, G. L., Weise, V. K., and Kopin, I. J. 1978. *J. Nerv. Ment. Dis.* **166,** 731–737.

Redmond, D. E., Jr., and Huang, Y. H. 1979. *Life Sci.* **25,** 2149–2162.

Rudolph, C. D., Kaplan, S. L., and Ganong, W. F. (1980). *Neuroendocrinol.* **31,** 121–128.

Satterfield, J. H., Cantwell, D. P., Saul, R. E., Lesser, L. I., and Podosin, R. L. 1973. *J. Aut. Childh. Schizo.* **3,** 36–48.

Schanberg, S. M., Breese, G. R., Schildkraut, J. J., Gordon, E. K., and Kopin, J. 1968. *Biochem. Pharmacol.* **17,** 2006–2008.

Seifert, W. E., Foxx, J. L., and Butler, I. J. 1980. *Ann. Neurol.* **8,** 38–42.

Shekim, W. O., Dekirmenjian, H., and Chapel, J. L. 1977. *Am. J. Psychiatry* **134,** 1276–1279.

Shekim, W. O., and Dekirmenjian, H. 1978. *Am. J. Psychiatry* **135,** 490–491.

Shekim, W. O., Dekirmenjian, J., and Chapel, J. L. 1979a. *Am. J. Psychiatry* **136,** 667–671.

Shekim, W. O., Dekirmenjian, H., Chapel, J. L., Javaid, J., and Davis, J. M. 1979b. *J. Ped.* **95,** 389–394.

Shekim, W. O., Daniel, A. E., Koresko, R. L., and Dekirmenjian, H. 1980. *Pediatrics* **65,** 154–157.

Silver, L. B. 1979. *Basic Handbook of Child Psychiatry* (J. D. Noshpitz, ed.), Vol. II, pp. 416–439. Basic Books, New York.

Svensson, T. H., Bunney, B. S., and Aghajanian, G. K. 1975. *Brain Res.* **92,** 291–306.

Swann, A. C., Maas, J. W., Hattox, S. E., and Landis, H. 1980. *Life Sci.* **27,** 1857–1862.

Sweeney, D. R., Maas, J. W., and Pickar, D. 1979. *Catecholamines: Basic and Clinical Frontiers* (E. Usdin, I. J. Kopin, and J. Barchas, eds.), Vol. II, pp. 1917–1919. Pergamon Press, New York.

Sweeney, D. R., Leckman, J. F., Maas, J. W., Hattox, S., and Heninger, G. R. 1980. *Arch. Gen. Psychiatry* **37,** 1100–1103.

Tietz, N. W. 1976. *Fundamentals of Clinical Chemistry.* W. B. Saunders, Philadelphia.

Wehr, T. A., Muscettola, G., and Goodwin, F. K. 1980. *Arch. Gen. Psychiatry* **37,** 257–263.

Wender, P. H., Epstein, R. S., Kopin, I. J., and Gordon, E. K. 1971. *Am. J. Psychiatry* **127,** 1411–1415.

Work, H. H. 1979. *Basic Handbook of Child Psychiatry* (J. D. Noshpitz, ed.), Vol. II, pp. 402–415. Basic Books, New York.

Young, J. G., Cohen, D. J., Brown, S.-L., and Caparulo, B. K. 1978. *J. Am. Acad. Child Psychiatry* **17,** 671–678.

Young, J. G., and Cohen, D. J. 1979. *Basic Handbook of Child Psychiatry* (J. D. Noshpitz, ed.), Vol. 1, pp. 22–62. Basic Books, New York.

Young, J. G., Cohen, D. J., Caparulo, B. K., Brown, S.-L., and Maas, J. W. 1979. *Am. J. Psychiatry* **136,** 1055–1057.

Young, J. G., Cohen, D. J., Anderson, G. M., and Shaywitz, B. A. 1981a. *The Psychobiology of Childhood: A Profile of Current Issues* (B. Shopsin and L. Greenhill, eds.). Spectrum Publications, New York, in press.

Young, J. G., Cohen, D. J., Hattox, S. E., Kavanagh, M. E., Anderson, G. M., Shaywitz, B. A., and Maas, J. W. 1981b. *Life Sci.* **29,** 1467–1475.

Young J. G., Cohen, D. J., Kavanagh, M. E., Landis, H. D., Shaywitz, B. A., and Maas, J. W. 1981c. *Life Sci.* **28,** 2837–2845.

Index